THE BAR BOOK

THE BAR BOOK

ELEMENTS OF COCKTAIL TECHNIQUE

JEFFREY MORGENTHALER
with **MARTHA HOLMBERG**

photographs by **ALANNA HALE**

CHRONICLE BOOKS
SAN FRANCISCO

Text and illustrations copyright © 2014 by Jeffrey Morgenthaler.
Photographs copyright © 2014 by Alanna Hale.

Library of Congress Cataloging-in-Publication Data available.

ISBN 978-1-4521-1384-5

Manufactured in China

Designed by Alice Chau

The photographer wishes to thank Arlo Jamrog and Helynn Ospina.

10 9 8 7

Chronicle Books LLC
680 Second Street
San Francisco, California 94107
www.chroniclebooks.com

This book is dedicated to the countless men and women all over the world whose bars I have sat at over the years, asking questions, borrowing ideas, and stealing recipes. It is your combined knowledge that fills these pages, and it is you who continually inspire me to work harder, learn more, and share with the rest of the world so that we can continue to keep growing this thing together.

CONTENTS

WHY I MAKE COCKTAILS, AND WHY I WROTE THIS BOOK 8

ANY GOOD COCKTAIL NEEDS THESE THREE ELEMENTS 10

I'VE ORGANIZED THE BOOK THE WAY I BUILD MY COCKTAILS 11

CHAPTER № 1
CITRUS JUICE 13

CHOOSING YOUR FRUIT 16

CHOOSING THE RIGHT JUICER 19

JUICING TECHNIQUE 22

CITRUS PROFILES 27
Daiquiri No. 3 28

CHAPTER № 2
OTHER JUICES 31

TYPES OF JUICERS 33

IMPROVISATIONAL JUICE EXTRACTION 34

APPLE JUICE 38
Flannel Shirt 40

PINEAPPLE JUICE 42
Kingston Club 42

TOMATO JUICE 43

POMEGRANATE JUICE 44

GINGER JUICE 45

FRUIT PUREES 46
Bellini 49

CHAPTER № 3
SODAS & MIXERS 51

A HISTORY OF CARBONATION 53
Tom Collins 56

SODA WATER 57

TONIC WATER 58
Quinine Syrup 59

Gin and Tonic 62

Ginger Beer 65

Dark and Stormy 68

SPARKLING WINE 70
French 75 71

CHAPTER № 4
SIMPLE SYRUPS 73

SELECTING THE RIGHT SUGAR 75

MEASURING YOUR INGREDIENTS FOR SIMPLE SYRUP 78

SUGAR SYRUPS IN COCKTAILS 81
House Old-Fashioned 82
Rum Old-Fashioned 82
Oaxaca Old-Fashioned 83
Maple Old-Fashioned 83

CHAPTER № 5
COMPOUND SYRUPS 87

SWEET SYRUPS WITH ADDED FLAVOR 90

FLAVORLESS BUT FAMILIAR: GUM SYRUP 90
Gum Syrup 93

HERB SYRUP 94
Mint Syrup 96

FRUIT SYRUPS 97
Grenadine 98
Jack Rose 100
Raspberry Syrup 102
Clover Club 102
Ginger Syrup 103
Pineapple Syrup 103
Hotel Nacional Special 107
Oleo Saccharum 108
Philadelphia Fish House
Punch 111

ORGEAT 112
Japanese Cocktail 113

SHRUBS 114
Strawberry-Mint Shrub 114

CHAPTER № 6
INFUSIONS, TINCTURES & BITTERS 117

INFUSIONS 119
    Tequila por Mi Amante 122
    Thyme-Infused Cointreau 127
    Chinese Five-Spiced Dark
      Rum 128
    Nocino 129
    Limoncello 130
WOOD INFUSIONS, A.K.A. BARREL AGING 132
TINCTURES 133
    Cinnamon Tincture 134
    Autumn Leaves 135
BITTERS 136
    House Orange Bitters 138
    Revolver 140

CHAPTER № 7
DAIRY & EGGS 143

CHOOSING THE BEST DAIRY PRODUCTS AND EGGS 145
CREAM 146
    Alexander Cocktail 146
    Irish Coffee 150
EGGS 152
    Cynar Flip 153
    Clyde Common Eggnog 154
    White Lady 161

CHAPTER № 8
ICE 163

HOW ICE BEHAVES 165
WHY ICE CLARITY MATTERS 165
STORING ICE 168
TRANSPORTING ICE 168
HANDLING ICE 168
TYPES OF ICE 170
    Mint Julep 176

CHAPTER № 9
MEASURING 183

WHY DO WE MEASURE? 185
MODERN MEASURES 186
MEASURING TOOLS 188
SPEED AND FREEDOM 191
    Vesper 196

CHAPTER № 10
STIRRING & SHAKING 199

CHILLING AND DILUTION 201
STIRRING 203
    Martini 210
SHAKING 213
    Sidecar 220

CHAPTER № 11
OTHER MIXING METHODS 223

BUILDING IN THE GLASS 225
ROLLING 225
SWIZZLING 226
    Queen's Park Swizzle 226
BLENDING 227
    Piña Colada 229
MUDDLING 230
    Mojito 233
    Caipirinha 237
"MIXING" ABSINTHE 238
FLAMING DRINKS 239
    Blue Blazer 240
FIRE FOR TOASTING 241
    Café Brûlot 242
FIRE AS CARAMELIZATION TOOL 243
    Spanish Coffee 245

CHAPTER № 12
GARNISHING 247

DROPPED GARNISHES 250
    Daniel Shoemaker's
      Brandied Cherries 252
    Todd Thrasher's
      Pickled Onions 256
VISUAL GARNISHES 259
UTILITARIAN GARNISHES 266
RIMMED GARNISHES 268
    Margarita 272
AROMATIC GARNISHES 274
    Sazerac 278

INDEX 282

WHY I MAKE COCKTAILS, AND WHY I WROTE THIS BOOK

I'll never forget the first time I stepped behind the bar. It was the night of April 25, 1996, which was a Thursday. I'd somehow convinced the manager to give me a job, though I had no experience and was about ten times cockier in the interview process than I was in real life—or a hundred times more than I should have been, given my limited social skill set.

The place had been around since the repeal of Prohibition, with smoke-stained walls and Naugahyde booths. It was pretty rough-and-tumble, over in the sketchier part of town, opposite the university district, where I lived. I was nervous as hell, and my hands shook as I wrote down every order for the only drink we served there: one of three beers on tap. That night, and for pretty much every night the first summer I spent there, at least ten people told me I was the worst bartender they'd ever seen.

But I honestly didn't much care. I was at the University of Oregon, getting my degree in interior architecture, and bartending at night to make some money, meet some ladies, and have a little fun. Little did I know the job would grow on me, and that I would begin to grow on those people who thought I was the worst bartender ever.

It was just supposed to be a summer job, but when the fall quarter rolled around, the owners asked me to stay. And so I did. I worked at the Tiny Tavern in Eugene, Oregon, for four years while I went to school, and that time spent behind the bar there, serving the same three beers every night, laid the foundation for a life-long love affair with bars and bartending.

I started my first architecture job the summer after I graduated. It wasn't entirely full-time work, so I kept a few shifts behind the bar to pay the bills. It was fine, and I was happy to be finally working in the field I thought I wanted to be in, but over the course of several years I realized that I'm not really the type to sit behind a desk.

I also realized something else, something far more important: bars, bartending, and cocktails were my hobby. I found myself coming home every night and reading up on classic cocktails. I spent my time at work online, bidding on out-of-print cocktail books, rare bar tools, and even rarer liquors. I had cocktail parties and regaled my friends with tales of the daiquiri, sidecar, and Manhattan while we sipped and swilled.

Eventually it became clear to me that my real interest lay in spending time behind the bar, and I slowly phased out the architecture—much to the chagrin of my friends and family. I became involved in the world of restaurants, climbed higher and higher up the ladder of fine dining, and learned more and more every day about the craft of tending bar.

I started my own blog, mainly so our guests could have access to my cocktail recipes. I became more connected in the growing worldwide community of people interested in cocktails. People began to look to me for information, and at some point someone called me an expert.

It's all very surreal to think about. When I'm not actively behind the bar, I spend my time managing, traveling, speaking at seminars and conferences, and training the next generation of bartenders. And these days, it's only once a month that someone refers to me as the worst bartender they've ever seen.

ANY GOOD COCKTAIL NEEDS THESE THREE ELEMENTS

When I train bartenders, I begin by teaching them one basic rule, and here it is: There are three things, of equal importance, that make a great cocktail. And unless all three are given their due respect, the drink you make isn't going to reach its full potential.

The first of these is the **RECIPE** that you choose. Let's say we're going to make a whiskey sour in this example. Well, if you really start doing your research, you're going to find that there are about a thousand different recipes out there for a whiskey sour. Check the Internet if you don't believe me. One old book might tell you to begin with 1 oz/30 ml of whiskey and 2 oz/60 ml of sour mix, but some guy's blog might argue that it's gotta be 2 oz/60 ml of whiskey, with fresh lemon juice and a dollop of egg white. Another recipe might be too sweet, and yet another might not be sweet enough. Choosing the right recipe is exactly one-third of the battle.

The second thing that's going to make or break our whiskey sour is the **INGREDIENTS** we choose. Some whiskeys are better suited to the drink than others. A higher-proof bourbon whiskey is going to shine through the other ingredients better than a lower-proof Irish whiskey. If we're using lemon juice, is it fresh or frozen? If we're using egg whites, are they pasteurized and packaged or fresh from a local farm? All of these decisions are as important as the recipe we've spent years researching and perfecting.

But the third thing, the one that's so often overlooked by bartenders and home mixers, and the thing that's the subject of this book, is **TECHNIQUE**. Everything from juicing those lemons properly, preparing your egg whites, and measuring the ingredients to how the drink is shaken, strained, and served in a perfectly chilled glass is as important as the recipe and ingredients you've selected.

As you might guess, there are plenty of books out there about recipes. And there are more and more volumes on bookstore shelves every day about cocktail ingredients. But this book aims to be among the first in what will hopefully become an ongoing conversation about technique.

I'VE ORGANIZED THE BOOK THE WAY I BUILD MY COCKTAILS

The chapters in this book are laid out a little differently than most other books. There is no chapter on vodka—in fact there are no chapters on alcohol at all. Instead, we have broken down the cocktail-making process as you would do it behind the bar. The first third of the book is all about prep: we'll teach you how to get your juices ready, prepare your syrups, make your bitters, and produce your ice. Next we'll show you how to put the drink together: how to measure and properly mix. And then we'll show you how the drink is finished and served.

I've included a few of my favorite recipes, which I've collected over the years—my own, some of my friends', and some of the best versions of the classics I've found—in order to illustrate some of the points we're making about technique, and to show you how these techniques are applied.

CITRUS JUICE

THE BRACING FOUNDATION OF A WIDE RANGE OF COCKTAILS

Every day at my bar, we typically juice in the neighborhood of one case of lemons, three-quarters of a case of limes, half a case of grapefruit, and half a case of oranges. That's every single day. When I see how much citrus we go through on an average busy day and night, I think back to the first cocktail bar I worked in. It was the daytime bartender's chore to head over to the grocery store across the street every morning and pick up a pack of Virginia Slims for the daytime cook, one of those big metal cans of grapefruit juice, and six limes and six lemons for garnishing gin and tonics and iced teas. And I remember clearly that at one point, the woman who was training me informed me that "limes and lemons are actually the same thing; limes are just unripened lemons." That wasn't really too long ago, but I feel like we've all come a long way.

Citrus is so ubiquitous in cocktails nowadays that it's often taken for granted. Back when I came of age and started hanging around in bars, drinks were being made with canned, neon-green sour mix, and nobody thought twice about it. These days we shouldn't think of using anything other than fresh-squeezed juice in our cocktails. And yet, as today's craft bartenders turn their attention to things such as apothecary herbs and esoteric tinctures, the basic lemon or lime *still* doesn't really get the attention it's due.

Citrus was pretty much treasured by earlier civilizations; it was used as a source of perfume and other beauty products, as a

medicine, and often in religious ceremonies. The satsuma, citron, and mandarin—three of the earliest ancestors of the citrus we know today—made their way from continent to continent, thanks to early explorers and traders (and sometimes conquerers, such as Alexander the Great, who was a big citron fan). Cultivation and consumption of the fruits spread from India to Persia (modern-day Iran), and eventually around the Mediterranean rim, including the Middle East, North Africa, and Europe.

Citrus made it to North America in the fifteenth century, supposedly arriving via Christopher Columbus (hey, at least he brought something other than just disease and genocide with him), and a half century later, explorer Ponce de León planted orange groves around St. Augustine, Florida. Those early trees have led to a multibillion-dollar orange industry in Florida.

The notion of mixing citrus with alcohol—which, as we've said, is a given nowadays—probably took millennia to catch on. Despite the use of citrus in pretty much every facet of daily life, the concept of citrus and alcohol didn't really become widespread until the early seventeenth century, when mixing spirits with citrus and sugar took hold in Britain and its colonies.

Variations on lemon or lime juice mixed with alcohol—punch—were being sipped in drawing rooms around England, but the pairing caught fire globally once the British Royal Navy got a taste for it and realized, after much trial and error, that citrus could stave off scurvy in its sailors. The Royal Navy–made beverage became a staple, and as the British sailors traveled, so did punch. That combination of hot and sour—mitigated by sugar, water, and spices—seems to be something our human physiology responds favorably to, because so many cocktails still use citrus as their backbone.

Citrus in all its forms brings much to the party: quarters are muddled, peels are zested, oils are extracted, and wedges are squeezed over the top. But it's the juice—sour, fresh, pungent, bracing juice—that brings the most to the world of cocktails. And so it's absolutely critical that you know how to choose, store, and handle citrus fruit, and then coax out the best quality juice from it, if you're going to be able to make a proper cocktail.

CHOOSING YOUR FRUIT

When we talk about citrus in cocktails, we're mostly discussing limes, lemons, oranges, and grapefruits. But yuzu, Buddha's hand, kumquats, and other exotics can all be found now in the modern bartender's toolbox.

As with everything that you'll use to make a cocktail, the first criterion when choosing citrus is freshness. With pretty much every other food type, I would advocate working with a local grower, but unless you're living in a climate along the lines of California's, Costa Rica's, or Morocco's, that may not be feasible.

Fortunately, most citrus has a moderately long shelf life and will stay bright and delicious for up to a week after you buy it. The specific characteristics that you need to look for when choosing citrus will depend on what you're going to do with it. When we select citrus at our bar, we place the fruit into one of two categories: fruit for juicing or fruit for garnishes.

Citrus fruit that is to be juiced should be plump, on the soft side, and heavy for its size, with the thinnest and smoothest skin possible, which is an indication of more juice-producing contents. And a thin, supple skin just makes it easier to squeeze. The skin color of juice fruit doesn't matter much; nor do a few blemishes. To evaluate fruit for juice, you need to heft quite a few to find the heavy, plump ones.

For garnishes, I want citrus with thicker skin or a pebbled surface, and a bright, even color. I also want fruit that hasn't been treated with pesticides and isn't coated with wax. (Learn more about making and using citrus garnishes in chapter 12.) Unfortunately, you usually don't get it all in the same piece of fruit, but for both juice and garnish fruit, choosing organic is always a good start.

BUYING IN BULK

The professional bartender has the convenience of a daily fresh produce delivery to the restaurant or barroom door. But this isn't the case for the average, or home, bartender. When planning for just a few cocktails, sourcing citrus is just a matter of going to a decent grocery store. But if you're planning a large event, or making cocktail components that use a lot of citrus (such as House Orange Bitters, page 138), having access to wholesale prices can make a big difference.

Some restaurant-supply wholesalers will sell to the general public, but finding them can take a little sleuthing. A good practice is to contact your favorite locally owned restaurant (chain restaurants often have their own internal supply avenues) or bar and ask whom they procure citrus from. Contact the front office of that particular distributor and ask if they'll sell to the general public.

A far simpler alternative is to contact your local supermarket or grocer and simply ask the produce manager for bulk-buying options. Often a produce manager will be able to offer a discount for purchasing citrus by the case, so it never hurts to ask about your options there. Plan on ordering several days in advance.

Another option is finding a large Asian or Latin market, which can be found in most sizable cities. After just a short drive and a friendly conversation with the market's produce manager, you may leave with a whole lot of fresh, gorgeous citrus at bargain prices. Plus, I find these markets offer an exciting array of other products that aren't found at traditional American supermarkets. I enjoy browsing around them and gleaning inspiration for new cocktail combinations.

Once you get your fruit home or to your bar, you want to store it in a way that will keep it fresh, which in the case of citrus, is in the refrigerator. There's a myth out there that chilling citrus will reduce the yield of juice, so some bartenders leave it on the counter, but you can trust me when I tell you that this is a load of bull. Check out the experiment we did on page 24.

HOW MUCH JUICE CAN YOU EXPECT?

Now that you've found a source for the least expensive, freshest citrus in your town, it's time to determine how much to buy. Obviously, different varieties of citrus are going to yield different quantities of juice at different times of the year, but here's a rough guide, which can at least help you make your shopping list.

FRUIT	AVERAGE YIELD OF JUICE
Lime	1 oz/30 ml
Lemon	1.5 oz/45 ml
Meyer lemon	2 oz/60 ml
Navel orange	3 oz/90 ml
Grapefruit	8 oz/240 ml

CHOOSING THE RIGHT JUICER

The bartender has several choices of equipment to use when juicing fruit, and the choice will be a matter of what kind of fruit and how much juice is needed.

HAND PRESSES

The simplest option for juicing at home or in a small-scale bar program is what we refer to as a hand press (also called a clamshell-type) juicer. There are two main types, with minor stylistic differences between them. Both require the fruit to be placed cut-side down in the unit. At first, this seems counterintuitive, given the shape of the juicer, but I repeat (probably several more times): *place the citrus cut-side down.*

The first type of hand press is an older style; it has no holes in its flat base, but merely a small reservoir around the cone and a pour spout on either or both sides. You place a half lemon or lime on the base cut-side down, swing the hinged top half over to embrace the fruit, and then squeeze the handles together to put pressure on the fruit and release the juice, which flows out of the pour spout.

Sadly, this type of press is nearly extinct, but vintage cast-iron or aluminum models can be found at online auction sites or antiques malls. The best ones were once made by Ebaloy, and I think they're worth seeking out for their ease of use and durability. As an aside, I would think twice before using one of these antiques in a professional bar setting, as antiques have a hard time handling repeated use.

The other, more common, type of hand press also consists of two parts hinged together. The base has holes in it to allow the juice to flow out, and the top half has a bulbous protrusion that pushes into the cut fruit and turns it onto itself so that the juice can flow through the holes. There are inexpensive cast-iron models from Mexico, which are usually fairly small. But, while good for juicing small limes, they may be worthless when you're juicing anything larger.

The best all-around hand press is an enameled aluminum juicer made by Amco. They make four: a small green model meant for limes, a medium yellow model for lemons, and an orange model for, well, oranges. There's also a two-in-one model with a plastic insert made for both lemons and limes—skip it. And also skip the green lime model as well. The lemon and orange models will suit all of your needs just fine; they cost about as much as a cheap bottle of wine.

But my favorite is a gorgeous solid stainless-steel juicer made by Norpro, which I've fallen in love with in recent years. It's around three times the cost of the Amco enameled aluminum models, but if it's style you're going for, there is no rival.

MECHANICAL PRESSES

Moving up the technology scale, the mechanical citrus press, or manual stand juicer, is the go-to for bartenders looking to juice a larger amount of juice, for either a party or medium-scale cocktail program.

There are two basic types: The first is a gearless unit that operates with levers and has a handle mounted on the front. The most popular producer of this style is Ra Chand, which makes a variety of cast-aluminum juicers. While the lack of gears and interchangeable parts makes this type of juicer a sturdier, longer lasting piece of equipment than others, I find the front-mounted handle a bit clumsy; it's difficult to get proper leverage unless you can position the juicer below counter or bar-top level.

The more common stand juicer used by the professional bartender is the Hamilton Beach 932 commercial citrus juicer. This is a side-mounted juicer with a geared handle and is by far the most comfortable to use for large jobs. The biggest drawback I find with this unit is that you can't replace the gears and tighten the individual parts. If you're going to be juicing a very large quantity of produce a day, plan on replacing the unit every three to six months. For the more casual user, it'll last a good long while.

ELECTRIC PRESSES

The most complex type, an electric press, commonly referred to as an electric juicer, is also the best option for a program that will be serving a large number of guests. The initial cost is, obviously, higher than the preceding two types of manual juicers, but these commercial-grade juicers will endure years of abuse, many more than their manual counterparts.

BARTENDER'S CHOICE: ELECTRIC JUICER

My favorite electric juicer, and the one that's widely preferred by professional bartenders, is the Sunkist juicer, model J1, which runs around $600/£650. This ¼-horsepower monster wrapped in a chrome-plated housing and topped with a domed plastic shell has been around for years, and it will be around for many more.

JUICING TECHNIQUE

When we talk about citrus behind the bar, we often use an earth-inspired metaphor: On either end of the (usually) oblong fruit is a "pole." The stem end (North Pole) is where the fruit was formerly attached to the tree; that's the end with the little brown nubbin. The stylar end (South Pole) is at the opposite end of the fruit, with no indentation or stem remainder, but often with a nippled end. The equator encircles the fruit and is equidistant from the North and South Poles.

CUTTING YOUR FRUIT FOR JUICING

All citrus to be juiced should be cut along the equator, perpendicular to the membranes that separate the individual segments inside. Bisecting in this direction opens the interior of the fruit completely and maximizes the juice extracted. If you're prepping a lot of citrus for juicing, you can do this beforehand; there's no need to cut each fruit immediately before juicing. Cut your fruit up to 2 hours before juicing, and keep it in the refrigerator once it's been cut.

HOW TO JUICE CITRUS FRUIT WITH A HAND PRESS

You can juice citrus to make just a single cocktail using a process that the kitchen calls *à la minute* (pronounced ah lah mee-NOOT), which is a culinary term that basically means "to order." In this case, you'll juice the fruit using a hand press and then measure it directly in the jigger. (More about measuring in chapter 9.)

To use the modern hand press, or clamshell-type, juicer (such as the colorful ones), put your citrus half into the bottom half of the press, cut-side down. This might not feel correct at first, because the concave shape of the press makes you think you should nestle the fruit right into it, but you shouldn't. Swing the top half over and

squeeze the two together, over your glass or jigger. This will push the bulb in the top half into the citrus, in effect forcing it inside out as it squeezes out the juice.

However, the professional bartender or home entertainer will most often be preparing a larger quantity of juice in advance. There are several advantages to this: First, juicing a lot of citrus makes a mess, which you don't necessarily want on display for your guests; keeping the bar looking clean and tidy is part of the job. Second, you can store your fresh-squeezed juice in plastic or glass bottles and then measure it out on a cocktail-by-cocktail basis, expediting the drink-making process—always a bonus when you're faced with a large, thirsty crowd.

HOW TO JUICE IN VOLUME

When juicing in larger quantities, it's really best to use a mechanical or electric press, although I have spent more occasions than I care to remember with a group of bartenders huddled around cardboard cases of precut citrus, hand pressing fast and furiously into a large bucket as we prepped for one event or another. It's not fun, and it's not pretty, but it works in a pinch.

Start by cutting all your citrus, and then set the mechanical or electric juicer in place. Next to the juicer, set a large container (a bowl or plastic bucket) and position a fine-mesh strainer over the top. The object of the strainer, and I feel very strongly about this, is to catch any pulp or seeds, leaving you with smooth, uniform citrus juice ready to be bottled.

Once you've juiced your fruit, seal it in clean bottles or containers, label it, refrigerate right away, and keep it as cold as possible.

HOW LONG WILL CITRUS JUICE STAY FRESH?

Fresh-squeezed juice changes over time, and strangely enough, that change doesn't go in a straight line from fresh and delicious to old and stale. While all juice is very good in the first moments after you squeeze it, lemon, lime, and grapefruit are actually a bit better for cocktails once they've got a few hours of age on them. Orange juice is a different story, however.

Oranges contain flavorless substances called LARL (limonoate A-ring lactone) and NARL (nomilinoate A-ring lactone). During and after squeezing, those substances are converted by an enzyme, which is also present in oranges, into limonin, which is very bitter. The earlier in the season the fruit is picked, the more LARL and NARL there will be. Ideally, you should squeeze oranges to order, or definitely use the juice within an hour at most.

FRUIT JUICE	OPTIMAL AGE	MAXIMUM AGE
Grapefruit	4 to 12 hours	48 hours
Lemon	4 to 12 hours	24 hours
Lime	4 to 12 hours	24 hours
Orange	0 to 1 hour	4 hours

GETTING THE MOST FROM YOUR CITRUS

There's a lot of conjecture these days about which trick extracts the most juice from citrus fruit. Some people swear by rolling and pressing the fruit on the counter, to crush the juice sacs inside. Some think a warmer piece of fruit yields more juice than a straight-from-the-fridge one, and some people even recommend microwaving the citrus in order to extract more juice (I definitely passed on this method). Rolling the fruit and bringing them to room temperature both made sense to me in theory, but I'd never really investigated these options myself. So I set out to do a little experiment.

I gathered sixty lemons and divided them into four groups of fifteen lemons. I weighed each group of lemons, making small adjustments between the groups so that each group weighed more or less the same, and then I gave each group a different treatment.

GROUP 1: I left these in the refrigerator; this was to be my control group. After all, the fridge is where most of us at home (and all of us in the bar and restaurant business) keep our fruit.

GROUP 2: The second group I left out in a bowl on my kitchen counter overnight (about nine hours).

GROUP 3: I refrigerated these, but I also rolled the fruit firmly on the counter with the palm of my hand before juicing.

GROUP 4: This last group I left out in another bowl on the counter, but as with Group 3, I rolled them firmly on the counter before juicing. This last group was the one I had the most confidence in; after all, I'm applying both tricks, so this should give us the greatest yield, right?

When I was ready to juice, I recorded the average temperature of each group with a digital thermometer, and then I cut and juiced each group and strained, measured, and weighed the results.

The results were rather surprising.

And if you take a close look at the results, you see some pretty good news: going through the extra step doesn't make a whole heck of a lot of difference. You can keep the fruit fresher, colder, and spare yourself some effort—while still ending up with the best yield—by simply storing it in the fridge.

	GROUP 1: REFRIGERATED, NOT ROLLED	GROUP 2: ROOM TEMPERATURE, NOT ROLLED	GROUP 3: REFRIGERATED, ROLLED	GROUP 4: ROOM TEMPERATURE, ROLLED
Number of lemons	15	15	15	15
Average temperature	43°F/6.1°C	67°F/19.4°C	45.7°F/7.6°C	65.7°F/18.7°C
Net weight before juicing	5.0 lb/2.3 kg	5.0 lb/2.3 kg	5.0 lb/2.3 kg	5.0 lb/2.3 kg
Total volume of juice	31.95 oz/945 ml	31.78 oz/940 ml	29.72 oz/879 ml	30.50 oz/902 ml
Total weight of juice	2.19 lb/994 g	2.18 lb/992 g	2.05 lb/929 g	2.08 lb/942 g
Percentage of juice by weight	43.9%	43.5%	40.7%	41.1%
Juice per lemon	2.13 oz/63 ml	2.12 oz/62.6 ml	1.98 oz/58.6 ml	2.03 oz/60.1 ml

CITRUS PROFILES

BITTER ORANGE: The most well known is the Seville. All varieties are too bitter to eat out of hand and instead are frequently used to make marmalades. Their essential oils flavor foods and liquors, such as curaçao.

BLOOD ORANGE: These are in the same family as the Valencia and the navel, but their color is much more dramatic. The most common are Moro oranges. The peel will often, though not always, be flushed with red, but the interior of a blood orange is a deep magenta, and the juice retains that color. Blood oranges are very sweet, with some berry notes to the flavor.

BUDDHA'S HAND: With its startling shape, Buddha's hand looks nothing like its essentially round citrus cousins. The multifingered, fragrant fruit is a type of citron, an ancient citrus that is long on rind and short on flesh. The Buddha's hand has no flesh or juice at all, just lots of zest to pare or grate, and the white pith underneath is very mild.

KEY LIME: A smaller relative of the Persian lime, key limes are thinner skinned, and somewhat more fragrant, and are mostly used in desserts. But the juice is fantastic and should be considered for cocktails.

KUMQUAT: The Shetland ponies of the citrus world, these marble-size fruits are all about the peel, which is candy-sweet, in contrast to the sour-bitter flesh and seeds inside. You can't juice a kumquat, but we've seen drinks in which the fruit has been muddled.

LEMON: The two main varieties—the Lisbon and the Eureka—are so similar that even most produce experts can't tell them apart. Within these varieties, however, there is plenty of variation, from thick skinned and somewhat dry to thin skinned and juicy.

MEYER LEMON: Meyers are a cross between a lemon and a type of orange, probably a mandarin. They have thin, tender skin that's very deep yellow, heading toward orange. They're super juicy, and the flavor is sweet, less acidic, and almost floral.

NAVEL ORANGE: While these are mostly destined to be eating oranges, they produce delicious juice and are often more brightly colored than Valencias, which means they're also good for garnishing. Navel orange juice will become bitter more quickly because they are at their peak in the winter months (see page 24). Look for Cara Cara navels, which have a beautiful pink color to the flesh.

PERSIAN LIME: This is the name for the common lime, but of course it's anything but common. Perfumed, sweet-tart, and moderately acidic, lime juice and zest play a huge role in cocktails.

RIO STAR GRAPEFRUIT: This is the "it" grapefruit of the moment. Grown in Texas and available from late winter through April, these thin-skinned grapefruits are fantastic for juicing, as well as eating. The flesh is a deep pink, and extremely sweet and juicy, especially as the season progresses; they're at their peak of sweetness in March. Other grapefruit varieties to look for are Honeygold and Oroblanco, which is a grapefruit-pomelo hybrid.

TANGERINE AND MANDARIN: There are multiple members of this family, and it's easy to get lost in the variations, but generally tangerine-type citrus has a loose, easy-to-peel skin, which is why they are primarily meant to be eaten out of hand. The juice is delicious, however, floral and very sweet.

VALENCIA ORANGE: These are the oranges most often used for juicing. They're thin skinned and juicy, but contain plenty of seeds. They're at their peak in late spring through summer.

YUZU: This is a somewhat exotic citrus native to China and greatly appreciated in modern Japan. The slightly wrinkly round fruit isn't good for eating—full of big seeds and not much juice—but the fragrance is extraordinary, like a combination of the best grapefruit and lemon.

DAIQUIRI NO. 3

By Constantino Ribalaigua Vert

MAKES 1 DRINK At the Floridita bar in Havana, Cuba, in the 1930s and 1940s, the daiquiri was king, and an extensive daiquiri menu was developed there, due in large part to bartenders like Constantino Ribalaigua Vert. His famed Daiquiri No. 3 was consumed in massive quantities by Ernest Hemingway, though he took his "without sugar and double the rum," which became the legendary Hemingway, or *Papa doble,* daiquiri.

Personally, I find the Hemingway daiquiri repulsive and instead prefer Constante's original.

2 oz/60 ml white rum

½ oz/15 ml 2:1 simple syrup (see page 78)

½ oz/15 ml fresh lime juice

¼ oz/7.5 ml grapefruit juice

1 tsp/5 ml maraschino liqueur, preferably Luxardo

Ice cubes for shaking

Crushed ice for serving

1 lime wedge for garnish

OLD-FASHIONED GLASS

Combine the rum, simple syrup, lime juice, grapefruit juice, and maraschino liqueur in a cocktail shaker or mixing glass. Shake with ice cubes and strain over the old-fashioned glass filled with crushed ice. Garnish with the lime wedge and serve with a straw.

2

OTHER JUICES

TECHNIQUES FOR A
WIDER ARRAY OF FLAVORS

So, as I mentioned before, I slowly phased out my career in architecture in exchange for a career behind the bar. And I've never been happier about a choice, because I essentially get paid to do my hobby every day now. But a big part of me still loves the study of the built environment—the design process and construction. So it's natural that I look for parallels to draw between my two fields, but it's not always that easy.

When I was looking for a way to introduce this chapter, it finally came to me as I sat thinking about the other types of juice, besides citrus, that we use behind the bar: citrus juice is like a wooden two-by-four. It's the most basic material out there when you're talking about the construction of a cocktail. But there are other building materials that need to be considered. Some of them are classic and sturdy, like masonry. Others are more exotic, like bamboo. But they all have their time and place, and knowing how to use each one is a hallmark of a well-trained bartender.

Fruit juices other than citrus have been used in cocktails for a long time. I mean, the United States was pretty much built on boozy apple juice. Ethan Allen and his Green Mountain Boys knocked back cider dosed with copious amounts of rum on the eve of the raid on Fort Ticonderoga, which succeeded in cutting off a key supply route for the British.

As colonial settlers moved west, they needed orchards in order to stake a claim on the land. John Chapman—the real Johnny Appleseed—planted apple nurseries that allowed settlers to get a jump on their orchards. Those apples were most likely used to make alcoholic apple cider or applejack—apple brandy, essentially.

The exotic pineapple had been cut up and used to flavor syrups and punches, or to decorate juleps, for some time, but it wasn't until around the Prohibition period that we began to see pineapple juice making an appearance in American cocktails. Now it is the most often-used juice in drinks, aside from citrus. Tomato juice made its debut in Bloody Marys at about the same time. What corner bar would think twice about stocking tomato juice as a necessary staple these days?

Now that bartenders have begun to work more closely with the kitchen—hell, some of the best bartenders in the world started back there—they have embraced the wide world of fruits available to them and given us all a huge leg up by showing us how to work with fruits and vegetables in a more culinary way.

Since only a few products are actually "juice-able" (that is, you can press or squeeze them and then extract a more or less clear liquid), we're also considering fruit purees, in which the solids are blended with the liquid inside the fruit—another technique perfectly suited to cocktails. All of these methods are another foundation upon which you'll be able to construct sturdy, well-executed cocktails.

TYPES OF JUICERS

There are three main tools that we use to juice fruits and vegetables. My choice is based on both the character of the produce (is it soft, hard, fibrous, mushy?) and the quantity of juice that I need to make.

FOOD MILL

The most basic tool for making juice, or technically, a puree, is a food mill, which is a sort of stainless-steel strainer fitted with a plate that you crank in order to push the food through. A food mill is large and unwieldy—certainly not what we want to use to make drinks to order—but it does have the advantage of straining out skins and seeds as you process the fruit. Food mills are best for creating purees of soft fruit, such as berries or stone fruits, rather than clear juices. You can achieve nearly the same effect with a strainer and a small ladle or spoon (see page 34), provided you're working with a small quantity of really soft fruit, such as raspberries.

FOOD PROCESSOR

A regular food processor makes for a really good juicer. Unlike a blender, the food processor's blade is wide, while the bowl is shallow, maximizing the contact between food and steel. The food processor destroys the cell walls of the fruit or vegetable to release the juice, so you need to take further steps to strain and filter out any fiber. At home I use the MacGyver centrifuge method (see page 36) when I'm juicing apples or other fruits with a lot of membrane, such as pineapples.

JUICE EXTRACTOR

The tool that works best for everything is, of course, the most highly engineered, and the most expensive. A juice extractor works in an entirely different manner than a food processor. Spinning blades grind the food into a pulp, which is then thrown against a spinning perforated drum, forcing the juice through the drum screen, and the pulp out through a chute in the back of the unit. You get the benefit of horsepower, centrifugal force, and fine screening all in one, which is great if you're trying to juice "stalky," fibrous vegetables such as celery or rhubarb, or harder roots and rhizomes such as beets or ginger.

The biggest drawback here is cost: a professional model can run upward of $300/£350. The good news is that every decade or so, the nation goes through a sort of fresh juice/smoothie diet craze, so juice extractors are plentiful at your local thrift shop. These used home models might not withstand intense juicing in a large-scale bar program, but they'll cost one-tenth of the price of new models, making them well worth a shot.

BARTENDER'S CHOICE: BREVILLE JUICE FOUNTAIN ELITE

This is a beautiful machine with a lot of power, and a serious price tag of about $300/£300. For a professional situation, the price is money well invested. For home use, this juice extractor may be a splurge, but you won't regret it if you're looking for a professional-grade piece of equipment that will last for years.

IMPROVISATIONAL JUICE EXTRACTION

For smaller jobs, like when you're entertaining at home, there is good success to be had without the price tag of a powerhouse juice extractor. Following are two ways of making juices at home:

Strainer Method

If it's a matter of a small quantity of really soft fruit, such as berries or kiwis, I'll simply force the fruit through a large strainer using the back of a metal ladle.

1. Place a large mesh strainer over a container, put a small amount of the fruit into the strainer, and, with the back of a medium stainless-steel ladle or a large spoon, mash the fruit in a circular motion to push it through the strainer.

2. After you've mashed a bit, scrape the juicy pulp from the underside of the strainer into the container. The inside of the strainer will eventually get clogged with seeds or skin, depending on your fruit, so scrape out that spent pulp from time to time also, and discard.

3. If needed, give your juice a final strain through another strainer with a finer mesh. For freshest flavor, use juice immediately.

MacGyver Centrifuge Method

For fruit that doesn't easily collapse into a puree—such as an apple or pineapple—I always use my food processor in conjunction with a little something I like to call the MacGyver centrifuge.

1. Cut two 36-in/91.5-cm lengths of cheesecloth (sold in packs at good grocery or kitchen supply stores). Rinse the cheesecloth, wring it out, and then refold it so you have a double layer.

2. Lay one piece across the basket of a salad spinner, so that the excess length hangs evenly over two sides. Lay the second piece perpendicular to that, to form a cross (one piece running north-south and one running east-west). Tuck and pull the cloth so that there are no gaps, in order to contain all the fruit you will place in the cheesecloth.

3. Cut your fruit into 1-in/2.5-cm pieces, put into a food processor fitted with a single blade, and process until you have a pulpy mixture. You might have to stop and push down the chunks that have crawled up the sides of the work bowl from time to time. Once you've got a puree about the consistency of applesauce, stop and scrape everything into the center of the salad spinner. Fold the ends of the cheesecloth to encase the fruit.

4. Operate your salad spinner—very slowly at first. As you spin, watch the juice that begins to accumulate. Pause and decant into another container as needed. Spin until the pulp runs dry. For freshest flavor, use juice immediately.

APPLE JUICE

In North America, there wouldn't be much reward for suffering through autumn and winter if it weren't for apple cider— spiced with orange peel and cinnamon and served piping hot to sip while picking pumpkins in October, or ice-cold in apple cider cocktails to dull the pain on New Year's Day. Cool temperatures and winter flavors have a natural affinity for the flavor of fresh-pressed apples.

The term *apple cider* can be confusing, because in Europe it refers to a fermented, slightly alcoholic cider (as was imbibed by American settlers heading westward), while generally in the States these days, it means fresh-pressed juice containing no alcohol. And then there's the not-to-be-mentioned apple *juice*, which is the highly filtered, clear golden juice from concentrate that often comes in a little box with a straw attached. Apple juice is for children; apple juice is not for cocktails.

Thanks to a serious outbreak of *E. coli* in some bottled fresh juices, virtually all apple cider sold in the United States and Canada since about the year 2000 has been pasteurized or treated by some other antimicrobial process. This, of course, robs cider of much of its fresh complexity, so it makes sense for technique-oriented bartenders to want to fashion their own. Fortunately, it's a simple task and the reward is a more interesting, fresher ingredient for your cocktails.

EQUIPMENT FOR MAKING APPLE CIDER

For the price of a nice dinner out, you can pick up a new cider press, the kind with the wood-slat pressing tub. It's got some disks inside, and a big metal screw that you turn to slowly press the juice out of the apples. If you want to go this Pennsylvania Dutch route and are planning on going through tubs and tubs of the stuff at a time, be my guest. For the rest of us for whom a cider press will only take up space and collect dust most of the year, I recommend a juice extractor or the MacGyver centrifuge method (see page 36).

PICKING APPLES FOR JUICING

Whole apples are always in season somewhere in the world, so they are on supermarket shelves year-round. But to pick a really good, bright apple, pay attention to where the apple is from. In North America, the season is late August through about November. Apples store well, but beyond, say, February, you may be better off choosing apples from the Southern Hemisphere, where autumn apple season is just revving up. If you don't want to use apples from halfway around the world, find a local producer who stores his apples properly, keeping them quite cold, with proper humidity and ventilation.

Once your apples are at your bar or house, store them in the refrigerator, away from any strong-smelling foods, as they absorb odors easily. Stored in the cold, apples will stay in great condition for up to 10 days.

How much juice will you get? Apples tend to be, at most, about one-third juice, which is a decent yield. Over the years I've learned that 1 lb/455 g of apples will yield just over 5 oz/150 ml of cider; knowing that allows me to plan my prep list accordingly.

APPLE BLEND

The juice of a single variety of apple is going to result in a single apple note in your cocktails. A better solution is a carefully selected blend of apples, which will bring a richer, more nuanced flavor to the drink. My strategy when selecting an apple blend is much like the orchestration of a well-balanced cocktail: I start with a strong apple flavor, balance sweet apples against the tart ones, and add in some accent flavors for complexity and depth.

This is a combination that has never let me down:

2 parts Red Delicious apples for their classic sweet apple flavor

2 parts Granny Smith apples for tartness

1 part Braeburn apples for a rich, dark, spicy component

1 part Honeycrisp apples for crisp, complex brightness

KEEPING THE JUICE FRESH

Once you've made your cider, use it immediately or store it in the fridge, tightly sealed and labeled with a date. Fresh apple cider, with its high sugar content, will begin to ferment in less than a week, even under refrigeration, so I toss it after 4 days.

SHOULD YOU WORRY ABOUT THE SEEDS?

Should you remove the apple seeds before juicing? You'll hear people say that apple seeds are poisonous, as they contain cyanide, but fortunately, that's not entirely correct. Apple seeds (and the seeds of stone fruits, such as apricots, plums, cherries, and peaches) contain a glycoside (basically a sugar molecule bound to another group) called amygdalin, which is broken down by enzymes in the small intestine to produce cyanide gas. That's the bad news.

The good news is that we're talking about incredibly small amounts here, and the human body is equipped to detoxify itself in the event of normal amygdalin consumption. You'd have to eat a gargantuan quantity of apple seeds to do any real harm, but if you're the paranoid type, feel free to take the extra step and discard the seeds before juicing.

FLANNEL SHIRT

MAKES 1 DRINK I developed this recipe with Highland Park Scotch for the StarChefs Rising Star Awards in Portland, Oregon. The event took place in December, and I knew I wanted to do something with Scotch and apple cider that would be served cold. So after coming up with the apple blend described on page 39, I set out to build a cocktail whose other ingredients would play a supportive role in expressing how beautifully Scotch whisky and fresh apple cider pair together.

1¾ oz/50 ml Scotch

1½ oz/45 ml fresh apple cider

½ oz/15 ml Averna amaro

¼ oz/7.5 ml fresh lemon juice

1 tsp/5 ml 2:1 Demerara syrup (see page 78)

½ tsp/2.5 ml St. Elizabeth Allspice Dram

2 dashes Angostura bitters

Ice cubes for shaking

Cracked ice for serving

1 orange peel for garnish

CHILLED OLD-FASHIONED GLASS

Combine the Scotch, apple cider, Averna amaro, lemon juice, Demerara syrup, St. Elizabeth Allspice Dram, and bitters in a cocktail shaker or mixing glass. Shake with ice cubes and strain over the old-fashioned glass filled with cracked ice. Twist the peel over the surface of the cocktail and drop in the drink to serve.

PINEAPPLE JUICE

Pineapple juice practically defines the tiki cocktail category, and fresh pineapple juice is a must if you want to make an honorable tiki drink.

PICKING PINEAPPLES FOR JUICING

This can be slightly tricky, because the skin of a pineapple is thick, rough, and doesn't give a lot of clues. And pineapples are picked ripe; they won't get any riper on your counter. But, fortunately, these days most pineapples are really high-quality and reliably sweet. Look for ones that feel heavy for their size, have a slight give when you squeeze them, and—most important—have a noticeably sweet perfume when you smell them. Del Monte Gold is a variety that you can count on. And don't rely on that old trick of pulling out a leaf, which supposedly will come out easily if the pineapple is ripe. There's no truth to that.

A 3-lb/1.4-kg pineapple should yield about 16 oz/480 ml of juice. Store your pineapple juice in the refrigerator at all times—it's quite perishable—and toss it after 3 days.

KINGSTON CLUB

MAKES 1 DRINK Palates tend to be pretty advanced here in Portland. Maybe it's the weather, maybe it's our intense love for coffee and big, bitter beers. But whatever the reason, I found myself in a bit of a conundrum while trying to put something tiki-inspired on my drink menu: Portlanders demand more depth of flavor than you'll find in most rum-based tropical drinks.

Herbal liqueurs to the rescue. I've always loved working with herbal liqueurs such as Drambuie, and Fernet-Branca makes a solid chunk of their sales from the staff at our restaurant. And behold, the Kingston Club was born.

1½ oz/45 ml Drambuie

1½ oz/45 ml fresh pineapple juice

¾ oz/22.5 ml fresh lime juice

1 tsp/5 ml Fernet-Branca

3 dashes Angostura bitters

1 oz/30 ml chilled soda water

Ice cubes

1 orange twist for garnish

CHILLED COLLINS GLASS

Combine the Drambuie, pineapple juice, lime juice, Fernet-Branca, and bitters in a cocktail shaker or mixing glass. Shake with ice cubes and finish with the soda water. Strain the mix into the chilled collins glass filled with fresh ice, and garnish with the orange twist to serve.

TOMATO JUICE

Oh, to know the joy of a Bloody Mary made with . . . well, no, *not* with fresh tomato juice. This category of juice is the one that goes against the general rule of "fresher is better." There's something odd about a tomato: a truly ripe one is so luscious and intensely flavorful when you eat it out of hand, but once you process it into a puree and then extract the juice, it becomes vegetal, weak, and weirdly frothy. Tomatoes need some sort of heat application to break down the cells in a way that will yield the sweet juice, rather than the other flavors.

This can be good news for the bartender, however, because there are canned tomatoes that will produce a delicious juice that is much better than actual canned tomato juice. And it's easier than procuring and handling fresh ripe tomatoes. Muir Glen organic brand tomatoes are perfect for juicing. Just puree them in a food processor and then strain. Use within 2 days.

Another option, more time-consuming, is to roast fresh tomatoes. Cut ripe tomatoes in half, arrange cut-side up on a rimmed baking sheet, and roast in a 375°F/190°C oven until the tomatoes start to shrivel a bit, about 1 hour (sometimes more, if the tomatoes are really juicy). Slide the tomatoes and their juices into a blender and process until you have a smooth puree. Strain through a fine-mesh sieve to remove seeds and bits of skin.

THE SAN MARZANO HOAX

You may find other canned tomato brands that are equally delicious, but please be wary of so-called San Marzano tomatoes. This is a fabled plum tomato variety from Italy that is said to be incredible; it even has a D.O.P. (*denominazione d'origine protetta*) designation. And the real San Marzanos are in fact great—grown in ideal soil and climate and harvested and processed when fully ripe. Delightful. But there is a brand of canned tomato that calls itself "San Marzano" that is sold in many stores in the United States, mainly because the labeling is attractive (graphically bold white, red, and green). They are in fact from California, and every can I have ever tasted is full of stringy, pale, tasteless tomatoes. Read the label!

POMEGRANATE JUICE

That noble and ancient fruit, the pomegranate, has been the subject of much popular discussion in recent years due to its alleged antioxidant qualities. Originating in Persia, the pomegranate spread across Asia and the Mediterranean in ancient times. Its sweet, dark juice, encapsulated in tiny seeds, figures prominently in Greek mythology; Persephone's unwitting consumption of the fruit and resulting banishment to the underworld for half the year was the Greeks' explanation for the seasons.

PICKING A POMEGRANATE

Pomegranates are in season for only a few months a year (the peak season is November to January), so get them while you can. Pick a smooth-skinned pomegranate, with no cracks or splits, that feels heavy for its size. You'll need to heft a few to find the heaviest.

HOW TO JUICE A POMEGRANATE

Getting the juice out of a pomegranate (say, for Grenadine, page 98) has for a long time confounded and frustrated bartenders. I can't tell you how many professional and home bartenders I've spoken with about the hard work and low yield of fresh pomegranate juice and the tedium of dealing with the seemingly endless number of tiny juice-filled seeds, each waiting to spill a meager drop or two of its messy, staining juice.

I've seen all kinds of methods, usually starting with separating the seeds from the flesh in some laborious process, followed by a multitude of variations on the same theme: getting the juice out of those tiny seeds. I've seen strainers deployed over bowls, while ladles mashed the seeds to separate the juice from the hulls. I've seen pomegranate-filled zip-top bags and rolling pins brought out from the cupboard (no joke), and my personal favorite: boiling the seeds in a shallow pan of water until they popped from the heat and gushed their guts, effectively turning the water a pale shade of pink.

It shocked me that almost nobody I spoke with had tried the obvious: cut the whole pomegranate in half along the equator and place it in a mechanical citrus press (see page 20), as you would a grapefruit. Press to yield a tremendous amount of fresh, dark juice with a minimum of mess and effort required by the bartender.

How much juice will you get? With the mechanical citrus press method, a 12-oz/340-g pomegranate should yield 8 oz/240 ml.

KEEPING THE FRUIT AND JUICE FRESH

You can keep whole pomegranates at room temperature (choose a cool spot) for a few days, and for up to 3 months in a plastic bag in the refrigerator. The juice will last in the fridge up to 3 days and in the freezer for 6 months.

GINGER JUICE

The flavor of fresh juice from ginger is potent and exciting, but not easy to produce. Ginger is tough and extremely fibrous, and the best way to get more than a few drops is by using a juice extractor. Chances are that if you want ginger juice, it's because you want to make ginger syrup. I have an effective and easy method for juicing ginger intended for syrup. See the recipe on page 103. The rest of the time you'll likely be using the juice to make Ginger Beer (page 65).

CHOOSING GINGER FOR JUICE

Ginger dries out quickly, and much of what you'll find in an ordinary grocery store is pretty leathery, and therefore isn't going to yield a lot of juice. Your best source for young, fresh, juicy ginger is an Asian grocery store. Look for hands (that's what the clumps are called) with fat sections and very thin, almost pinkish skin. If you can scrape it off with a fingernail, that's a good sign. If the skin is thicker and more like a brown paper bag, just be sure it isn't shriveled.

HOW TO JUICE GINGER WITH A JUICE EXTRACTOR

If the skin is very thick and tough, you should peel off most of it, just so its woody flavor doesn't taint the juice. For younger, thinner-skinned ginger, you can toss the whole thing into a juice extractor, because the built-in strainer will remove any skin and fiber.

KEEPING GINGER AND ITS JUICE FRESH

There's a lot of debate about how to store ginger to keep it fresh—in a plastic bag, in a bowl of sand (yes, really), or steeped in vodka. I find that more conventional methods, like a plastic bag, keep the ginger fresh for just as long and are a lot less messy than the others.

For a short period, you can just leave the unpeeled hand of ginger on the counter, but for more than 1 or 2 days, wrap it first in a paper towel, and then in a plastic bag and store in the fridge. If you leave out the paper towel, the ginger can get moldy because of the condensed moisture. The juice itself will stay fresh for up to 3 days.

FRUIT PUREES

When the texture of a fruit is very soft, it's difficult to separate the juice from the rest of the cell material. Instead of clear juice running from fibrous pulp, you end up with a homogenous puree—which is delicious and totally appropriate for certain cocktails. A perfect example of fruits that produce a nectar or puree, rather than a clear liquid, are the so-called stone fruits or drupes (peaches, nectarines, apricots, plums, etc). The best way to use this family of summer fruits is by making them into perfectly smooth purees that you can then mix into cocktails.

HOW TO MAKE A FRUIT PUREE

When pureeing small amounts of soft fruit such as raspberries, kiwi, very ripe pear, or grapes, the first option is always the hand-powered one, avoiding the need for electricity or cleanup. A food mill, or even a strainer and ladle, is perfect. See page 34 for the how-to.

To puree fruit such as mangoes, melons, or peaches, or to puree soft fruit in large quantities, you need some power, as in a food processor. It's fast, it's easy, and the results are perfectly acceptable. Simply dump a bunch of fruit into a food processor, puree until smooth, and strain the results through a fine-mesh strainer into the container of your choice.

How to Make a Stone Fruit Puree

This method will work for any stone fruit, including plums, nectarines, peaches (shown here), and of course white peaches, used in the Bellini (page 49).

Start by selecting the ripest, freshest white peaches you can find. Each peach should bring you about 2 oz/60 ml of puree. Peel each peach with a paring knife (I do this over the sink) and remove the pit and stem.

Puree in a food mill if you have one; otherwise puree them in a food processor until smooth. You'll need to run the puree through a sieve or mesh strainer if you're using the processor (see page 34).

Peaches tend to lack the right amount of sugar content unless picked at the height of the season, so sweeten the puree to your particular taste with a little 2:1 simple syrup (see page 78). Bottle in a squeeze bottle and refrigerate until ready to use.

STORING FRUIT PUREES

The luscious texture, fresh flavor, and vibrant color of a newly made fruit puree is perishable, as you can imagine. So as soon as you make one, store it in a sealed container. I keep small amounts of fruit puree in labeled and dated plastic squeeze bottles for ease of measurement later.

Fortunately, fruit purees freeze very well, so you can make large batches when the fruit is at its peak season. Pack them into small freezer bags, label and date, and freeze for up to 6 months, although they will start to lose some quality after around 3 months.

BELLINI

MAKES 1 DRINK There is no classic cocktail that takes advantage of fruit puree quite like the Bellini, a concoction of sparking wine and white peach puree. The drink reflects the same philosophy that Italians have toward food: use only the best ingredients at their peak season, and don't muck them up—let the ingredients speak for themselves.

Unlike so many classic cocktails, there is no dispute over who invented the Bellini, though the date is still fuzzy. Giuseppe Cipriani, founder and owner of the fabled Harry's Bar in Venice, adored the delicately fragrant white peaches that were plentiful during the Italian summer. He "squeezed" one (must have been mighty ripe) and blended the puree with some prosecco. The flavor was like summer in a glass, and the drink had a gorgeous pale pink blush to it, thanks to the little tinge of red flesh that's closest to the pit of a white peach. The drink never left Harry's menu, and in fact he subsequently named a New York restaurant Bellini.

The risk you run with the Bellini is the drink becoming too thick, so that it feels as if you're slurping down peach puree touched with a hint of wine. After toying around with the proportions at my bar for years, we've finally settled on the ratio of 1 part puree to 3 parts prosecco. It's the perfect balance. In an 8-oz/240-ml Champagne flute, this works out perfectly to 1½ oz/45 ml of puree finished with 4½ oz/135 ml of prosecco, leaving a 2-oz/60-ml head space at the top of the glass.

I gotta admit that I'm not the world's biggest fan of prosecco, as it tends to be a little sweeter, simpler, and more one-dimensional than the French or even Spanish sparkling wines I typically seek out. But for this drink, there is absolutely nothing that will work like prosecco. Trust me on this one, as a lot of dry, complex depth is not what you're looking for in this cocktail.

1½ oz/45 ml white peach puree

4½ oz/135 ml chilled prosecco

CHILLED CHAMPAGNE FLUTE

Pour the peach puree in the Champagne flute. Top up slowly with the chilled prosecco. I like to give this one a stir with a chopstick rather than a metal bar spoon, as the Champagne flutes I have at home and in my bar are too delicate to handle with steel implements.

SODAS & MIXERS

LENGTHENING COCKTAILS WITH CARBONATION AND VOLUME

Walking up and down the aisles of your local grocery megastore, and pretty much any run-of-the-mill grocery store in the country, you'll eventually come across an aisle labeled "Mixers." While a lot of the newer, hipper stores with incandescent lighting and the word *organic* plastered all over the place will choose a more elegant label, such as "Sodas" or "Beverages," for their mixers aisle, the big-box stores still hang on to that word: *mixers*.

You take a lap through that aisle and think to yourself, "What in the hell am I supposed to mix with this?" Diet cherry vanilla cola. Grape-flavored soda. Packets of brightly colored powder that you're supposed to pour into your water bottle in order to turn water into a hydrating beverage. And sports drinks, which no one has ever seen being consumed by people who participate in sports.

And then you get to that place we've all seen a million times: It's a skimpy section of shelving somewhere near the end of the aisle, and it's where the real "mixers" live. There are a few bottles of Angostura bitters here, and some bright red maraschino cherries. There's definitely a jar or two of olives, and depending on how fancy the surrounding neighborhood is, there might be some specialty olives stuffed with roasted garlic or something. Neon red grenadine, brighter neon green lime cordial. And then there are the sodas.

They used to always stock something generically labeled as "collins mix" here, but I think that was before everyone figured out it was the same thing as Squirt, or right about the time that people stopped drinking vodka collinses in favor of vodka sodas, heralding the modern quest for fewer calories and even less flavor.

There's tonic water here, as well as diet tonic water, which is not only made with the same artificial quinine as regular tonic water, but sweetened with artificial sweetener to boot. Sour mix was pretty much born and raised in this little section of grocery store shelving, and sometimes it's still referred to by that name, but most often these days it goes by "margarita mix." It's usually sold right next to a small plastic container of kosher salt festooned with a plastic sombrero, labeled "margarita salt."

The unfortunate thing is that even though I'm an experienced bartender with the knowledge and skills to make perfectly executed classic cocktails from fresh ingredients, I'm still conditioned to think of this sad little section of the grocery store any time I hear anyone say the word *mixers*. And I think most other people do, too—which is terrible news for cocktails—because unlike you and me, some people actually make a point of shopping here when it comes time to mix their alcohol with other ingredients. I hope this chapter will change that behavior.

A HISTORY OF CARBONATION

The cultural shift toward intellectualism during the Age of Enlightenment in eighteenth-century Europe encompassed a number of disciplines, from philosophy to ethics, physics to chemistry. Enlightenment-era chemists were obsessed with, and made major advancements in, the search for the fundamental building blocks of the universe, or as we now know them, the elements.

One of the many scientific disciplines that arose at this time was the study of different states of matter. One such state was (and, um, still is) gas. At the time, scientists believed that there were three elemental types of gases, or as they were known at the time, "airs." The first was called "common air," which we now think of as Earth's atmosphere, or the air we breathe—a mixture of nitrogen, oxygen, argon, and other trace gases. The second was named "inflammable air" by Henry Cavendish; we now know it as the element hydrogen. And the third became known as "fixed air" and was observed blanketing fermentation tanks at breweries by a Unitarian minister named Joseph Priestley.

Priestley, unsuccessful at sermonizing thanks in part to a debilitating stutter, was quite the aspiring scientist. In 1767 he published *The History and Present State of Electricity*, partly encouraged by American statesman Benjamin Franklin. That same year, Priestley moved to Leeds, in England, into a house next door to a brewery, where he continued his scientific edification, conducting experiments in and around those fermentation tanks.

He discovered a layer of "air" above the fermentation tanks that held some interesting properties. He noticed that a lit candle, when moved into this layer of air, would quickly and inexplicably extinguish. His next experiment involved mice, often plentiful in and around the sacks of grain found in breweries. He discovered that his poor, unwilling subjects died when exposed to this "air" for several minutes. But it was his greatest experiment that changed the way we drink forever. Priestley noted that when water was poured back and forth between two glasses held in the "air," it became full of tiny bubbles. Joseph Priestley had discovered carbon dioxide.

In 1772, Priestley published a book titled *Impregnating Water with Fixed Air*. In the book he described an intricate process in which "oil of vitriol"—or, as it's called now, sulfuric acid—was dripped onto limestone to produce carbon dioxide gas, which was then to be dissolved in water. It was the world's first process to carbonate water artificially. But why go to all that trouble for what we now think of as a refreshing, yet still unnecessary, in the grand scheme of things, beverage? Quite simply, Priestley was convinced that the carbonated water was medicine, a possible cure for scurvy, a common ailment among sailors who often spent months at a time at sea. We now know that scurvy is the result of a vitamin C deficiency, a consequence of having no access to fresh fruits and vegetables on long voyages. Priestley tried, unsuccessfully, to sell the new process for carbonating water to the Royal Navy. Instead, he ended up teaching the crew of James Cook's second South Seas voyage the process after being turned down for the position of ship's astronomer. They likely still suffered from scurvy, but at least they had some delicious sparkling water on their voyage.

CARBONATED WATER AS HEALTH TONIC

At around the same time, the German town of Niederselters had something very special on its hands. The city possessed a unique mineral water spring, which was, oddly enough, lightly carbonated. My personal theory is that there was, deep underground, a mixture of sulfuric acid and limestone mixing with the water to infuse it with carbon dioxide gas, much like in Joseph Priestley's artificial carbonation process.

As early as 1728, the town's water was sold across Europe as a sort of tonic in the newly popular health spas. The spring water was bottled in earthenware jugs and sealed with tar to keep the carbonation intact. Spas had been enjoying a recent resurgence in Europe, as a sort of destination cure for all manner of ailments, from arthritis to pneumonia. The town's "Selters water" soon became all the rage in such resorts, eventually giving rise to the generic term *seltzer water*.

MECHANICAL CARBONATION

Johann Jacob Schweppe, a German watchmaker living in Switzerland, learned of Priestley's method of dripping sulfuric acid onto limestone to produce carbon dioxide gas and, using his machinist's skills, became the first to develop a manufacturing process to artificially carbonate mineral water. The Schweppes Company was founded in Geneva in 1783 and is still operating today, as part of a larger company.

Europe's thirst for carbonated water remained unquenched, and in 1813 a man named Charles Plinth created the first portable soda siphon, which could be mounted onto horse-drawn carts, spreading the popularity of the drink around London. As early as 1814, a waiter working at Limmer's Hotel on Conduit Street, in London, had a very popular gin punch on his hands. The recipe called for gin, lemon juice, and sugar, and was lengthened with soda water, quite possibly provided by one of Plinth's portable soda carts.

The waiter's name was John Collins, and the punch was named after him. Supposedly, the drink was originally made with Holland or Jenever gin, which is a maltier, richer, and more oily version of the dry gins we consume today. As illegal home distilling became more common and gave rise to the Old Tom style of sweetened English gin, the drink took on a slight name change, which would become a permanent one: Tom Collins.

HOW CARBONATION WORKS

Carbonation is the common term for the dissolution of carbon dioxide (CO_2) into water. Carbonation being a chemical reaction, there are some basic rules to know, and knowing those rules will help you make your drinks better.

The first rule is that carbon dioxide is much more soluble in cold water than in warm water. So what does this mean for us? Well, it means that we'll want to keep any carbonated beverages or ingredients, be they beer, sparkling water, Champagne, or Coca-Cola, as cold as possible to ensure that as much of that CO_2 stays in solution once the bottle's been opened.

Carbonation also relies on pressure to maintain solution, and since CO_2 wants to be at equilibrium with its system, a low-pressure system such as Earth's atmosphere will result in a loss of carbonation. In layman's terms, this means that once that bottle has been opened and exposed to the atmosphere here on Earth, the carbon dioxide wants to escape. So keep those bottles closed until they're ready to be used.

It's important to remember that a carbonated drink served over ice contains billions and billions of places for bubbles to form, which are called nucleation sites. As a result, the drink will lose its carbonation more quickly than one served in a bottle or a glass without ice, which has fewer nucleation sites.

It's also important to note that when carbon dioxide (CO_2) is dissolved in water (H_2O), there is a reaction that takes place that produces a small amount of carbonic acid (H_2CO_3). This is applicable to cocktails, because it means that carbonated drinks are slightly more acidic, and therefore taste less sweet than noncarbonated drinks. Adjust your recipes as needed.

Carbonation reaches equilibrium with its system

TOM COLLINS

MAKES 1 DRINK The first recipe for a single-serving Tom Collins appeared in the 1876 edition of Jerry Thomas's *The Bar-Tender's Guide*. By this time, sparkling cocktails such as collinses and fizzes were a mainstay of American bar culture.

I can't think of many more refreshing drinks than a perfectly carbonated Tom Collins. It's the sort of thing I'll whip up at a party when the only things on hand are a little gin, some fresh lemons, sugar, and soda water. A Tom Collins is just one of those drinks that always seems to wow people when made correctly.

I find that adding soda to the glass once the drink has been shaken and strained over ice merely results in a layer of cocktail and a layer of soda. I always add the soda directly to the shaker once I'm done shaking the drink, and I never double-strain; the fine strainer provides too many nucleation sites, which help dissipate that carbon dioxide too quickly.

2 oz/60 ml gin, preferably in the Old Tom style, such as Hayman's

¾ oz/22.5 ml fresh lemon juice (see page 22)

½ oz/15 ml 2:1 simple syrup (see page 78)

Ice cubes

2 oz/60 ml chilled soda water

1 lemon peel for garnish

CHILLED COLLINS GLASS

Combine the gin, lemon juice, and simple syrup in a cocktail shaker or mixing glass. Shake with ice cubes and add the soda water to the contents of the shaker.

Strain into the chilled collins glass filled with fresh ice. Twist the peel over the surface of the cocktail and drop in the drink to serve.

SODA WATER

Today the modern bartender has a number of options for carbonated water in cocktails. The simplest, and certainly least sustainable, method is to purchase bottled soda water, also known as sparkling water. There are a number of companies willing to separate you from your money in this department, each touting a long-standing European tradition of mineral-rich water textured with all manner of carbonation and bubble size. Take your pick and choose your favorite if heading down this road, but always remember to keep your bottles well chilled in the fridge in order to maximize the life of the carbonation.

MAKING YOUR OWN SODA

Carbonating your own water means less wasted plastic and less transportation energy. It also means you can make exactly as much soda you want, when you want it—not to mention the additional control it gives you over your costs.

How to Use a Soda Siphon

A good, though somewhat involved, technique is to use a soda siphon, such as the type made by Liss or iSi. Begin by filling the siphon according to the manufacturer's instructions with cold filtered tap water. This first step is important to remove any lingering impurities or flavors in the municipal water system. At home I lean toward the Brita system, although there are certainly many other options out there for both commercial and home use.

Next, attach the head to the canister and fit a CO_2 cartridge into the unit. You'll hear the hiss of gas as it fills the unit; once you can't hear it any longer, make sure the gas is completely dissolved in the water by shaking the canister hard for 10 seconds. Don't worry, the unit isn't going to explode on you.

At this point, you're ready to rock. Simply depress the lever on the side of the head gently to dispense carbonated water, much like a circus clown. Just make sure you don't hit anyone in the face. These soda siphons are great for quickly carbonating water and keeping it fresh, but I do find that discharging requires a gentle touch if you're trying to fill a jigger to measure.

Other Ways to Carbonate

Pouring from a bottle is a more gentle way to dispense carbonated water, and, fortunately, these days there are companies that make such contraptions for bottling water at home. Sodastream is one such company, and although their unit is somewhat bulky (taking up as much counter space as a small coffee machine), it fills sealable glass carafes with the water, which makes for nicely bottled water in a beautiful package.

The Fizz Giz makes a pretty cool portable unit that I like to throw into my bar tool bag. The carbonator is handheld and fits into a custom-designed bottle cap, which should screw onto some standard plastic water or soda bottles, though finding one whose threads exactly match those of the Fizz Giz can be a frustrating game of trial and error.

TONIC WATER

Quinine, the bitter compound that forms the base for tonic water, has a mythical and turbulent past. The bark of the quinquina tree was known to Peruvian Incas to have a very special property: when ground and mixed with hot or cold water and consumed as a sort of tea, it stopped the body from shivering in the cold. We now know that quinine is a mild muscle relaxant.

I would argue that Jesuit missionaries, exploring the New World and grabbing everything they could get their hands on, took notice of this peculiar phenomenon. Since shivering was one of the symptoms of malaria, a disease that had been ravaging Europe for centuries, they probably figured that whatever stopped the shivering would stop the disease. Their guess proved to be sound, even if their reasoning wasn't: quinine kills the microorganism in the blood that causes malaria. The shivers are merely a symptom.

Regardless, the bark quickly became a well-known malaria preventative in Europe, worth its weight in gold as Peruvian supplies quickly dwindled. By 1862, the Dutch had smuggled seeds out of Peru and set up cinchona (as it became known) plantations in Java, Indonesia. By the 1930s, Java grew to be the world's primary source of quinine to the tune of a 95 percent market share.

Quinine was consumed by those working for the British East India Company in India. The tonic was made more palatable by the added novelty of carbonated water. Since the most common liquor imbibed by the British at the time was gin, it became a natural addition to the medicinal tonic. In the early 1800s, the gin and tonic was born.

MAKING TONIC WATER

I began my first experiments with house-made tonic water in 2007. I was looking for a tonic with more assertive flavors and natural ingredients than those found in commercial tonic water. A glance at the standard-issue tonic available at most bars and restaurants reveals the lack of flavor even before you open the bottle. Just look at the ingredients: water, high fructose corn syrup, citric acid, sodium benzoate, and quinine. I thought we could do better.

Conversely, my issue with most homemade tonic water was that it had *too* assertive a flavor profile for the general public. Even my own first recipe, which was lauded by bartenders and home mixologists all over the Internet and in newspapers, I personally found to be muddy, dirty, earthy, and, quite frankly, a bit tough to drink.

I set out, yet again, in search of a tonic recipe that I could be proud of, and that I would enjoy drinking. It finally dawned on me that if I made a tincture of quinine, and then made a quinine syrup, I could have more control over the flavor of the whole drink. This is the formula I landed on:

Mix 1 part Quinine Syrup (facing page) to 3 parts soda water. Or mix 1 part Quinine Syrup to 3 parts still water and carbonate using a carbonator.

QUININE SYRUP

MAKES 28 OZ/830 ML, WITH ENOUGH TINCTURE LEFT OVER FOR 2 MORE BATCHES You can buy cinchona, whole gentian root, and soft-stick cinnamon in bulk from retailers of herbal medicine and other specialty herb shops. And please use a scale for measurement; it makes a difference. I'm keeping the quantities in metric weights because it's important to be precise. Any electronic scale will have a setting for metrics as well as U.S. weights.

Quinine Tincture

6 g powdered cinchona bark (red will be more assertive, yellow is milder and less bitter)

150 ml vodka

Aromatics

20 g citric acid

10 g whole gentian root

2 g Ceylon soft-stick cinnamon, broken by hand into small pieces

30 g lemon peel, peeled with a vegetable peeler

30 g grapefruit peel, peeled with a vegetable peeler

400 g sugar

500 ml water

To make the tincture: Dissolve the powdered cinchona bark in the vodka. Mix well, and then strain through a paper coffee filter fitted into a strainer (or a filter cone, if you have one) and suspended over a large enough container to accommodate the final volume of vodka. This process could take up to 1 hour, so don't worry if it seems like nothing is happening. (The tincture lasts forever.)

To make the aromatics: Combine all the ingredients for the aromatics in a medium saucepan. Heat over medium heat just until boiling, reduce the heat to low, and simmer, covered, for 20 minutes. Strain out the solids and let the liquid cool.

Stir 1½ oz/45 ml of the quinine tincture into the cooled aromatics, and then bottle. Seal tightly and store in the refrigerator for up to 2 weeks.

GIN AND TONIC

MAKES 1 DRINK There are gin and tonics, and then there are Gin and Tonics. This is one you won't be embarrassed to serve your guests. I make pitcher after pitcher every summer for friends to sip in the backyard.

2 oz/60 ml London dry or
Plymouth gin

½ oz/15 ml Quinine Syrup (page 59)

1½ oz/45 ml chilled soda water

Ice cubes

1 lime wedge for garnish

OLD-FASHIONED GLASS

Combine the gin, quinine syrup, and soda water in the old-fashioned glass and fill with ice cubes. Garnish with the lime wedge to serve.

GINGER BEER

MAKES 1 GL/3.8 L Back in that supermarket mixers section, there are probably a couple of brands of ginger ale, which is more often than not an artificially flavored beverage, sweetened with high fructose corn syrup and best served to children with upset tummies. I even keep a can or two of the stuff in the fridge for when I'm not feeling well.

But ginger *beer* is a completely different animal. The early predecessor to Canadian-born ginger ale, ginger beer first began life in England as a fermented, slightly alcoholic beverage made of fresh ginger, lemon, sugar, water, and a yeast and bacteria compound commonly known as "ginger beer plant." Ginger beer plant is a live organism composed of *Saccharomyces florentinus* yeast and *Lactobacillus hilgardii* bacteria, and is in the same family of bacteria that are used to make kombucha tea, vinegar, and sourdough bread.

It would probably be very "authentic nineteenth-century England" to find or culture ginger beer plant and use that for fermentation, but I've grown to really like the results I've gotten from Champagne yeast. It's easy and inexpensive. I reach for the Red Star Premier Cuvée brand when I'm at the home-brew shop.

Over the years I have developed a series of ginger beer recipes for use at home and in my bars, one of which I published on my website in 2008, and got a great response. But the version we've used for the past several years is the one I'll publish here, a lighter, slightly drier style of the one on my website.

I've always advocated the use of 16-oz/480-ml flip-top bottles, available at any home-brewing supply store. But these days we bottle in 12-oz/360-ml amber beer bottles, and cap them with a bottle capper, also available at home-brew shops. I find that the rubber gasket that comes with the flip-top bottles tends to wear out, resulting in a flat bottle here or there, so the bottle cap route should be the professional's choice.

Since most bartenders and enthusiasts aren't going to be making a single bottle at a time, I'm providing a recipe that makes 1 gl/3.8 L of ginger beer. Doing a little math reveals that this will yield eight 16-oz/480-ml bottles, or eleven 12-oz/360-ml bottles. Make sure you've got enough of whichever bottle size you choose on hand before starting this project.

9¼ cups/2.2 L warm water

10 oz/300 ml ginger juice, juiced from approximately 1 lb/455 g fresh ginger (see page 45)

16 oz/480 ml fresh lemon juice, finely strained (see page 22)

28 oz/840 ml 1:1 simple syrup (see page 78)

1 packet Champagne yeast

EIGHT 16-OZ/480-ML BOTTLES OR ELEVEN 12-OZ/360-ML BOTTLES

continued

If you don't really want to measure out the 9¼ cups/2.2 L of warm water you will need, and I know I don't, you can simply combine the ginger juice, lemon juice, and simple syrup in a 1-gl/3.8-L container and top the whole shebang off with enough warm water to bring the volume to 1 gl/3.8 L. Or you can combine the the ginger juice, lemon juice, and simple syrup in a large container and add exactly 9¼ cups/2.2 L of water. It's your choice.

Next, mix that up very, very well. We definitely don't want this mixture to be anything but perfectly homogenous. Stir it for a couple of minutes, or if you're using a 1-gl/3.8-L container with a lid (I find that used water jugs with screw-on lids work well for this project), give it a shake for a minute or two.

The next trick is the yeast. You don't need much to get the job done, so I take a small paring knife, dip the knife point into the yeast packet until I've got about ½ in/12 mm of yeast covering the tip of that blade (a small paring knife is a perfect tool for this), and then slip the yeast into the neck of each clean, dry bottle.

Now, using a funnel, fill each bottle with your ginger beer mixture and cap or seal. I like to make sure everything's well mixed, so once I've got that bottle sealed, I give it a good, hard shake for at least 10 seconds. Find a warm, dark space (under the kitchen sink works well) and let the bottles sit for exactly 48 hours.

During this time your ginger beer is going to undergo a little transformation. The yeast will soon spring to life and begin devouring those sugar molecules, converting them into the three by-products of the fermentation process: a little bit of heat, a trace amount of alcohol, and a whole lot of carbon dioxide gas. After 48 hours you should have enough gas in the bottles to warrant stopping the fermentation process, so your bottles don't explode.

Popping your ginger beer into a cold fridge will stop this process. Once cold, your ginger beer is ready to enjoy. Be sure to keep your ginger beer refrigerated at all times; it will last up to 1 week.

I might suggest using your Chinese Five-Spiced Dark Rum (page 128) and mixing up a spiced Dark and Stormy (page 68).

DARK AND STORMY

MAKES 1 DRINK A Dark and Stormy is one of my favorite drinks in spring, when the weather here in the Pacific Northwest is warm, but the clouds are heavy and full of rain. Sitting out on a covered porch watching the rain clouds roll in is always better with one of these sunny refreshers in hand.

But sometimes, during our long, dark, cold winters, we need a little refreshment, too. So we came up with this version, "winterized" slightly with the Christmas-y scent of Chinese five-spice powder.

Cracked ice

2 oz/60 ml Chinese Five-Spiced
Dark Rum (page 128)

4 oz/120 ml Ginger Beer (page 65)

1 lime wedge for garnish

CHILLED COLLINS GLASS

Fill the glass with cracked ice and add the spiced rum and ginger beer. Stir with a chopstick or bar spoon, and garnish with the lime to serve.

SPARKLING WINE

But what about that other sparkling beverage so wonderful in cocktails: sparkling wine? There's a whole category of cocktails built around sparkling wines, whether actual Champagne, prosecco, cava, or one of the many crémants from France, or a less traditional sparkling wine, such as those from California.

When you use sparkling wine as a mixer, as opposed to serving it as a stand-alone beverage, you're more likely to have some left over in the bottle. Dumping out a plastic 2-liter bottle of generic soda water hurts a hell of a lot less than a bottle of French sparkling wine, but as it turns out, there are a couple of options to help keep the carbon dioxide in the liquid, where it belongs.

Your first option is the cheapest and the simplest. For next to nothing you can pick up a good Champagne stopper. Look for the stainless-steel type with two wings, which fold down and clamp on to the neck of the bottle. I usually pick up a few different types to accommodate bottle variations, and go with the one that feels like it locks down the tightest to prevent any gas from escaping. Using this method should keep your bubbly, uh, bubbly for a day or so.

A better, albeit more expensive, option is made by Perlage System. The unit is basically a three-piece Lexan shell that screws together at the base and completely encapsulates the open bottle of sparkling wine. A valve allows carbon dioxide to be pumped into the bottle, which keeps the wine at the same pressurized state as before it was opened. The company claims that freshness and carbonation will last weeks or even months.

FRENCH 75

MAKES 1 DRINK The 1919 edition of Harry MacElhone's *Harry's ABC of Mixing Cocktails* contains the first printed recipe for a drink surprisingly similar to a Tom Collins, but calling for sparkling wine in place of the sparkling water. Made with London dry gin, which was prevalent at the time, the drink is named the French 75 and credited to a bartender by the name of Malachy McGarry, of Buck's Club in London.

For me, nothing epitomizes the use of sparkling wine in a classic cocktail like the French 75. But for the longest time, I didn't really see the drink's appeal; it's a little gin, a little lemon, and a little sugar thrown into a Champagne flute, with some sparking wine on top and maybe a sad little lemon peel floating around. But then I realized something while perusing old bar books: the French 75 is basically a dressed-up Tom Collins! And once I took the collins approach and served it on the rocks as the original recipe states, I began to see what a truly refreshing and inspired cocktail this is.

1 oz/30 ml London dry gin

1 oz/30 ml fresh lemon juice
(see page 22)

½ oz/15 ml 2:1 simple syrup
(see page 78)

Cracked ice

2 oz/60 ml Champagne or
sparkling wine

1 lemon peel for garnish

CHILLED COLLINS GLASS

Combine the gin, lemon juice, and simple syrup in a cocktail shaker or mixing glass. Fill with cracked ice and shake. Add the Champagne to the shaker. Strain into the collins glass. Twist the peel over the surface of the cocktail and drop in the drink to serve.

SIMPLE SYRUPS

THE PARADOX OF SIMPLICITY

A simple syrup is the original, the most basic, and generally one of the most common ways to add sweetness to a cocktail. And on the surface, simple syrup lives up to its name: measure water, measure sugar, mix together. Simple, right?

Not exactly. I can't even begin to tell you how many bartenders I've met who don't make simple syrup correctly. Sometimes it's because they're not paying attention to detail, but usually it's because they don't understand the basic principles behind it, the ones you're about to learn here. More often than not, it's some rock star mixologist who creates works of art behind his own bar but has a hell of a time figuring out why his drinks taste so different when someone else is making them. Not using the right technique at home, when you're making a drink for yourself and adjusting to taste, probably will not have any far-reaching consequences, but in a professional bar, where consistency is of paramount importance, it most certainly will.

So why go to all the trouble of making a syrup when you should just be able to toss in a spoonful of sugar? As anyone who's ever tried stirring a packet of sugar into a tall glass of iced tea on a warm summer day knows, the best one can hope for is a slightly sweeter beverage and a sad little layer of undissolved crystals at the bottom of the glass. Sugar doesn't dissolve well in cold liquid, and it definitely doesn't dissolve in alcohol, so when we're sweetening cocktails, we use simple syrup instead. In this form, the sugar is already dissolved, so the sweetener will be incorporated quickly and completely into the drink and produce a smooth, uniform cocktail.

SELECTING THE RIGHT SUGAR

You can choose from a range of sugars when making your simple syrup. We keep a variety of syrups made from most of these sugars on hand at my bar, as do many cocktail bars around the world. Their primary purpose is to sweeten, of course, but we find that each one brings some subtle flavor nuances of the source sweetener to the cocktail.

WHITE SUGAR

The most common bar simple syrup is made from refined, granulated sucrose; it's the white stuff you find in bags and boxes, and packets and shakers, all over the world. White sugar is made from either sugar beets or sugarcane and is cheap, sweet, and almost flavorless—the economy car of sweeteners. It doesn't interfere with other ingredients in a cocktail by bringing any of its own flavors to the party, so I use it when making simple two- or three-ingredient cocktails and want to highlight those basic flavors without adding another dimension to the drink.

There are two types of white sugar: granulated sugar, which is the stuff you're probably most familiar with, and superfine sugar, which is granulated sugar that's been ground into finer crystals. Also known as "caster sugar" or "baker's sugar," superfine has the same volume-to-weight ratio as granulated. For example, 1 cup equals 7 oz/200 g for both granulated and superfine.

We typically don't use powdered or confectioners' sugar in simple syrups, because it contains about 3 percent cornstarch, which is added to prevent clumping. Using powdered sugar is going give you a slightly thickened, scummy syrup—definitely not what you're looking for.

BROWN SUGAR

Despite a somewhat rustic look and flavor, brown sugar is even more processed than white sugar, because it's actually highly refined white sugar with molasses added at the end of the process for flavoring and moisture.

Light brown sugar is 3.5 percent molasses, and dark brown sugar is 6.5 percent. Both are suitable for cocktails; make your choice according to how much molasses flavor you'd like. I prefer a dark brown sugar syrup, and I use it almost exclusively when making an Irish Coffee (page 150).

RAW SUGAR

Turbinado sugar and Demerara sugar are the two common names for what is essentially unprocessed sugar. They are both light amber sugars with fairly large crystals made from pressing sugarcane to extract the juice, letting the cane juice dry to become syrupy, and then crystallizing it. The name Demerara comes from the former Dutch colony in what is now Guyana, but these days Demerara sugar is mostly produced in Mauritius, an island in the Indian Ocean.

Turbinado sugar, named for the centrifuge used to extract the cane juice, is made primarily in Hawaii. You'll find this style of sugar sold under the brand name Sugar in the Raw, which is how many people now refer to it. Both of these sugars have more flavor than white sugar, with just a hint of caramel and molasses. Raw sugars are great in spirit-driven rum drinks.

MUSCOVADO SUGAR

This brown sugar has the most character. It's not always easy to find, but it's worth seeking out at specialty grocery stores for its more complex, deep molasses flavor and aroma.

Muscovado is produced by pressing fresh cane juice and then cooking it a bit before drying and crystallizing it, giving it a deeper caramel flavor than regular raw sugars. The texture is both fine and very moist, and the color is the darkest brown of all the sugars. Muscovado is used in the production of some rums and brings with it an exotic aura. It shines beautifully in tiki-style drinks.

HONEY

Even though honey technically comes from the hive already in syrup form, it's so thick that it won't dissolve in a cocktail without further dilution. So I like to prepare it as a simple syrup.

Be aware that the flavor of honey can vary radically, depending on its source. A generic honey in a little plastic bear from the grocery store will offer mostly sweetness with a touch of characteristic honey flavor. But single-source honeys range from the citrus-y notes of an acacia honey to the downright husky and grainy flavor of a buckwheat honey— delicious and fun to pair with other flavors. Just be sure to taste your farmers' market honey before making your syrup, so that you know what flavors you're bringing to your cocktails.

AGAVE SYRUP

Agave syrup, also called agave nectar, is made from two varieties of agave plant, which is also the source of tequila and mezcal. Agave syrup is about one and a half times sweeter than white sugar, and it's also sweeter than honey, though thinner and less viscous.

In recent years, agave has developed a reputation among health-conscious consumers for being more healthful than cane or beet sugars. This comes from the misconception that agave syrup is less processed than sugar. Actually, although it does have a lower glycemic index than sucrose products, most agave syrup is a highly processed, industrially produced sweetener that is no better than high fructose corn syrup. If you're okay with that, go ahead and use whatever you can find. But you can also seek out smaller producers who work with local farmers to provide an organic, less processed, lower fructose product. Your taste buds will thank you. Light agave syrups are fairly neutral in flavor, but some of the darker, more artisanal versions taste something like a blend of honey, caramel, and stewed pineapple. The syrup is showing up in cocktails around the world; it adds another layer of agave flavor to tequila and mezcal cocktails.

MAPLE SYRUP

Perhaps less common in cocktails than any of the previous sweeteners, maple syrup can bring a fantastic character to a drink, provided you know how to use some restraint. As with honey and agave syrups, we need to dilute maple syrup to create a component that's easily incorporated into a cocktail and delivers a consistent dose of sweetness.

Maple syrup is sold in two grades—A and B—and paradoxically, grade B is the favorite among those of us who care about flavor. Deeper, and slightly smokier than the premium grade A, grade B is just more interesting and complex. Unfortunately, it's not always easy to find in grocery stores, so you may need to seek out a specialty grocer or shop online.

CALORIE COUNTS FOR SUGARS

TYPE OF SUGAR	CALORIES PER TEASPOON
White sugar	16
Raw sugar	15
Brown sugar	15
Muscovado sugar	15
Honey	20
Agave syrup	20
Maple syrup	17

A SUGAR IS A SUGAR IS A SUGAR

Despite very different appearances and flavors, all sugars are quite similar chemically. Whether golden honey, moist brown sugar, or sparkling white superfine granulated, the sweeteners are some combination of two simple sugar molecules: glucose and fructose. White and brown sugars are a combination of both, while more "natural" sugars such as honey, maple syrup, and agave syrup are mostly fructose (as is corn syrup, which we don't generally use in cocktail making).

Some people feel that the less-refined sugars and syrups are more healthful—for example, that honey is better than granulated sugar. It's true that our bodies process each type of sugar slightly differently—glucose goes directly into the bloodstream, while fructose is metabolized first in the liver to become glucose. But most of the science indicates that sugar is sugar is sugar as far as nutrition is concerned. You do get added minerals or other beneficial ingredients from minimally processed sugars, but not enough to be significant, other than from a philosophical point of view.

MEASURING YOUR INGREDIENTS FOR SIMPLE SYRUP

Simple syrup is generally found in two strengths: Equal parts sugar and water, the most common strength in U.S. bars, is referred to as "one-to-one" (1:1). Two parts sugar to one part water is, as you might guess, referred to as 2:1, which is the standard syrup in U.K. bars; in the States, you'll often hear 2:1 syrup being referred to as "rich simple syrup."

You can measure your syrup ingredients by volume (with a measuring cup) or by weight (using a scale). Volume is certainly the most common method in the States, and by far the easiest to describe: Use the same 1-cup/240-ml measure for the sugar and hot water, and stir them together until the sugar is dissolved into the water. But the volume method doesn't really allow for enough precision for my obsessive-compulsive tastes. First off, 8 fl oz/240 ml (the volume measure) of sugar *weighs* closer to 7 oz/200 g, so our 1:1 ratio is actually ⅞:1.

WHY CRYSTAL STRUCTURE MATTERS

Mathematics aside, let's think about what those sugar crystals look like close up. Picture a measuring cup full of little blocks, and in between each little block is a gap of air. You can imagine that some of those little blocks are going to line up better than others, and that the number of blocks in the measuring cup is going to depend on how well aligned all those blocks are.

For granulated or superfine sugar, alignment isn't a big issue, because the crystals are small and they fill the volume measure pretty much the same way each time. However, chunkier sugars and the moist brown sugars can be hugely variable. A very fluffy brown sugar will take up more space in the measuring cup than one that has been compacted through sitting on the shelf for some time. The 1-cup/240-ml measure of fluffy sugar would yield less actual sugar—and more air—than the same measure of packed sugar.

Different Densities of the Same Volume of Sugar

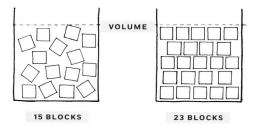

15 BLOCKS   23 BLOCKS

A more accurate method is to measure your sugars and water by weight. Stick a cup or bowl on a scale, tare it out to 0, and then weigh out 8 oz/225 g of sugar and 8 oz/225 g of water.

DISSOLVING THE SUGAR IN THE WATER

Once you've weighed ingredients, the next step is to dissolve the sugar in the water. As with so many things in bartending, there are two schools of thought:

Hot Process

This is the method I prefer, as do most bartenders I know. All you do is gently heat the sugar and water while stirring to dissolve

the sugar, and promptly remove from the heat once all the sugar is dissolved. (Remember from our iced tea example, sugar is more soluble in hot liquid than in cold.) Take care not to let the syrup actually boil, as this will evaporate the water and change the ratio of water to sugar.

Sterilize your bottle or jar by filling it with boiling water; pour some over the lid, too. Dump the water out right before you fill with the hot syrup.

Cold Process

With this method you make the simple syrup with room-temperature water, usually through agitation such as stirring or shaking. You'll hear bartenders advocating for cold-process simple syrup because it prevents the sucrose from separating into glucose and fructose molecules. I even read an interview with one guy who stated firmly that he uses only cold-processed simple syrup to retain that "fresh, uncooked cane flavor" as if that weren't absolute b.s. Sure, sucrose breaking down into glucose and fructose is what happens to some extent during cooking, but it takes a hell of a lot of time and heat to do it. I've yet to hear any real convincing arguments in favor of cold-method mixing, and in blind taste tests I've always chosen the hot-processed simple syrup. It's less work and has a longer shelf life because it has been sterilized by the higher temperature. Skip the cold process and use a little heat.

STORING THE SYRUP

Sugar is used in cooking as a preservative—think jams and jellies, which are also called preserves. So simple syrups have a decent shelf life, when prepared and stored properly: made with very hot water and stored in a sterile container in the refrigerator.

But *decent* doesn't mean interminable—left too long, your syrup can get moldy, so make only quantities that you're likely to use within a reasonable time frame. Stored in the refrigerator, 1:1 hot-process simple syrup should last 1 month, while 2:1 simple syrup should last 6 months. Cold-process syrups can become moldy in as little as half that time.

SUGAR SYRUPS IN COCKTAILS

Back in the eighteenth and nineteenth centuries, there were, as there are today, many different types of drinks. There were punches. There were juleps. There were cobblers and smashes, crustas and sangarees, flips and noggs. And there were cocktails. A legacy of these early cocktails is our frequent use of sugar syrups today.

The first printed definition of the word *cocktail* came from the Hudson, New York, newspaper *The Balance and Columbian Repository* in 1806. When asked by a subscriber what this (relatively) new word *cock-tail* meant, the editor replied:

> Cock-tail is a stimulating liquor, composed of spirits of any kind, sugar, water, and bitters—it is vulgarly called bittered sling, and is supposed to be an excellent electioneering potion, inasmuch as it renders the heart stout and bold, at the same time that it fuddles the head. It is said, also to be of great use to a democratic candidate: because a person, having swallowed a glass of it, is ready to swallow any thing else.

Hilarious political commentary aside, this crude formula—any type of spirit, sugar, water, and bitters—is not a bad formula for a family of drinks. Jerry Thomas's *The Bar-Tender's Guide* (1862) was the first book of drink recipes ever published in the United States. He describes how to make a whiskey cocktail within:

3 or 4 dashes of gum syrup [see page 93]

2 dashes of bitters (Bogart's)

1 wineglass of whiskey, and a piece of lemon peel.

Fill one-third full of fine ice; shake and strain in a fancy red wineglass.

If the drink is beginning to sound at all familiar, it is because it is the same drink we typically think of as an old-fashioned today. It is believed that once the word *cocktail* took hold, all drinks became known as *cocktails* (as they still are), and old-timers looking for that original formula might ask the bartender for a cocktail "in the old fashion."

One trick that many cocktail-minded bartenders like to keep up their sleeves these days is the old-fashioned variation. Put simply, we'll make an old-fashioned cocktail with a base spirit, and then match the sweetener to the base.

HOUSE OLD-FASHIONED

MAKES 1 DRINK This is the standard old-fashioned we make at my bar. The formula has never disappointed even the most discerning classic cocktail drinker, but then again it's pretty much cribbed word for word from Jerry Thomas (save for the Bogart's bitters, which are sadly still extinct at the time of this writing).

1 tsp/5 ml 2:1 simple syrup
(see page 78)

2 dashes Angostura bitters

2 oz/60 ml bourbon whiskey

Large ice cubes

1 orange peel for garnish

CHILLED OLD-FASHIONED GLASS

Combine the simple syrup, bitters, and bourbon in a mixing glass and stir with ice cubes. Strain over fresh ice into an old-fashioned glass. Twist the peel over the surface of the cocktail, rub the rim of the glass with the peel, and drop in the drink to serve.

RUM OLD-FASHIONED

MAKES 1 DRINK Occasionally we'll encounter rum drinkers who may have been exposed to the spirit only through tropical fruit-based concoctions. So when we're asked to whip up something different with rum, this is often the first drink we'll turn to.

1 tsp/5 ml 1:1 Demerara syrup
(see page 78)

2 dashes House Orange Bitters
(page 138)

2 oz/60 ml 12-year rum

Large ice cubes

1 lime peel for garnish

CHILLED OLD-FASHIONED GLASS

Combine the Demerara syrup, bitters, and rum in a mixing glass and stir with ice cubes. Strain over fresh ice into an old-fashioned glass. Twist the peel over the surface of the cocktail, rub the rim of the glass with the peel, and drop in the drink to serve.

OAXACA OLD-FASHIONED

MAKES 1 DRINK There are few people in the world as passionate about Mexico's native spirits as Phil Ward. Proprietor of Mayahuel, in New York, Phil lives, eats, and breathes agave. He created this drink in 2007, at the New York bar Death + Company, to rave reviews. It was certainly one of the most ingenious uses of tequila and mezcal I'd ever heard of, and it's tucked into many bartenders' back pockets as a go-to agave cocktail these days.

1½ oz/45 ml reposado tequila

½ oz/15 ml mezcal

1 tsp/5 ml 2:1 agave simple syrup
(see page 78, made with agave syrup)

2 dashes Bittermens Xocolatl Mole
bitters

Large ice cubes

Wide swath of grapefruit peel for
garnish

CHILLED OLD-FASHIONED GLASS

Combine the tequila, mezcal, simple syrup, and bitters in a mixing glass and stir with ice cubes. Strain over fresh ice into an old-fashioned glass. Twist the peel over the surface of the cocktail, rub the rim of the glass with the peel, and drop in the drink to serve.

MAPLE OLD-FASHIONED

MAKES 1 DRINK Sometimes pairing the sweetener with the base spirit is about using the same raw ingredient, as is the case with the Rum and Oaxaca Old-Fashioned (at left). But at other times it's about invoking a range of flavors that are familiar to the region, as is the case with this drink. Maple syrup and whisky work wonderfully together, and the high cinnamon content of the bitters ties up the whole package.

2 oz/60 ml Canadian whisky

1 tsp/5 ml 2:1 maple simple syrup
(see page 78, made with maple syrup)

2 dashes Fee Brothers Old Fashion
Aromatic Bitters

Large ice cubes

Wide swath of lemon peel
for garnish

CHILLED OLD-FASHIONED GLASS

Combine the whisky, simple syrup, and bitters in a mixing glass and stir with ice cubes. Strain over fresh ice into an old-fashioned glass. Twist the peel over the surface of the cocktail, rub the rim of the glass with the peel, and drop in the drink to serve.

CHAPTER Nº

5

COMPOUND SYRUPS

**BLENDING SWEETNESS,
FLAVOR, AND TEXTURE**

Locked away in a commissary kitchen, deep in the heart of Emeryville, California, surrounded by the rich agricultural bounty of Northern California, stands my friend Jennifer Colliau. It's hot and humid in the kitchen, and today it's pretty cramped because of all of the crates of fresh produce stacked high. And Jen's right there in the middle of it all, working hard.

Today she's taking apricot kernels she found in a Chinese apothecary, soaking them in water, and pressing them with a large screw press. A ton of work for very little payoff, but Jen's making orgeat syrup—one of the classic cocktail ingredients she's known for among bartenders—and it's got to be right.

Jennifer Colliau followed the same haphazard path that many of us in the business wandered. She picked up her first gig at an Irish bar in Los Angeles in the mid-'90s pretty much by just hanging around. She poured some beers, saw some Flogging Molly shows, and put a few bucks in her pocket. And, you know, she liked it. So she moved up to a solid Southwestern joint with a killer tequila program and spent some time delving into agave spirits. Blind tasting to learn the difference between Lowland and Highland tequilas. Getting to know artisan mezcal production methods. Confronting sales reps about the use of diffusers in mass-market joven tequilas. That sort of stuff. Because that's the sort of obsessive freak my friend Jen is: when she's interested in something, she makes certain that she's the world's foremost expert on it.

But regardless, if you asked her what she did for a living back then, she probably would have told you she was a student, not a bartender.

Los Angeles was eventually traded for the Bay Area, and her attentions slowly morphed into cabinetry and furniture design. Tending bar supported her while she picked up the odd woodworking commissions, but being the ultimate sort of craft-oriented worker, she was quickly excelling at both.

Jen and I followed similar career paths, and we often talk about that moment that happens to some of us, if we're extremely lucky: It's when the work you went to school for, studied for, and paid for is no longer your main focus and someone's paying you to do your hobby.

She began working at the Slanted Door, on the waterfront in San Francisco's Ferry Building, in 2005. The bar is world renowned for a cocktail program every bit as sophisticated and ingredient driven as the food from the much-vaunted kitchen. And it was here that Jennifer developed her deep-seated frustration with the lack of availability of high-quality classic cocktail ingredients.

It all started with the mai tai. After learning of the drink's early origins in neighboring Emeryville, Jen and bar manager Erik Adkins decided they needed to put one on the menu. But a proper mai tai calls for orgeat, a syrup made with bitter almonds or with fruit pits (see page 112). It's called for in some of the earliest classic cocktails, and the commercial versions just weren't working for Jen.

"Have you had the one they use for coffee, that almond-flavored coffee syrup? It tastes like hand soap," says Jen while we're on the phone one day. "They're all just made with high fructose corn syrup and almond flavoring. It's disgusting." So Jen being Jen, she set out to make her own.

She made her own orgeat, and a few other syrups for the bar, with her usual all-consuming pursuit of quality. Before long, the Bay Area cocktail community came knocking at her door, and for a year she supplied her fellow bartenders with her beautiful house-made syrups. Then in 2008, she started Small Hand Foods, making gum syrup, raspberry gum syrup, pineapple gum syrup, grenadine, and, in extremely limited quantities, orgeat.

So when it came time for me to write this book, I called up the one person on my speed dial who knows more about compound syrups than anyone else in the business. And without hesitation she flew up to Portland, sat at my kitchen counter, and smiled as I begged her to teach me 1 percent of what she knows.

SWEET SYRUPS WITH ADDED FLAVOR

A compound syrup is just another way to bring sweetness to a cocktail. But unlike simple syrups, which deliver sweetness with little to no flavor, a compound syrup adds another layer of flavor—or sometimes texture—to your drinks. So, instead of storing quantities of fresh esoteric ingredients, you can stock a selection of compound syrups with the same flavors.

You see, a syrup also has the advantage of preserving flavors. A raspberry syrup will maintain its vibrant flavor and perfume longer than fresh raspberry juice or puree alone, because the sugar acts as a preservative. And that sort of thing is important to bartenders who want to provide an ever-growing array of flavors for their guests.

SWEET-AND-SOUR SYRUPS

Two other forms of compound syrup have gained prominence recently—shrubs and gastriques. Both are vinegar-based, and both have long histories that began in the kitchen before they migrated to the bar.

FLAVORLESS BUT FAMILIAR: GUM SYRUP

There is one compound syrup, the most basic, that doesn't have any flavor at all. It's called gum syrup, and other than the sweetness and nuances of flavor from whatever sugar you use, it's flavorless. Gum syrup isn't about how it tastes, it's about how it feels.

Gum syrup would have been familiar to any bartender working before 1920. A standard ingredient in cocktails back then, gum syrup (also spelled the French way, *gomme* syrup) consists of a 2:1 (rich) simple syrup mixed with gum arabic. Also called gum acacia, this natural substance was originally intended to prevent the sugar syrup from crystallizing, but it also gave the syrup a silky mouthfeel. Gum syrups fell out of favor because the gum arabic powder is tricky to use, but in recent years we've seen a revival as bartenders make an effort to seek out authentic pre-Prohibition cocktail ingredients or make them themselves.

Gum syrup is mainly used in spirit-driven cocktails whose natural consistency can be on the thin side. It's typically not used in citrus-based drinks, such as daiquiris, where many of the textural nuances of gum syrup would be lost. But it certainly doesn't hurt in those applications, either. The amount of syrup you use is often quite small, but it has just enough thickening power that your cocktails take on a subtle silkiness not present in drinks made with a regular simple syrup.

Gum syrup likely fell out of favor with bartenders because it can be, quite frankly, a huge pain to make. *The Gentleman's Table Guide*, by E. Ricket and C. Thomas, published in 1871, gives the following instructions: "Dissolve 1 lb. of the best white gum arabic in 1½ pints of water, nearly boiling; 3 lb. of white sugar or candy; melt and clarify it with half pint cold water, add the gum solution, and boil all together for two minutes." Sounds like a piece of cake, until you actually try to make it and end up with a hot, sticky mess that is roughly the consistency of peanut butter.

The main issue is that gum arabic clumps badly in hot or warm water. I've even tried running a batch through my commercial blender, which can make anything homogeneous in seconds, but I still came up with clumps. What I needed was a gum syrup recipe that could be made easily, wouldn't clump, and didn't involve a hot cobra slithering out of a pot on my stove top.

My solution takes a bit of advance planning, but it's the easiest and most foolproof way you'll find for making gum syrup. Allowing gum arabic to sit for 48 hours in room-temperature water ensures that all the lumps dissolve beautifully. It is then blended with simple syrup.

GUM WHAT?

If you've heard of gum arabic already, it's more likely in connection with your art supplies, rather than as a cocktail staple. Gum arabic is a powder derived from the sap of two types of acacia tree, and it has an enormously broad range of uses. The salient quality of the stuff is its ability to control the consistency of ingredients, so in food manufacturing it's used as a stabilizer, and in the printing world it's used to control ink viscosity.

But gum arabic is indeed used most in the beverage world, since it's a key ingredient in Coca-Cola and other sodas, where it creates the right amount of surface tension for the best texture and long-lasting fizz.

The two trees from which gum arabic comes are the *Acacia senegal* and the *Acacia seyal*, which are related. Most of these trees are grown in the area of Africa just below the Sahara. If you look on a map, you'll see that this area includes part of Sudan, the major producer of gum arabic.

Shortly after the 9/11 terrorist attacks, a story began circulating on the Internet that Osama bin Laden owned most of the gum arabic production in Sudan, and there were calls for a boycott of all products using it. Bin Laden's holdings had already been divested by the Sudanese government six years earlier, and fortunately the story died quickly— but not before many commercial food producers changed their ingredient lists to read "gum acacia" rather than "gum arabic" in an attempt to distance themselves from this myth.

GUM SYRUP

MAKES ABOUT 13 OZ/385 ML Gum arabic
(or gum acacia, as it is often referred to these
days) is easily purchased online from retailers
of herbs and spices. It's important to be precise, so measure carefully.

2 oz/55 g gum arabic (gum acacia)

6 oz/180 ml water

12 oz/340 g superfine sugar

In a small plastic container, combine the
gum arabic and 2 oz/60 ml of the water. Stir
with a chopstick to blend, and cover. Let
sit for 48 hours, or until the gum arabic is
completely dissolved in the water.

In a small saucepan, combine the sugar and
remaining 4 oz/120 ml water. Heat gently
until the sugar begins to dissolve, and then
fold in the gum arabic mixture. Remove from
the heat immediately, let cool, and bottle in
a plastic squeeze bottle. Store in the refrigerator indefinitely.

HERB SYRUP

I desperately wanted to put a Mojito on the cocktail menu at my first restaurant job back in 2001. It was a big, busy place and after a couple of hectic weekends, I realized we needed a faster way to prepare this labor-intensive drink. And thus the mint simple syrup was born. The problem was that steeping fresh mint leaves in hot simple syrup, as we did, resulted in a syrup that turned brown after only a few hours and left us with a rather unappetizing-looking cocktail.

Hilariously, our solution back in those days was to add Midori for a little green coloring and name the drink an "Asian Mojito." Had I known better, we could have saved more than a few palates from that sickly sweet concoction we were serving.

The reason herb syrups prepared in this fashion turn dark is because of a process called enzymatic browning: substances in plants called polyphenols allow enzymes to cause browning when they come in contact with oxygen. Your herb syrup may look clear or a lovely shade of light green when you first make it, but once you've exposed it to oxygen, it can darken to an unappealing shade.

The way to stop those enzymes from doing their thing is by subjecting them to a little heat. For that, we use a cooking technique called blanching. Blanching is simply boiling something for a few seconds (or up to a few minutes for vegetables) to deactivate the enzymes, and then stopping the cooking process by plunging the ingredients into ice water to maintain their fresh flavor.

HOW TO BLANCH HERBS FOR SYRUPS

Bring a large pot of water to a boil (cover the pot to speed things up). In the meantime, put some cold water and ice into a medium bowl, and arrange a double layer of paper towels on the counter.

Once the water is boiling, gather your herbs. Don't pick the leaves; simply leave them on the stalk for now. Holding them by the ends, plunge the stalks into the boiling water. I blanch softer, more delicate herbs, such as mint, tarragon, and basil, for 15 seconds, and hardier herbs, such as thyme and rosemary, for 30 seconds.

Once the time is up, remove the herbs from the boiling water and plunge them immediately into the ice bath. Let them stay there for a full 1 minute, remove them from the water, and pat them dry with the paper towels.

The next step is easy: Remove the leaves, throw them in a blender with premade simple syrup, and blend on high speed for about 1 minute. All that's left to do is strain out the solids using a fine-mesh sieve, and bottle.

MINT SYRUP

MAKES ABOUT 12 OZ/360 ML While I
always prefer the single-serving method for
making a Mojito (page 233), this little trick
is a great way to make a big group happy
(say, while hosting a summertime Cuban
cookout) and avoid spending the entire
evening in the kitchen making drinks. Simply prepare your Mojitos the normal way,
omitting the muddled mint and substituting
this mint syrup for the plain simple syrup.
This amount of syrup plus a full fifth (750 ml)
of rum will make exactly 12 drinks. Plan
accordingly.

12 oz/360 ml 1:1 simple syrup
(see page 78)

5 large sprigs or 7 medium sprigs
fresh mint

Bring a large pot of water to a boil. Meanwhile
put some ice cubes in a medium bowl and fill
with water for an ice bath.

Grasping the stem ends of the mint sprigs,
immerse the leafy ends completely in the
boiling water for 15 seconds. Remove from
the water and immediately submerge
in the ice bath for 1 minute.

Remove from the ice bath, pat dry with paper
towels, and pick the leaves from the stems.

Blend the blanched mint leaves and simple
syrup on high speed in a blender for 1 minute.
Strain through a fine-mesh strainer or cheesecloth, pour into a plastic squeeze bottle, and
refrigerate; it will keep for about 1 month.

FRUIT SYRUPS

Fruit is a more common flavoring ingredient for a compound syrup than herbs—many drinks want the flavor of fresh fruit, and syrup captures the essence of the fruit without adding any extra volume to your drink.

I use three different methods to make my fruit syrups, depending on the character of the fruit itself. Highly juicy fruits such as pomegranate don't need any added water in order to make a syrup. Most other fruits need a little additional water, and superfibrous ingredients such as fresh ginger need a whole lot of added water in order to temper their small quantity of powerfully flavored juice.

SOFT FRUIT SYRUPS

The idea behind a fruit syrup is to extract as much flavor and color as possible, while leaving the physical fruit and any cellulose fiber behind; your final product should be crystal clear. Most fruit needs to be combined with water in order to get the desired result. (Pomegranates are an exception.)

With raspberries and other soft fruit, I find the best way to effect extraction is by simmering the fruit in water, straining out the solids, and then mixing in sugar to create the syrup. Many recipes out there will direct you to simmer the fruit in sugar syrup, but I find it difficult to control the juice-to-sugar ratio using that method. Inevitably, some of the sugar gets absorbed by the fruit and stays there, throwing off your balance.

Another reason for not simmering fruit with sugar is that we're going to be filtering the whole product through a coffee strainer, and believe me, water and berry juice is a hell of a lot easier to filter than a syrup. What takes a few minutes without sugar will end up taking you hours with sugar, so filter your results before mixing the still-hot liquid with sugar.

When straining soft fruit, such as raspberries or peaches, press on the solids in your strainer, and then filter to obtain the proper clear consistency. For fruit that's slightly more fibrous, such as pineapple, I like to press it gently with a potato masher before simmering in order to coax out more juice and even more flavor.

SYRUP FROM FIBROUS INGREDIENTS

I use a more aggressive technique for ingredients that are extremely tough or fibrous, such as fresh ginger or rhubarb. Here we're not just chopping the ingredient before using it; we're actually processing it in a blender with hot water and sugar—essentially simmering with pulverization as well as heat. Note that, unlike the recipes for Raspberry Syrup (page 102) and Pineapple Syrup (page 103), in which I strained out the solids and then filtered the fruit liquid before I added sugar, in the Ginger Syrup recipe (see page 103), I simply pass the syrup through a fine-mesh strainer and forget the filter. Given the fact that ginger syrup will never be crystal clear because of the nature of ginger juice, I decided to forego the coffee-filtering method and live with a touch of cloudiness.

GRENADINE

MAKES 16 OZ/480 ML We're all familiar with the bottled, neon red grenadine that you can find at the grocery store: high fructose corn syrup with "natural and artificial flavors," preservatives, and artificial red coloring. Which is sad, because classic grenadine is, or used to be, anyway, nothing more than pomegranate syrup with the addition of a few other ingredients.

I've found that even the higher-end commercial grenadines, packaged in sexy apothecary-style bottles and sold for outrageous sums at specialty shops and gourmet grocery stores, are still crap—nothing more than that awful neon syrup made with some fresher ingredients but still processed to the point of being unrecognizable as a fresh-fruit syrup.

Bartenders, these days, prefer to make their own, but there seems to be some confusion about how the syrup should look and taste. Someone should inform these folks that grenadine isn't pale pink, and it certainly isn't brown. Grenadine is a beautiful deep red color, because it's made from fresh juice.

Pomegranates can seem slightly inaccessible because getting the juice out of those hundreds of tiny seeds can feel daunting, but with the proper method (see page 44), it's easy to extract loads of juice from a pomegranate. If you're not lucky enough to currently be enjoying the three months out of the year when fresh pomegranates are available, I strongly recommend the 100 percent pomegranate juice made by POM

Wonderful. It's the closest commercial product you're going to find to fresh pomegranate juice. Don't be tempted by the glass bottles with labels touting organic or all-natural in the juice aisle; I've tried them all, and they all suck.

So now that you've got a bunch of fresh pomegranate juice, either from a fruit or a bottle, it's time to turn it into grenadine. Many recipes you'll come across will tell you to concentrate those rich, fresh flavors by boiling down the juice, but I find that this results in an end product that's about as delicious as, well, boiled juice. Skip it, and gently heat the juice until it's just warm enough to dissolve the sugar, which is well below the point of boiling. You'll still retain the fresh flavor of the pomegranate.

You can do this in a small saucepan, or you can just throw it in the microwave for 1 to 2 minutes. Next, we'll add sugar to dissolve, a little pomegranate molasses for some richer, deeper flavors, and a touch of orange blossom water for some lighter floral notes.

The only step left is to add 1 oz/30 ml of vodka, if you like; this is an optional preservative. If you're not planning on using up your grenadine over the course of a month, then add it. But if you're serving it in a bar and plan on going through it pretty quickly, as I do, then you can just skip it.

If you decide to make a big batch of the stuff in the winter, when pomegranates are in season, it should last about 1 month. You can also juice more pomegranates, freeze the juice, and then make grenadine later in

the year. The frozen juice will retain much of its original fresh character, so your syrup will be good even out of season.

16 oz/480 ml fresh pomegranate juice (approximately 2 large pomegranates) or POM Wonderful 100% pomegranate juice

16 oz/455 g raw sugar

2 oz/60 ml pomegranate molasses

1 tsp/5 ml orange blossom water

Heat the pomegranate juice slightly, either in a microwave-safe bowl or in a small saucepan, so it's just warm enough to allow the sugar to dissolve easily. Add the sugar, molasses, and orange blossom water, stirring until the sugar is dissolved. Allow to cool, and then bottle. Seal the bottle and refrigerate; the grenadine will last for up to 1 month.

JACK ROSE

MAKES 1 DRINK Your grenadine will be great in all manner of classic cocktails, and, hell, even in a Shirley Temple if that's your thing (I know I treat myself to one at least once a year). But the one drink in which I think grenadine really shines is the Jack Rose.

There are a number of stories circulating about the origin of the name Jack Rose, most of which I'm sure are a load of b.s. The best one I've heard yet is that *Jack* was inspired by the applejack, and *Rose* by the rose color of the drink, from the grenadine. Regardless, it's a delicious classic.

1½ oz/45 ml applejack, preferably Laird's bonded, if you can find it

¾ oz/22.5 ml fresh lemon juice (see page 22)

½ oz/15 ml Grenadine (page 98)

Ice cubes

1 lemon peel for garnish (optional)

CHILLED COCKTAIL GLASS

Combine the applejack, lemon juice, and Grenadine in a cocktail shaker or mixing glass. Fill with ice cubes and shake.

Strain into the chilled cocktail glass. Twist the peel over the surface of the cocktail and drop in the drink, if desired, to serve.

RASPBERRY SYRUP

MAKES 2¼ CUPS/540 ML In the world of cocktails, there are fewer things more evocative of summer than a syrup made from fresh raspberries. This one adds another layer of farmers' market freshness to your drinks.

2 cups/335 g fresh or good-quality frozen raspberries

8 oz/240 ml water

1 cup/250 g granulated sugar

In a medium saucepan, simmer the raspberries in the water until the juice has leached from the fruit and the water and berries are approximately the same color, 5 to 10 minutes. Strain through a strainer, pressing on the berries and then discarding them. Filter the juice through a coffee filter to clarify. While still hot, add the sugar, stirring until dissolved. Let cool, then bottle and refrigerate. The syrup will last about 3 weeks.

CLOVER CLUB

MAKES 1 DRINK There's probably a deep historical story to this drink . . . but I don't know it. What I do know is that when you make this variation of a gin sour with raspberry syrup, it's one of the most beautiful things you can put in your mouth.

1½ oz/45 ml gin

¾ oz/22.5 ml fresh lemon juice (see page 22)

¾ oz/22.5 ml Raspberry Syrup (at left)

½ oz/15 ml egg white (see page 154)

Ice cubes

CHILLED COCKTAIL GLASS

Combine the gin, lemon juice, raspberry syrup, and egg white in a cocktail shaker or mixing glass. Shake until the egg white is frothy and the ingredients are combined. Add ice cubes and shake again. Strain into the chilled cocktail glass, and serve.

GINGER SYRUP

MAKES ABOUT 1½ CUPS/360 ML This method of making ginger syrup is probably one of the best bartender's tricks I've picked up over the years. It's fast, it's easy, and it's actually really delicious, especially given the fact that raw ginger juice is so much more potent than ginger that's been cooked. I know a lot of bartenders who use this little trick, and it's something of a secret handshake when I see someone else using it. You can replace the sugar with an equal quantity of honey to make ginger-honey syrup, which is also beautiful in cocktails.

Note that this method also works beautifully for another tough, fibrous plant: rhubarb. I always make a lot of rhubarb syrup in the spring, when it's first coming into season.

½ lb/250 g fresh ginger, washed and cut into ½-in/12-mm chunks

1 cup/240 ml boiling water

½ lb/250 g sugar

Put the ginger in a blender and add the boiling water and sugar. Blend thoroughly, and then strain through a fine-mesh sieve. Your syrup won't be perfectly clear; that's okay. Bottle, label, and store in the refrigerator for up to 1 week.

PINEAPPLE SYRUP

MAKES 12 OZ/360 ML Pineapple syrups are important in the cocktail repertoire, especially in the world of tiki drinks. Pineapples need a bit more work to liberate the juice from their fibrous flesh.

One 1-lb/480-g pineapple, both ends trimmed

12 oz/360 ml 1:1 simple syrup (see page 78)

Cut the pineapple crosswise into ¾-in/2-cm slices, and then cut each slice into six wedges. Cut off the peel .

Combine the pineapple and simple syrup in a large bowl and leave to macerate for at least 4 hours, or up to 24 hours, in the refrigerator. Stir or mash the fruit lightly from time to time. Strain the syrup into a clean bowl through a fine-mesh strainer and press on the pineapple with a ladle to extract as much liquid as possible. Let cool, bottle, and refrigerate for up to 1 week.

HOTEL NACIONAL SPECIAL

By Charles H. Baker. Adapted by Erik Adkins.

MAKES 1 DRINK Charles H. Baker's incredible 1939 account of his encounters as a gadabout, *The Gentleman's Companion: Being an Exotic Cookery and Drinking Book,* is full of breath-taking cocktail recipes from around the world. His offering from the Hotel Nacional in Havana, Cuba, calls for fresh pineapple juice, but my friend Erik Adkins, the bar manager at the Slanted Door, in San Francisco, put a spin on the drink that has always seemed so right: using pineapple syrup in place of the juice.

I've gone on record in the press as saying that I kinda hate Erik Adkins. I struggle with rec-ipes, and I sorta feel like every second spent behind the bar for me is a tense moment, as I desperately try not to screw up people's drinks. But Erik isn't like that at all; his drinks are always, always, always perfect. As one mutual friend so eloquently put it, "Erik sprinkles magic pixie dust on top of his drinks. No matter how hard you try, you can never make the same drink as well as he can." And it's true. I've followed his ver-sion of this recipe to the letter, but I still enjoy it more when he makes it for me. Good for you if you can make it the way Erik does; otherwise, you'll have to be con-tent to be a mere mortal, like the rest of us.

1½ oz/45 ml aged rum

¾ oz/22.5 ml fresh lime juice

¾ oz/22.5 ml Pineapple Syrup (page 103)

½ oz/15 ml apricot brandy

1 drop Angostura bitters

Ice cubes

1 lime wheel for garnish

CHILLED COUPE GLASS

Combine the rum, lime juice, pineapple syrup, apricot brandy, and bitters in a cocktail shaker or mixing glass. Fill with ice cubes and shake.

Strain into the chilled coupe glass. Garnish the rim with the lime wheel and serve.

OLEO SACCHARUM

MAKES ENOUGH FOR 1 BATCH OF PUNCH

One of the key elements in a classic punch recipe is a proper oleo saccharum. Making oleo saccharum the traditional way involves peeling citrus, gently muddling it into superfine sugar, and letting it rest for an hour or more until the sugar essentially dissolves in the citrus oil as it leaches from the peels, creating what is basically a citrus oil compound syrup. The oleo saccharum needs occasional tending during that hour, but what you're eventually left with is a sweet, aromatic base for a tasty bowl of punch.

The biggest drawback for people who, like me, make a lot of punch, is that this amount of time and effort is just too much. I needed a method that would cut out all of the steps in this process, leaving me free to perform the many other prep chores that my bar requires. And that's when we came up with the vacuum seal technique for making oleo saccharum.

In a nutshell, all of the ingredients are placed into a vacuum seal bag and sealed under vacuum. Since the peels and sugar are placed in such close contact, the oils begin dissolving the sugar almost immediately. Within hours, the sugar has been converted into oleo saccharum with no additional tending or stirring needed.

One 1-lb/455-g box superfine sugar

Zest of 12 lemons (pared with a vegetable peeler)

Place the sugar and lemon zest into a vacuum seal bag and seal according to the manufacturer's instructions. (We use the inexpensive FoodSaver vacuum sealer, and 1-qt/960-ml size bags at our bar.)

Let the bag rest at room temperature for at least 4 hours (or up to overnight), until the sugar is soaked in lemon oil. Date the bags and refrigerate. The oleo saccharum will last for 1 month, unopened and stored in the fridge. Alternatively, if you don't have a vacuum sealer, gently muddle the lemon peel with the sugar and let rest for 1 hour. Store in a resealable plastic bag or tight container in the refrigerator for up to 2 weeks.

PHILADELPHIA FISH HOUSE PUNCH

MAKES ABOUT 5½ QT/5.2 L Likely the most storied of all American punches is the Philadelphia Fish House Punch. Created some time around 1732 at the Schuylkill Fishing Club, in Philadelphia, this potent punch is rumored to have kicked off every meeting. Given the unavailability of unsweetened peach brandy at that time, we present our version, using David Wondrich's solution, a 3:1 ratio of American apple brandy to French sweetened peach liqueur.

1 batch Oleo Saccharum (page 108)

16 oz/480 ml Appleton Estate rum

8 oz/240 ml Smith & Cross rum

12 oz/360 ml cognac

3 oz/90 ml crème de pêche

9 oz/265 ml applejack

16 oz/480 ml fresh lemon juice (see page 22), finely strained

3 qt/2.8 L cold water

Ice ring mold (see page 178)

PUNCH BOWL AND SMALL PUNCH GLASSES

Combine the Oleo Saccharum, both rums, the cognac, créme de pêche, applejack, lemon juice, and cold water in a punch bowl and chill. Add the ice ring mold when ready to serve.

ORGEAT

If there's one important syrup that's better left to the pros, it's orgeat. Orgeat (OR-zhah) belongs to a family of syrups that originally were barley based—the Latin word for barley is *hordeum*. The sweetness came from the barley sugars and the flavoring came from almonds. Eventually the barley dropped out but the almond flavor remained.

Orgeat seems to have been the first compound syrup used in cocktails. It first showed up in Jerry Thomas's *The Bar-Tender's Guide* (1862) in a drink called the Japanese cocktail, which follows the original nineteenth-century definition of a cocktail: spirit, sugar, and bitters. He uses the almond-flavored sweet syrup instead of plain sugar syrup.

The main flavoring in orgeat is almonds, both sweet (the kind of almonds we eat and use in cooking) and bitter almonds. The latter are slightly controversial because they include a substance called amygdalin, which breaks down into cyanide or hydrocyanic acid, which is toxic in large quantities and useful in assassinations. Cyanide shouldn't be totally scary, however, because it's present in a lot of natural foods we eat, but in very small and manageable quantities. Bitter almonds were also thought to cure cancer, however, so pick your poison.

The intense almond flavor originally derived from bitter almonds is also found in the pits of stone fruits, such as apricots, peaches, and plums, and some orgeats are made with those fruit pits instead of the bitter almonds.

Now, me being me, whenever I'm at a cocktail convention or on the road, I always meet people who want to foist their (mostly) odd house-made ingredients on me. I don't know how I became the DIY poster boy, but if I never taste another awful bottle of home-made orgeat again, it'll be too soon. Making orgeat—good orgeat—is a royal pain, and this is one occasion where I do suggest using commercially available brands. My friend Jennifer Colliau, at Small Hand Foods, makes the best one on the planet, if you can find it (see page 88). Another good orgeat is made by a friend of mine here in Portland, Blair Reynolds, the proprietor of B.G. Reynolds' Hand-Crafted Syrups. Blair's orgeat doesn't go through a process quite as painstaking as Jennifer's, so the flavor is less intense. I mainly use his in recipes that call for a larger quantity of orgeat, more than ½ oz/15 ml.

JAPANESE COCKTAIL

MAKES 1 DRINK I'm not really a history guy, but from what I've read, Jerry Thomas came up with this drink to commemorate the visit of a Japanese dignitary to New York. Or something. Ask David Wondrich if you run into him, and tell him I told you to bug him. What I do know is that it's a cocktail in the classical sense—spirit, bitters, and sweetener, in this case orgeat.

2 oz/60 ml cognac

½ oz/15 ml orgeat

2 dashes Angostura bitters

Ice cubes

1 lemon peel for garnish

CHILLED COUPE GLASS

Combine the cognac, orgeat, and bitters in a cocktail shaker or mixing glass. Fill with ice cubes and shake.

Strain into the chilled coupe glass. Twist the peel over the surface of the cocktail and drop in the drink to serve.

SHRUBS

Like many things that we obsess over today, shrubs began as a simple expediency. In the old days, fresh fruit was precious in colder climates, such as in colonial America. There were no refrigerators, so to preserve fruit, a frugal housewife would pile it into a crock and add some vinegar. That would essentially pickle the fruit, but it was still edible and delicious in its own way.

The soaking liquid, of course, was the real prize. As the fruit macerated, the process of osmosis drew most of the flavor and sweetness out of the fruit and into the vinegar. Once the fruit had been consumed, the liquid was served, lengthened by adding some cool water. Eventually, someone had the bright idea to add alcohol, and the fruity drink was born. Asian drinking vinegars are essentially the same as shrubs, though they're coming out of the Asian tradition rather than the American colonial one.

We now use a method for this sweet-tart syrup that speeds things up and makes a more deeply flavored product. Instead of macerating fruit in vinegar and then adding sugar, I simmer fruit in vinegar for just a few minutes, and then strain, filter, and add sugar.

The beauty of a shrub lies in its tension between sweet and sour; it's sweet enough to bring balance to cocktails, but it comes with a high acidity, which provides a strong structure to your drinks.

STRAWBERRY-MINT SHRUB

By Neyah White.

MAKES 48 OZ/1.4 L If there's anyone who could win an international sherry competition by using fresh, homemade ingredients, it's a San Francisco bartender. And the San Francisco bartender who actually did so is Neyah White. God bless him.

1 qt/680 g very ripe strawberries, hulled and halved
Leaves from 10 sprigs fresh mint
4 cups/800 g sugar
1 tbsp kosher salt
4 cups/960 ml cider or white wine vinegar, or a combination of the two

Put the strawberry halves in the bottom of a large bowl, layer the mint leaves on top, cover with the sugar, and sprinkle with the salt. Let this macerate covered at room temperature for a few hours, stirring occasionally, and then refrigerate for about 8 hours, stirring a few more times to be sure the sugar is making contact with the fruit.

After a syrup has formed, add the vinegar and stir to dissolve any undissolved sugar. (To speed the process, transfer to a pan and simmer for a few minutes.) Use immediately or let sit for a few days to allow the flavor to deepen. I find my sweet spot is just 1 day. Once you are satisfied with the flavor, filter the mix through a double layer of cheesecloth, pour into clean bottles, and cover tightly. The shrub is essentially pickled now and can be stored in the refrigerator for up to 4 months.

INFUSIONS, TINCTURES & BITTERS

EXTRACTING AND INTENSIFYING FLAVORS

In 2001, after having tended bar for five years in various dives (pool halls and night-clubs), someone finally took a chance on me and put me in charge of a real restaurant cocktail program: chef-owner Stephanie Pearl-Kimmel's new pan-Asian concept, Bamboo, in Eugene, Oregon.

Bamboo was awesome. Our intense, wiry Malaysian chef ran the volatile kitchen, while a white boy from Santa Cruz held down the sushi bar out front. And off to the side of the restaurant was my tiny bar. This being 2001, my bartenders and I put out huge, colorful cocktails with flavored-sugar rims and all manner of fruit puree and nectar in the glass. And like at so many other places at that time, four large infusion jars sat proudly on the back bar.

There was a blueberry gin infusion for the blueberry gimlet. The vodka infused with whole vanilla bean went into about a hundred vanilla lemon drops every night. The Thai chile pepper vodka spiced up our take on the Bloody Mary, and the pineapple-habanero tequila made the most famous margarita in town.

Today's mustachioed, arm-gartered mixologists will laugh in derision at those old days of infused alcohol, perhaps instead preferring to tease your drink with a dash of their house-made celery root bitters, or maybe finishing it off with a cocoa nib tincture.

But at their core, pineapple-and-habanero-infused tequila, celery root bitters, and cocoa nib tincture are all essentially the same thing: flavorful compounds suspended in an alcohol solution for use in cocktails. And when done properly, any of these three can be very effective at adding layers of flavor to your drinks.

INFUSIONS

HOW INFUSIONS WORK

The infusion of alcohol with food flavors occurs via two physical processes: osmosis and dissolution. Osmosis is what happens when the universe strives for balance. When two liquids containing water are placed next to each other and separated by a cell wall, there's a drive for equilibrium. Water wants to move from the side that has more water to the side that has less water, in an effort to even things out. Fresh fruit and vegetables contain a lot of water, while vodka, for example, contains a lot less.

Water and Alcohol Reach Equilibrium through Osmosis

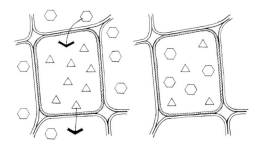

Frat boys will tell you that the pieces of fruit in their tub of jungle juice contain a higher level of alcohol than the drink itself, but thanks to osmosis we know that the concentrations of alcohol and water inside and outside of the fruit are exactly the same. Alcohol flows into the cell walls, water flows out, until equilibrium is reached. The sugar and other flavor compounds that are inside the cell come along with the water, which is ultimately why our liquor becomes flavorful and our fruit becomes alcoholic.

The second process, dissolution, is the action of the solvent (in our case, alcohol) by which it unlocks and releases the compounds found in a flavoring ingredient (the solute). There is no water to be exchanged; the process is simply all about dissolving those compounds into the alcohol.

For alcohol to work effectively as a solvent, it needs to be in high concentrations, at least 40 percent alcohol. At that level, there are enough alcohol molecules to connect with the solute and do the job; at lower concentrations, there is more water, and the water bonds with the alcohol and interferes with its ability to engage with those flavor compounds.

Here's an easy way to think of these two processes in action: For infusions involving fresh ingredients —fruit, vegetables, herbs, flowers—osmosis is the primary action taking place. For infusions involving dried flavorings—spices, dried citrus peel, roots—dissolution is the main driver of the flavor exchange, as there's no water left in those cell walls for osmosis to take place.

THE COMPLEXITIES OF FLAVOR AND INFUSIONS

Flavor is a complicated thing. Some of what we taste when we eat or drink is our mouth's response to the five basic flavors: sweet, sour, salty, bitter, and umami. But on top of those fundamental five are all the subtleties that make a pear taste like a pear and Islay Scotch taste like Islay Scotch. Most of those flavor compounds are actually "tasted" by us through receptors in our nasal passages.

When we're cooking, we want to release those many flavor compounds so that they can blend with others and we can taste them more fully. Some flavor compounds are soluble in water, some are soluble in fat, and some are soluble in alcohol.

The best example of how this works is making a vegetable soup. You could put all your vegetables in a pot, add water, and simmer, and the soup would be, you know, fine. But if you first sautéed those ingredients in some fat before simmering them, your soup would be richer and more complex, having both water-soluble and fat-soluble flavors in the pot.

Relatively recently, chefs and bartenders have been experimenting with a form of infusion called *fat washing*. A fatty ingredient in its liquid state, such as warm bacon grease or melted butter, is blended with a spirit (bacon and bourbon is a popular combination) and left to infuse. The fat releases some flavor compounds and the alcohol dissolves others, so that you're left with the smoky, porky, salty flavors of the bacon. About 24 hours at room temperature with frequent agitation should do the trick.

Now the only thing left to do is remove the fat from the alcohol to reclaim the consistency of the original spirit. For that, we use the method any cook who has made gravy or chicken stock knows: we pop it in the freezer or refrigerator. The fat will rise to the surface and congeal and can be lifted off in big pieces and discarded. The alcohol will still need to be strained through a coffee filter to remove all the grease, but the flavors that came along with the fat will indeed stay behind.

Of the infusions, tinctures, and bitters that we use behind the bar, infusions are the least intensely flavored. Your goal when making an infusion is to add flavor from the fruit, spice, or herb you've chosen, while preserving the flavor of the original alcohol, since you'll likely be using this as a base spirit in your cocktails, and not simply as an accent.

For this reason, we want to start with as high quality a liquor as possible. Even though eventually some of the nuances of the liquor will be masked by the infused flavors, I always follow one simple rule: Garbage in, garbage out. This is no time to skimp on ingredients.

CHOOSING YOUR INGREDIENTS

For the most flexibility in terms of creating a successful combination, choose an unaged spirit such as gin, vodka, white rum, or blanco tequila. The flavors of these more neutral liquors will pair with just about anything you dream of.

A spirit with a bigger flavor profile such as bourbon, Scotch, or dark rum will need a more considered pairing, because a collision of flavors is a greater possibility. But when the spirit and the infusion ingredient have a natural affinity, such as bourbon and peaches, the results just feel right.

As you're deciding what ingredients to infuse into your liquor, practice some restraint; it can be tempting to create multiflavored combinations, but too many flavors will just taste muddy, especially if they're similar. If I'm going to use more than one flavor, I want them to be contrasting flavors, such as a fruit and a chile, rather than similar ones, such as blackberry and plum.

Soft fruits and vegetables such as cherries, peaches, pineapple, plums, raspberries, strawberries, and tomatoes have relatively mild flavors and so need to be used in large quantities in order to deliver enough flavor to the alcohol. Look for spirits that weigh in at around 100 proof when infusing, as the water contained inside the cell wall of the fruit is going to lower the alcohol content of your spirit.

How to Infuse Liquor

I use a ratio of 2 parts fruit or vegetable to 1 part alcohol, by weight. The important exception is when I'm using hot chiles; see page 124 for advice on those.

1. Rinse your fruit and remove any stems or leaves (they'll add bitter or vegetal notes, which you typically don't want). Whether you peel or not is up to you; skins add a lot of their own flavor, so it's fine to leave them on.

2. Cut the fruit into thumb-size pieces to maximize the surface area, or cut small things like plums in quarters and strawberries in half (there's no need to cut really small fruit, such as blueberries).

3. Pile the fruit into your clean container—I usually use large Mason jars—and then cover with the alcohol and seal. (Don't use plastic because the alcohol can encourage substances in it to leach into your liquor. Not healthy.) Leave to infuse away from direct sunlight; unrefrigerated is fine.

4. Many methods call for highly disciplined agitation, on a precise daily schedule. I tend to agitate my infusing alcohols simply by occasionally picking up the jars and turning them over, out of curiosity more than any-thing. It probably does average out to once a day, but if you don't get around to it, don't stress yourself out over it. Militarily sched-uled agitation isn't needed. Three weeks is a typical amount of time for the flavor exchange to take place, but some ingredients may take a bit longer, so taste before proceeding to the next step to be sure you've achieved the con-centration of flavor that you want.

5. When the flavor is as you like, strain the mixture through a colander or mesh strainer, gently pressing on the fruit so it gives up as much of the juice and alcohol trapped inside the cell walls as possible, without pulverizing the remains in the strainer.

6. You need to filter the infusion, in order to make it crystal clear and free of any fruit sludge. Most experts recommend what's called *subsidence*—basically letting the mixture settle, skimming the clear stuff off the top, and leaving the solid stuff at the bottom. I prefer the coffee-filter method.

HOW TO STRAIN INFUSED LIQUOR

Suspend a large strainer over a bowl and line it with a large, flat-bottom coffee filter, (the type you'd use for a drip coffee machine at an office, such as the ones made by Bunn). You may have them already at your bar, but you can buy them in most grocery stores and definitely at a restaurant supply store. Pour the liquor through the filter. Once filtered, the infused spirit is ready to be bottled and used.

STORING INFUSED LIQUORS

Infused liquors last indefinitely, in terms of flavor quality, but their colors—which can be spectacular—will fade over time (probably within 6 months), especially if exposed to direct sunlight. As with all spirits, storing them in a dark place away from direct sunlight is best.

TEQUILA POR MI AMANTE

By Charles H. Baker

MAKES ABOUT 16 OZ/480 ML Infused alcohol might seem like a relative newcomer in the world of cocktails, but in his revolutionary 1939 chronicle of his gustatory world travels, *The Gentleman's Companion: Being an Exotic Cookery and Drinking Book*, Charles H. Baker describes a strawberry-infused tequila called Tequila por mi Amante, or "Tequila for My Lover," a creepy name for a drink, probably best left untranslated.

In September 1942, *Gourmet* magazine recommended serving 3 oz/90 ml of the luscious, rosy elixir in a collins glass with the juice of a small lime and finishing it with ice and soda. The tequila also makes the best strawberry margarita you've ever tried, but I find it to be a damn fine sipper straight out of the fridge, which is how I take mine.

1 qt/680 g ripe fresh strawberries, halved

16 oz/480 ml reposado tequila

Combine the berries and tequila in a 1-qt/960-ml canning jar and seal. Let sit for 3 weeks, agitating occasionally.

Strain through a mesh strainer, gently pressing on the berries to release their liquid. Discard the berries. Strain the entire mixture through a coffee filter suspended in a strainer set over a bowl. Bottle and store away from direct sunlight indefinitely, though the color may fade after 6 months.

INFUSING WITH HOT CHILES

Fresh chiles are worthy candidates for infusions. The combination of spicy heat and fruity, grassy flavors gives spirits like vodka or tequila a delicious dimension, which in turn makes for delicious cocktails. Just imagine a Thai chile Bloody Mary to perk up a dreary winter day, or a spicy jalapeño margarita at the height of summer.

But chiles do require some special handling in order to protect yourself and mitigate their serious heat. It might seem inconvenient, but I recommend you always wear food-service-grade latex gloves while cutting fresh chiles. They're cheap and they're multipurpose; I keep a box at home for everything from cutting chiles to handling things like paint or shoe polish.

Also, be sure to give your cutting board and knife a proper cleanup right away. The heat-producing compound in chiles—called capsaicin—is potent, and if it migrates to the wrong location, such as to your eyes or any other, uh, sensitive areas, you can develop some unfortunate problems—not to mention a considerable amount of pain.

Most of the heat is concentrated in the internal ribs of the chile, which hold the seeds. While the seeds themselves are hot, the whitish ribs (called the placenta) are the epicenter. As you prep your infusion ingredients, decide whether to include the ribs and seeds or not. An infusion containing seeds and ribs will take on more spice more quickly, while a seedless and ribless infusion will have beautiful vegetal flavors underneath the heat.

The tricky thing about infusing with fresh chiles is the wide variation in heat level among specimens of the same type of chile. You might be able to take a bite from one jalapeño but not get a second one past your lips without pain. Even chiles from the same plant can have radically different heat levels. That being said, there's a hierarchy of heat, expressed through the Scoville scale, with a poblano being one of the mildest and the fabled ghost chile being the hottest in the world . . . that we know of.

Scoville Scale

CHILE	AVERAGE SCOVILLE HEAT UNITS
Poblano	2,000
Jalapeño and chipotle	5,000
Serrano	17,000
Bird's-eye (Thai chile)	75,000
Habanero and Scotch bonnet	200,000
Naga jolokia (ghost chile)	1,000,000
Police-grade pepper spray	5,000,000
Pure capsaicin	16,000,000

You want your chile-infused spirit to be balanced—and not lethal—and because of a chile's variability, it's important to start tasting earlier than you would another type of infused spirit. I taste test my chile infusions after 1 day. If it's gone past the point of being comfortable to consume, I'll strain the infusion and cut back the heat by adding uninfused spirit until it's where I want it to be.

INFUSIONS OF HERBS, SPICES, AND OTHER INGREDIENTS

To infuse liquor with herbs or spices, you use the same process as with fruit: combine the flavoring with the spirit, wait, strain, filter, and drink. Since there is little to no water contained within the cell walls of these types of ingredients, however, the process for this sort of infusion is all about the dissolution of the potent oils and compounds contained within. Eighty-proof liquor should be sufficient since you won't be losing any alcohol strength to water content.

Infusing with Herbs

Tender fresh herbs are soft enough that their flavor will leach out without any additional prep such as chopping or grinding, and, in fact, doing so can lead to a murky infusion and bitter flavors. Hardier herbs can benefit from a gentle bruising to help release their oils.

All infusions are ultimately "to taste," in terms of how much ingredient to use and for how long to infuse them, but here are some guidelines for herb infusions.

Tender fresh herbs, such as basil, chives, cilantro, dill, mint, parsley, shiso, or tarragon: For one 750-ml bottle of vodka, use 2 cups/50 g lightly packed sprigs (no need to remove the stems). Steep for 1 week, agitating regularly, and then strain and filter.

Hardier, resinous herbs, such as marjoram, oregano, rosemary, sage, or thyme: For one 750-ml bottle of vodka, use 1 cup/40 g lightly packed gently crushed sprigs (remove large or woody stems only). Steep for 1 week, agitating regularly, and then strain and filter.

THYME-INFUSED COINTREAU

MAKES ONE 750-ML BOTTLE One little trick that I like to employ behind the bar is infusing flavored liqueurs with complementary flavors. Cointreau is an absolutely gorgeous orange liqueur that just happens to be 80 proof, and if any herb pairs beautifully with orange, it's thyme.

One drink that takes advantage of this natural pairing and highlights it beautifully is the white lady (see page 161), one of my favorite drinks made with Cointreau.

1 cup/40 g fresh thyme sprigs, gently bruised

One 750-ml bottle Cointreau

Combine the thyme and Cointreau in a 1-qt/960-ml canning jar and let sit for 1 week, agitating regularly. Strain the entire mixture through a strainer lined with a coffee filter, set over a bowl. Bottle the infused Cointreau; it should keep indefinitely.

Speed Infusion through Pressure

There's another very fast, and very cool, way to infuse herbs into liquor, and that's by pressurizing your ingredients with a cream whipper, such as the iSi Gourmet Whip. The intense pressure caused by the release of gas from a nitrous oxide cartridge forces the flavor compounds out of your flavoring ingredient and into the liquor rapidly. You can use any type of fresh herb, and you can even simulate barrel-aged cocktails by infusing a premade cocktail with wood smoking chips made from whiskey barrels found at barbecue specialty retailers. (For more on barrel aging, see page 132.)

To Infuse Using a Cream Whipper

Put your flavoring ingredient into the whipped cream canister, add your liquor, seal the unit, and charge the canister with nitrous oxide (N_2O).

Give the canister a gentle shake, wait for 1 minute or so for softer herbs, or 30 minutes for wood chips, and then slowly vent the gas from the whipper by gently squeezing the lever while the unit remains upright. Strain your liquor through a fine-mesh strainer and filter through a coffee filter if necessary.

Infusing with Spices

It can be much trickier to infuse with spices. The goal is a subtle, soft flavor; you don't want your rum tasting like a candle shop at the mall. The amount of spice you need and the infusing time it requires will vary, depending on the surface area of the spice and the intensity and character of its flavor.

The more surface area, the more accessible the flavor compounds are, and so the faster the infusion takes place. As an example, if you drop a whole nutmeg into a bottle of rum, you might be waiting for a year to get enough noticeable spice flavor. But if you were to add 1 tsp of ground nutmeg, which is essentially *all* surface area, the flavor exchange might take place within 24 hours.

I've found that most spices have a similar potency, and so I use about the same amount: 1 tsp freshly ground spice to one 750-ml bottle of liquor as a general rule of thumb. But some spices are crazy intense, such as cardamom and cloves. With these I find I need much less, about ⅛ tsp per bottle.

CHINESE FIVE-SPICED DARK RUM

MAKES ONE 750-ML BOTTLE Making your own spiced rum gives you greater control over the flavors in your cocktail than simply purchasing spiced rum off the shelf. For a wintery version of an island cocktail I love so much, I employ Chinese five-spice powder to infuse dark rum—a little trick I picked up while working at Bamboo. Try using 2 oz/ 60 ml of your spiced rum in a Dark and Stormy (page 68) with the house-made Ginger Beer (page 65).

1 tsp Chinese five-spice powder

One 750-ml bottle dark 80-proof rum, preferably Gosling's Black Seal

Using a small funnel, spoon the spice powder into the neck of the rum bottle and replace the cap. Shake to mix well. Allow to infuse for 24 hours, agitating regularly.

Strain the rum through a coffee filter and rebottle. This will keep forever.

NOCINO

MAKES ABOUT 2 QT/2 L Nocino, like limoncello, is an Italian liqueur and an infusion. It's an infusion of just about everything I've talked about in this chapter: citrus fruit, spices, and nuts—green walnuts. (A fresh walnut straight from the tree looks like a small lime; the best way to find them is to prowl your neighborhood and look in neighbors' yards, but sometimes you can find them at a farmers' market). You steep the green walnuts, lemons, cinnamon, cloves, and vanilla in Everclear or 100-proof vodka, along with some white wine and sugar. It's traditional to leave the nocino to steep in the sun in order to speed the process, so a back porch or patio is perfect; shake every few days. You could probably get good results indoors, as well, but it feels more Italian to put the jar outdoors.

Nocino is traditionally made on the day of St. John's Feast, June 24, which is when the walnuts should be ripe but still green; the infusion should be ready to strain and filter for Christmas presents. Nocino is quite sweet, but less so than limoncello, and much more complex, with layers of spice, nuts, and a faint bitterness. It's a nice winter sipper and is great with desserts and on ice cream.

30 fresh (still soft) green walnuts, quartered (pod and all)

One 750-ml bottle 100-proof vodka or grain alcohol, such as Everclear

One 750-ml bottle unoaked white wine, such as Pinot Gris or Sauvignon Blanc

2 cups/400 g granulated sugar

Zest of 1 lemon

3 cinnamon sticks

20 whole cloves

1 green cardamom pod, crushed

Combine the walnuts, vodka, white wine, sugar, lemon zest, cinnamon sticks, cloves, and cardamom pod in a 1-gal/3.8-L glass jar with a tight-fitting lid. Let the infusion sit in a window that receives as much direct sunlight as possible for about 5 months, shaking it every day. After 5 months, start tasting. When the flavor is deep and complex, it's time to bottle.

Strain the nocino into a large container through a colander first to remove the large ingredients; then strain again through a coffee filter or a super-fine-mesh strainer several times, until most of the sediment is gone. Let the strained nocino sit in a clean bottle for at least a day so that any leftover sediment will settle to the bottom, and then carefully pour it off into your choice of decorative bottles. Nocino keeps for a long time, at least 4 years.

LIMONCELLO

MAKES ABOUT 2 QT/2 L In recent years, house-infused liqueurs have become widely popular, especially those in the "cello" family. Limoncello—made from lemons—is the most popular, but other citrus cellos (pronounced like the musical instrument), such as tangerine and blood orange, are showing up on bar menus and as holiday gifts from crafty friends.

The process consists of infusing grain alcohol or high-proof vodka with citrus zest for about 3 months, and then mixing with simple syrup for sweetness. The Italians serve limoncello as a digestif, traditionally in a small chilled ceramic cup, but it shows up in cocktails and even desserts. Cellos are often oversweetened; I prefer to use them in moderation.

```
15 lemons
Two 750-ml bottles 100-proof vodka
4 cups/800 g sugar
5 cups/1.2 L water
```

Wash the lemons well under running hot water and pat dry. Peel the zest from the lemons in long, wide strips.

Combine the lemon peels and 1 bottle of vodka in a 1-gal/3.8-L glass jar with a lid. Cover the jar and store it at room temperature, away from light, for about 6 weeks. Give the jar a swirl every few days.

After the 6 weeks, make a sugar syrup. Combine the sugar and water in a medium saucepan. Bring to a boil and let the syrup continue boiling for 5 minutes. Let cool, and then add it to the limoncello mixture, along with the second bottle of vodka. Cover the jar and infuse for another 5 to 6 weeks, swirling the jar a few times during this period.

Strain the limoncello through a fine-mesh strainer into clean, decorative bottles; discard the lemon zest. Limoncello tastes best when very cold, so store your bottle in the freezer; it should be good for at least a year.

WOOD INFUSIONS, A.K.A. BARREL AGING

Barrel aging is essentially little more than infusing alcohol with wood, a process that has been part of the beverage world for centuries. Wines, spirits, and even beers take on some characteristics of the oak barrels they're stored in. By putting cocktails into oak barrels, we're taking advantage of two processes: using the alcohol as a solvent to wash the caramelized sugars, vanillin, and other organic compounds out of the wood, as well as exposing the cocktails to a small amount of air, which will slowly oxidize the drink over time.

In 2009, I met Tony Conigliaro at his bar ("the bar with no name") at 69 Colebrooke Row, in London. Tony served me a Manhattan that he'd been aging in a glass bottle for five years. The cocktail's flavors were more integrated, softer, and more delicate. I remembered an oak barrel I'd been seasoning with Madeira wine back home, and immediately set out to expand on Tony's experiment upon my return. Almost overnight, bars all over the world began their own barrel-aged cocktail programs.

Barrel aging a cocktail made with wine-based ingredients, such as sherry or vermouth, oxidizes the cocktail slightly. During this process, small amounts of ethylene are converted, via interaction with air, to acetaldehyde, contributing flavors of nut, mushroom, grass, and apple.

Drinks made with wine-based ingredients are also lower in alcohol and higher in acidity and are more efficient at extracting a compound known as hemicellulose. Found in plant matter (such as wood), hemicelluose is believed to break down the rougher edges found in spirits, resulting in a "softer" drink.

Small barrels can be purchased for very little over the Internet, though I do recommend breaking in unused oak barrels for some time with inexpensive sherry to flavor and season the wood. Here are some other tips for aging cocktails in oak:

Aging Cocktails Do's and Don'ts

DO	DON'T
check your cocktail regularly by opening the barrel and extracting samples (I employ a turkey baster dedicated solely to this purpose).	leave your cocktail in a barrel for too long, as it can result in the extraction of too much hemicellulose, which is found in oak, and lead to a flabby cocktail.
be careful about selecting your choice of cocktail to age. Spirit-driven cocktails are, of course, a natural choice for aging, as are cocktails that include a wine-based ingredient, such as vermouth or sherry.	age cocktails that contain ingredients such as fresh citrus, egg whites, or cream, as they are prone to spoilage and can lead to contamination.
choose cocktails made with spirits that have had little to no oak aging. Lighter, unaged spirits such as white whiskey, gin, vodka, unaged rum, and tequila fare the best with time spent in an oak barrel, particularly one that has been previously used to age whiskey.	as a general rule, age cocktails made from oak-aged spirits, as this will minimize the effect of the oak aging and provide you with a much less striking rendition than you would get with unaged spirits.

TINCTURES

Tinctures are similar to infusions, but on a much more concentrated scale. Where we might use 2 oz/60 ml of an infused vodka in a cocktail, we'd use only a dash or drop of a tincture. I like to think of a tincture as a very small, very portable way to add flavor to a drink. In fact, I often carry a few of my favorite tinctures in dropper bottles packed in a small zippered bag in my bar kit.

So why a tincture and not an infused liquor? Well, here's one example: If I have a whole fifth (750 ml) of something very specific, like, say, clove-infused vodka, I can only make those cocktails that call for clove-infused vodka, and there aren't that many. But if I have a small bottle of clove tincture, I can make clove-flavored drinks using any base spirit on my shelf. It's infinitely more versatile, plus it saves space and money— I don't need to commit a lot of resources to clove, since clove is a flavor I care very little about.

Because the purpose of a tincture is to add flavor without volume, it's made from intensely flavored ingredients, including some herbs, spices, citrus peel, chiles, and roots—sassafras, for example. We don't make blueberry tincture, because blueberries just don't have the intensity we need.

The way you get that intensity into the tincture is through controlling the amount of the flavoring agent and the length of steeping time. In other words, you can add a large amount of ingredients to your alcohol, which can get expensive, or you can leave your mixture to steep for a long time—but that requires patience.

To speed up the process while keeping it economical, I use a method similar to the one for making spice infusions (see page 127): I grind the fresh ingredient myself, add it to the alcohol, and it let steep for 1 week or so—or in some cases, for even less time. I always monitor the flavor development by frequent tastings, and I make sure to give it a good shake whenever I pass by, as that tiny volume of spice tends to settle at the bottom of the bottle.

CHOOSING ALCOHOLS FOR TINCTURES

The higher the alcohol content, the more effective the tincturing process. A 100-proof vodka does the job perfectly, and you can find it just about anywhere. Don't be tempted to make a tincture using anything less than about 80-proof spirits, however, because at a lower strength, there are too many water molecules bonding with the alcohol molecules, and they block the ability of the alcohol to release the flavor compounds from the ingredient.

How to Make a Tincture

The ratio I use for my tinctures, by weight, is 1 part flavoring agent to 4 parts alcohol. The method is similar to the others we've discussed in this chapter, but you'll probably be making a smaller quantity, something closer to 8 oz/240 ml at a time.

1. Measure your spice and alcohol and use 1 part spice or herb to 4 parts spirit, in the quantities you desire.

2. Finely mince your herbs, or grind your spice or other dried flavoring in a spice grinder or in a mortar with a pestle, until powdery, or at least quite granular.

3. Put your tincturing ingredient into a clean canning jar, and add your alcohol.

4. Leave for 1 week away from direct sunlight, gently agitating the jar about once a day.

5. Strain your tincture through a coffee filter and store in clean dropper bottles, which you have labeled, to make the tincture easy to administer. (You can find eye dropper bottles at most container stores and at many online sources.)

CINNAMON TINCTURE

MAKES ABOUT 6 OZ/180 ML Cinnamon is one of those flavors I like to use mainly in the fall, and always sparingly. So I keep a small dropper bottle of cinnamon tincture at the bar and at home to easily turn just about any cocktail into something seasonal.

About 2 sticks Ceylon soft-stick cinnamon

1 cup/240 ml 100-proof vodka

Grind the cinnamon in a spice grinder or with a mortar and pestle. In a small canning jar, combine the vodka and cinnamon. Cover and shake to combine. Let sit for 1 week, shaking occasionally to agitate. Strain through a coffee filter and store in a labeled dropper bottle. This keeps forever.

AUTUMN LEAVES

MAKES 1 DRINK We came up with this variation on the classic New Orleans cocktail the Vieux Carré as an autumnal offering at my bar. The drink was so popular when it debuted on our menu five years ago that it's still frequently requested by name.

¾ oz/22.5 ml rye whiskey

¾ oz/22.5 ml apple brandy

¾ oz/22.5 ml sweet vermouth

¼ oz/7.5 ml Strega liqueur

1 dash Cinnamon Tincture (facing page)

Ice cubes

1 orange peel for garnish

CHILLED SMALL ROCKS GLASS

Combine the rye whiskey, apple brandy, vermouth, Strega liqueur, and cinnamon tincture in a mixing glass. Add ice cubes and stir until chilled. Strain into the rocks glass filled with more ice cubes. Twist the orange peel over the surface of the cocktail, rub the rim of the glass with the peel, and then drop in the drink to serve.

BITTERS

What started out more than 200 years ago as a category of medicines is now one of the most talked-about and hotly debated subjects in bartending. It seems like every self-described cocktail geek these days crafts his or her own library of bitters for use at home and behind the bar.

Born in Europe and embraced by America, bitters were originally developed as cure-alls for a variety of ailments, mainly stomach. In fact, an eighteenth-century English hangover cure composed of Stoughton's bitters and fortified wine from the Canary Islands may have been one of the earliest predecessors of the cocktail.

Bitters are having a renaissance right now. Some bartenders are even using bitters as the base spirit in drinks, with surprisingly beautiful results. My friend Giuseppe Gonzalez, a New York bartender, is legendary for a drink known as a Trinidad sour, which calls for a whole 1 oz/30 ml of Angostura bitters, while bartenders Kirk Estopinal and Maks Pazuniak, at Cure, in New Orleans, make a drink called the gunshop fizz, with a whopping 2 oz/60 ml of Peychaud's.

Simply put, bitters are nothing more than a tincture, or combination of tinctures, with the addition of a bittering agent—typically a bitter root or bark. I like to think of them as the salt and pepper of cocktails. While they do bring their own flavor to the party, their main effect is to enhance all the flavors of the drink, making everything taste a bit more

like itself. If the ultimate goal is a drink with depth and complexity, the bitters I reach for are potent and deeply bitter.

ALCOHOL THAT'S TOO HARD TO DRINK?

If bitters are nothing more than blended and bittered tinctures, and tinctures have high-proof alcohol as their base, then why are bitters sometimes sold in places where liquor sales are prohibited? It turns out that even the government believes that some booze is just too difficult to drink on its own. The Alcohol and Tobacco Tax and Trade Bureau, or TTB, has deemed bitters "nonpotable" and therefore not a problem to sell, even to a minor. The flavor is so strong and bitter that it's inconceivable that someone could drink enough to get intoxicated.

Author and bar expert Gary Regan managed to make a bitters that crossed the line from unpalatable to quaffable, at least according to the TTB. They deemed his Regan's Orange Bitters No. 5 too potentially drinkable, and prevented it from being sold. Fortunately for Gary, twelve formulations later he was rewarded with a stamp of approval for a version less palatable on its own, and Regan's Orange Bitters No. 6 was able to make it onto store shelves.

COMMERCIAL BITTERS

Back when I was first getting started in the business, there was one dusty bottle of bitters hidden behind every bar, and it was inconceivable that a day would come when a guest would ask what bitters were available before deciding on a drink. Now, you can stock your bar with a new bottle of bitters every week, but there really are only three that you'll need in order to make the vast majority of classic cocktails: Angostura, Peychaud's, and orange bitters.

Angostura Bitters

These are the go-to bitters, the bottle that is found in every bar, grocery store, liquor store, and home liquor cabinet. Unmistakable, with its distinctive oversize paper label often scrunched around the neck, Angostura bitters have been around since the early 1800s. Angostura is pinkish-purple in color with a flavor profile that can be best described as potent, hinting at cinnamon and herbs.

The bitters have a rich history. Johann Gottlieb Benjamin Siegert was a German doctor who served at the battle of Waterloo before heading to Venezuela, where he became a surgeon general in Simón Bolívar's army. Siegert experimented with local herbs, roots, botanicals, and barks to develop a tonic to help the troops with all manner of digestive ailments.

Peychaud's Bitters

These were developed in the 1830s by Antoine Amédée Peychaud, a Haitian pharmacist living in New Orleans. Peychaud's is used in the very popular Sazerac cocktail, a drink that has kept Peychaud's prominent.

Its flavor is slightly floral, with a subtle hint of anise and notes of cherry and spice. Its bright red color will give your cocktails a beautiful rosy hue.

Orange Bitters

Orange bitters are, as you might guess, a tincture of orange peel and other spices blended with bitter barks and roots. Long extinct, you can find quite a few commercial brands on the market these days, though no single brand stands as the quintessential orange bitters.

When I'm not making my own (see page 138), I often adopt a trick favored by New York bartenders called the fifty-fifty, in which equal parts Fee Brothers and Regan's orange bitters are mixed together to take advantage of the best qualities of each.

HOUSE ORANGE BITTERS

MAKES ONE 750-ML BOTTLE Most bitters recipes you'll see out there call for neutral spirits, such as Everclear, but I prefer to use Wray and Nephew overproof white rum as the base for my orange bitters. It not only provides the necessary high proof I'm looking for but also contributes its own subtle flavor characteristics, unlike flavorless grain alcohol.

For maximum flavor, you can make your own dried orange peel by grating oranges with a Microplane and drying the grated peel on a parchment paper–lined baking sheet in a low oven. Or you can find a reputable spice trader whose product you trust and use pre-dried peel. After making nearly a hundred batches of dried grated orange peel over the years, I now just buy it from a place I like.

One 750-ml bottle overproof white rum, preferably Wray and Nephew

3 oz/85 g dried grated orange peel

2 whole cardamom pods, crushed

½ tsp caraway seeds, crushed

1½ tsp coriander seeds, crushed

1¾ oz/50 ml 2:1 Demerara syrup (see page 78)

Combine the rum, orange peel, cardamom pods, caraway seeds, and coriander seeds in a clean canning jar. Leave for 1 week, away from direct sunlight, gently agitating about once a day.

Add the Demerara syrup and let sit for 1 week more, again agitating daily.

Strain the mixture through a coffee filter and store in clean, labeled dropper bottles. The bitters will keep indefinitely.

REVOLVER

By Jon Santer

MAKES 1 DRINK My first encounter with the revolver went like this: A favorite regular of ours frequently traveled for business, and he enjoyed a good cocktail wherever he went. One night he came in and told us about a bartender he'd recently become enamored with on his latest trip to San Francisco: Jon Santer.

Jon Santer is a bartender's bartender, and something of a legend among those in the know. He now owns The Prizefighter in Emeryville, California, but before that he worked in bars all over San Francisco for years. It was while Jon was working at Bourbon & Branch that our regular enjoyed his cocktail, the revolver.

The drink was described to me by our man, and while I tried my best to replicate it using his instructions, he left unsatisfied. As luck would have it, the drink appeared in a *Wall Street Journal* article the following week, so I cribbed the recipe and surprised our regular with what I thought was a perfect version of his new favorite drink. Although he couldn't put his finger on why, he still wasn't satisfied with my version of the revolver.

Later that year I found myself bartending alongside Jon at a party in London, and eventually I got around to asking him what the secret to the drink was. As it turned out, the recipe in the newspaper was slightly off. I was able to return home and surprise one of our favorite guests with a good story and an even better cocktail, and Jon and I have been close friends ever since.

2 oz/60 ml dry, spicy bourbon

½ oz/15 ml coffee liqueur

2 dashes House Orange Bitters (page 138)

Ice cubes

1 orange peel for garnish

CHILLED NICK AND NORA GLASS

Combine the bourbon, coffee liquer, and House Orange Bitters in a mixing glass. Add ice cubes and stir until chilled (see page 206).

Strain into the chilled Nick and Nora glass. Using the orange peel, express flamed orange oil (see page 277) over the surface of the drink. Drop the orange peel into the drink to serve.

CHAPTER Nº

=7=

DAIRY &
EGGS

ADDING A LAYER OF TEXTURE
THROUGH FOAM AND FAT

—

If it weren't for whoever first used dairy in cocktails, the world very well might be without guilty-pleasure drinks. And that would make me very sad, because I don't want to live in a world without brandy Alexanders and White Russians. There's a chain restaurant around here, which shall go unnamed, that serves these boozy milkshakes full of Kahlúa and Oreo cookies and stuff. They're so good that about once a year I can't control my urges and I have to drive out to the nearest mall to have one.

My parents learned how to drink at a time when "guilty-pleasure cocktails" were simply referred to as cocktails. What we think of today as overly sweet, fruity, or creamy concoctions were the norm back in the '60s and '70s. Sex on the beach. Screwdrivers. The Bahama mama, whatever the hell that is. And then there were the creamy drinks. Piña coladas (which don't actually contain any cream, but are creamy anyway.) White Russians. Grasshoppers. The B-52.

If you wanted to rob my parents' liquor cabinet in, say, the mid-'80s, when I was in high school, you had a choice to make. You could drink what you saw the adults drinking, namely things like Irish cream and Kahlúa, and run the risk of them noticing some booze was missing. Or you could, as I would have done if I were the type who'd steal liquor from my parents, help yourself to the many bottles of Scotch that sat barely touched, all the while envious

of the forbidden: those creamy, fattening, caloric, guilty-pleasure drinks my parents got to enjoy.

But relegating dairy to the world of fatty, overly sweetened drinks minimizes the important role that dairy has played in cocktails since, well, before cocktails as we know them were invented. In the seventeenth century, a mixture of ale, rum, sugar, and raw eggs would be heated with a hot poker from the fireplace; it was a warm early prototype of an eggnog. A dollop of egg whites have been used for well over a hundred years by bartenders to lend drinks a creamier, silkier mouthfeel. Those classic New Orleans breakfast cocktails, the Ramos gin fizz and the brandy milk punch, are balanced and light enough to be consumed on even the muggiest Gulf Coast day.

The whole point is that bartenders have begun to turn back the clock on the use of dairy in cocktails, and we've all realized that there's more to milk, cream, and eggs than simply sweetened vanilla or chocolate milkshakes. And since we're going to be doing more with dairy than simply throwing it into a blender, we'll need to know a thing or two about the products we're handling.

CHOOSING THE BEST DAIRY PRODUCTS AND EGGS

Of all the ingredients you'll use behind the bar, dairy ingredients and eggs are the most perishable. They need to be chosen and handled with as much thought—and perhaps more care—than you'd give to any rare spirit or esoteric liqueur.

With dairy, the best way to choose prime ingredients is to buy from a local farm—directly, if possible, or through a farmers' market or a good grocer. The flavor of your drinks will be markedly better when you use dairy and eggs that have been produced in a more responsible and intelligent way. At the bar, we work with local farmers to get large quantities. For home, I simply pop in at the Saturday farmers' market and pick up what I need for the week.

Even though I advocate local and hyperfresh, there are, of course, limits: we don't ever serve raw (unpasteurized) dairy at a bar, because we don't want to take that kind of health risk with the public. But at the other end of the spectrum, we also avoid ultra-pasteurized half-and-half or cream. Oddly enough, a lot of the organic dairy on the market is ultrapasteurized, which just means that it's been heated to a higher temperature to kill more bacteria and extend the shelf-life. (Ultrapasteurization heats the milk to 280°F/138°C for two seconds; traditional pasteurization heats the milk to 165°F/74°C for fifteen seconds.) But the higher temperature kills not only more of the bacteria but also a lot of the flavor, giving the product a flatter, less fresh, and more, well, cooked taste, which I don't like. If I have to choose between organic ultrapasteurized and a nonorganic regular pasteurized, I'll choose the latter every time.

CREAM

When you're hanging out at home, perusing classic cocktail recipes (as I do) in books and on the Internet, you'll notice that they almost always call for cream. But real cream is rough to work with as an ingredient; it's simply too heavy and too rich to consume in a cocktail, and the greasy mouthfeel interferes with the rest of the drink. I use half-and-half when a recipe calls for cream as an incorporated ingredient, and every bartender I know does as well. Save the cream for whipping, as a garnish, and get the highest fat content you can find.

It's good to know the relative fat contents of the different types of cream and milk, so that you understand what's going into your cream-based drinks and make the right choice.

DAIRY PRODUCT	AVERAGE PERCENTAGE OF FAT
Heavy cream	39%
Whipping cream	35%
Half-and-half	12%
Whole milk	3.8%

ALEXANDER COCKTAIL

MAKES 1 DRINK If you ever have the good fortune to meet my father, ask him to tell you the story about the time he and his buddy Henry Reynoso had, like, fifteen brandy Alexanders each at the bar down the road from the cabin we owned back in the 1980s. My dad knows two things for certain, the first being that brandy Alexanders will make you sicker than anything you've ever had in your life, and the second being that they come from a blender full of ice cream.

All I know about the brandy Alexander is that it's sort of the sequel to an even older drink called the Alexander cocktail, which first appeared sometime around 1915 in New York, and is made with equal parts gin, dark crème de cacao, and cream. Of course, I use half-and-half because it's lighter than cream. It's also lighter than a carton of vanilla ice cream, which was never used in the original Alexanders.

1 oz/30 ml London dry gin

1 oz/30 ml dark crème de cacao

1 oz/30 ml half-and-half

Ice cubes

Freshly grated nutmeg for garnish

CHILLED COCKTAIL GLASS

Combine the gin, créme de cacao, and half-and-half in a cocktail shaker filled with ice cubes and shake for 10 seconds. Double strain into the chilled cocktail glass (see page 219) and garnish with a little fresh nutmeg to serve.

What Does the Sell-By Date Mean on a Carton of Cream?

All dairy products are stamped with something called a sell-by date. A lot of people think it means the contents will be good until that date. A nice promise, but one that's not really true. And it's really no fun to find out the hard way, trust me.

The sell-by date means that if the product is kept properly chilled and *unopened*, it should be good for about 1 week after that date (the store "sells by" and then you take home and keep longer). Once you open that carton or bottle, all bets are off, in the sense that the producer can't control what kind of bacteria may be hastening spoilage. How long you leave the carton on the counter in a warm room, whether someone takes a swig of milk right from the carton (as I usually do), or to what temperature your fridge is set all factor in.

You can assume that a product with a date that's further out will be fresher than one with a date only days away, so be sure to piss off your grocer and rummage around the selections, looking for the one with the latest date. Just remember that once you've opened it, it's up to you to store it optimally to keep it fresh. Opened milk products should be good for 7 to 10 days.

HOW TO STORE CREAM

To keep your cream and half-and-half free from bacteria and preserve flavor and freshness, keep them cold. Bacteria tends to grow around the carton spout and other oxygen-accessible spots. Transferring the cream to a clean plastic squeeze bottle, labeled with the date, minimizes that potential and makes the cream easy to pour and measure.

HOW TO WHIP CREAM

I do use actual cream, rather than half-and-half, when I want it whipped for garnishing a cocktail. To garnish a drink properly with whipped cream, you need to whip it to order. Once again, you've got a few options.

Using a Cream Whipper

While the equipment isn't necessarily cheap, it's certainly the easiest option. You fill the canister with cold cream, charge it with nitrous oxide, give it a shake, and press the lever to deliver whipped cream. You can load it, keep it in the fridge, and have it at the ready whenever you need it; just grab, shake, and go. (It's a good idea to write the date when you added the cream on a piece of masking tape and stick it on the side of the canister.) The biggest drawback—aside from the cost—is the texture of the cream: firm and tight, almost overwhipped. Cream whipped to that consistency might look nice as a swirl on a mocha or a piece of pie, but it doesn't incorporate well into a cocktail; it just sits on top and requires a straw to access the drink beneath.

Whipping Cream Manually

This option is a pain in the ass, but it produces a better whipped cream for use in cocktails. You pour some cold cream into a small stainless-steel bowl, take a whisk, and whip until the cream is thickened and has more volume but isn't yet at the stage where it holds its own shape. Don't be tempted to whip until you see billowy peaks—that's too much. Cream that's only thickened, rather than whipped so it holds peaks, will float nicely on the surface of a cocktail, yet will easily incorporate into the drink as it's sipped without the need for a straw. The cream provides a sort of cool pillow through which a hot coffee cocktail is sipped.

You have a lot of control over texture and consistency with this hand-whipped method, but it's problematic in a service situation for several reasons:

- The volume in the cream doesn't last forever, meaning you will need to rewhip before serving.

- In order to prevent the whipped cream from drying out and picking up flavors, it needs to be covered in plastic wrap.

- It needs to be refrigerated between uses to prevent spoilage.

- And finally, a bowl and whisk take up precious space behind the bar and in the fridge.

The Mason Jar Method

The best option is the one we've perfected at my bar: Take a canning jar, fill it halfway with cream, seal, and shake hard for 15 seconds. Pour the amount you need directly onto your cocktail. What's left over in the jar goes right back into the fridge, where it's ready for you to grab for the next drink. There's no need for messy whisks or bowls, and your cream is already in the dispensing vessel.

Knowing how much to shake the cream is key. The rule of thumb is to shake until the volume has increased by about half. So if you start with 8 oz/240 ml of cream, you want to shake until you have 12 oz/360 ml. Using a jar that has some calibrations on the side—most canning jars do—will help you eyeball the volume levels.

IRISH COFFEE

MAKES 1 DRINK Every year when I visit San Francisco, I perform a little ritual. I drop my bags at the hotel, walk down the street, and catch the streetcar for a ride over the hills to the Buena Vista Cafe for a couple of Irish coffees. The Irish coffee was invented at the Buena Vista, and while I'm sure they do make plenty of other drinks well, I've never ordered anything else. Judging by what the other guests are drinking, neither does anyone else. There's always a line of glasses down the bar, and the bartender cranks them out in assembly-line fashion and finishes them off with a metal tin full of the most delicate cream, lightly whipped in a milk-shake machine to just the right consistency.

If you want to make an Irish coffee as well as they do at the Buena Vista, you can do it without the milkshake machine. Simply shake the cream in a canning jar, using the method described on page 148.

You'll need the right glassware to be truly authentic: A real Irish coffee is served only in a 6-oz/180-ml Libbey Georgian Irish Coffee glass, model number 8054. The glass can be purchased directly from Libbey's website (Retail.libbey.com), but if you don't want to bother with that, you can use a small 6-oz/180-ml wineglass instead. Just know that it's a point of pride for bartenders to serve this one in the proper glass, and it's a joy to take a drink from it.

1½ oz/45 ml Irish whiskey

2 tsp/10 ml 2:1 brown sugar syrup (see page 78)

3 oz/90 ml hot freshly brewed coffee

Whipped cream (see page 148) for garnish

IRISH COFFEE GLASS

Heat the glass with hot water. Once the glass is warm enough, empty the contents and add the whiskey and brown sugar syrup. Stir in the hot coffee. Top with whipped cream and serve (without a straw).

EGGS

The difference in flavor between what I call a supermarket egg and a fresh local egg is remarkable. In part, it's a matter of actual freshness, with a farmers' market egg being probably a few days old at most, while a supermarket egg can be, under U.S. Department of Agriculture (USDA) regulations, up to 5 weeks old when you buy it. (The sell-by date must be no later than 30 days after the eggs are packed, and eggs must be packed no more than 7 days after they were laid.) But the quality of the feed, type of chicken, and other handling issues also affect the flavor and performance of the egg.

MEASURING EGGS

Each individual egg in a carton of eggs labeled "large" doesn't need to meet the USDA's criteria for a large egg; the whole dozen must meet a standard weight. In one carton you could have some undersize and some oversize. And most farmers' market eggs aren't graded by size at all.

Looking again at classic cocktail recipes, you'll often see the author call for "the white of 1 egg" rather than an actual measurement. Keep in mind that eggs were much smaller a hundred years ago than they are today, so when you encounter a recipe calling for 1 egg white, plan on using a volume of ½ oz/15 ml, as we do at my bar. Within a typical egg, you'll have twice as much white as yolk. So in a large egg, the volume of the white will average just over 1 oz/30 ml and the yolk just over ½ oz/15 ml.

As with raw milk and cream, raw unpasteurized eggs (most are unpasteurized) can carry a small risk of bacteria—in the case of eggs, salmonella. The best way to avoid having any problems is to be exquisitely sanitary when preparing, handling, and storing eggs. Once they're out of the shell, always keep them refrigerated. And while I've eaten raw eggs countless times and in countless forms and have never gotten sick, if you do have a compromised immune system, you might want to avoid raw-egg cocktails.

CRACKING EGGS

Whether you crack your egg by rapping it sharply on the edge of a bowl, or use Jacques Pépin's method of tapping the egg flat on the counter (he asserts the sharp edge will force shell into the egg, while the flat surface just creates a breach in the shell for you to pull apart), it's a pretty simple procedure, and one that you've done a hundred times without getting any shell in the egg. But the 101st time, you might not be so lucky. A tiny bit of shell can ruin a drink, and really ruin a large batch of eggs. The foolproof way to avoid getting shell in your egg is to crack the egg into a small bowl first, verify that there's no shell, and dump it into any other eggs, the drink, or whatever the destination is.

WHOLE EGG COCKTAILS

The most straightforward egg-based cocktail is called a flip. As that seventeenth-century mixture of ale, rum, sugar, and raw eggs heated with a hot poker from the fireplace evolved, it emerged in Jerry Thomas's *The Bar-Tender's Guide* (1862) as a cold cocktail without the ale and featuring a myriad of base spirit options such as brandy, rum, gin, or even port wine.

The key to all egg-based cocktails is getting the eggs to a consistency that allows you to combine them with other ingredients, so beating them well before using them in a cocktail is important. I typically use a small whisk and a metal bowl when I'm preparing a big batch of whole eggs or egg whites, or simply my bar spoon in a shaker tin when I'm making a single-serving egg cocktail.

CYNAR FLIP

By Ben Sandrof

MAKES 1 DRINK My friend Ben Sandrof is one of those bartenders who pushes the boundaries. He lives in Boston and has helped run some of the most progressive bar programs in the country. A few years ago he was making a sort of ice cream with Fernet-Branca, a very powerful Italian bitter, when the idea struck him to try making a flip with Cynar, another Italian *amaro*, made from artichokes. It was the first time I'd ever heard of such a thing, and I've been making them with great success ever since.

1 egg

2 oz/60 ml Cynar

2 tsp/10 ml 2:1 simple syrup
(see page 78)

Ice cubes

Fee Brothers Whiskey Barrel-Aged
bitters for garnish

CHILLED COUPE GLASS

Put the egg into the cocktail shaker, making sure no shell came along. Then, using your bar spoon, break up the yolk, and whip the egg vigorously to loosen up the whites.

Add the Cynar and simple syrup, fill the shaker with ice cubes, and shake. Strain into the chilled cocktail coupe. Using an eyedropper, drop bitters into the foam on top of the drink and drag a toothpick through the bitters to garnish before serving.

CLYDE COMMON EGGNOG

MAKES ABOUT 1 GL/3.8 L Eggnog is essentially a flip, with the addition of cream (read that as half-and-half, remember?). While you can technically make eggnog as you would the flip (see page 153), adding 2 oz/60 ml of cream to the mix, I find that eggnog is best shared with friends, and it also lends itself to aging for a day or so in the fridge.

Therefore, I always make my eggnog in a large batch and trade in my shaker and bar spoon for a blender. You simply blend the eggs for a few seconds on low speed, which will get the consistency fluid enough to play well with the other ingredients as you continue to build your cocktail.

The eggnog we serve at my bar, Clyde Common, in Portland, Oregon, has been immensely popular for years. The combination of sweet añejo tequila with dry amontillado sherry is a gorgeous pairing.

12 large eggs
2¼ cups/450 g superfine sugar
12 oz/360 ml añejo tequila
15 oz/450 ml amontillado sherry
36 oz/1 L whole milk
24 oz/720 ml heavy cream
Freshly grated nutmeg for garnish

SMALL CHILLED PUNCH GLASSES

In a blender or stand mixer on low speed, beat the eggs until smooth. Slowly add the sugar and blend or beat until all of it is incorporated. Slowly add the tequila, sherry, milk, and cream. Refrigerate overnight and serve in small chilled punch glasses. Dust with fresh nutmeg before serving.

EGG-WHITE COCKTAILS

Bartenders learned long ago that they could create a creamy mouthfeel in a cocktail, without the flavor and fatty feel of cream, simply by adding a dollop of whipped egg white. But don't listen to mustachioed speakeasy mixologists who might be inclined to tell you that the original whiskey sour recipe called for egg whites—it didn't. The white does give the drink a wonderful texture, however.

HOW TO SEPARATE AN EGG

You've got three options for separating the white from the yolk, from the simplest to the most culinary.

The Shell Method

This method uses the shell itself as the separating tool, and is quicker and more foolproof than the two methods that follow, but it takes some practice to get it right. Crack the egg sharply in the center, gently insert both thumbs, and pry the shell apart over a small bowl to catch the white. As you pull apart the egg shell, simultaneously invert the egg so the egg shell halves are open-side up, one in each hand. The egg will be in one half, and the white will be spilling over its sides and into the bowl.

Tip the full half to allow more of the white to begin dripping from the shell into the bowl. Use the other half to catch the yolk as it starts to slide out as well. Repeat the

process, letting as much of the white as possible fall into the bowl, but always catching the yolk before it falls.

Be careful not to let the edge of the shell pierce the yolk. The whites won't foam properly if they're contaminated with any type of fat, such as egg yolk or cream. After a few back-and-forths, the white will be in the bowl and the yolk in the shell; save it for another use or discard it.

The Hand Method

Holding the egg in your dominant hand, crack it in the center, at the widest point, sharply on the counter or on the edge of a bowl. Then, widen the crack by pulling one half of the shell with the thumb and forefinger of your dominant hand while gripping the other half with your palm and other fingers. You just need to open the two halves wide enough for the egg to fall out, into your nondominant hand, which is gently cupped over a bowl to catch the egg.

Now, open the fingers of your "catching hand" a bit to let the egg white slide between them, into the bowl, keeping the yolk in your hand. Dump the yolk into a second bowl, and repeat if you have more eggs, or wash your hands if not. This method can be very fast if you're good at it, but it does mean that your hands have to be immaculate before you start—not great if you wear rings and such—and you'll need to take a quick break to wash your hands afterward, too.

The Tool Method

There are tools designed for separating eggs, but they take up valuable space, have only one purpose, and are not as effective as the two other methods. One tool looks like a shallow cup with slots around the rim. You crack the egg into it, the yolk settles into the curved bowl, and as you tilt the cup, the white slides out the slots into another catch bowl.

The second design looks a little like a strainer, but instead of mesh, you have spiral wires. You crack the egg into the center, the white slides out through the wires, and the yolk is captured in the center. Sometimes. I strongly suggest skipping the tools and using one of the previous methods.

HOW TO PREPARE AND STORE EGG WHITES

Egg whites are mucilaginous (super slippery) and resist being divided or mixed. If you've ever tried to add just half an egg white to a recipe, you know what I mean: you start to empty a little bit of the white out of the shell, and before you know it the entire white slides into your bowl.

That gloppiness is the work of proteins in the egg white (whites are 90 percent water, 10 percent proteins). In their natural state, the proteins are curled up tightly in little balls, with bonds holding the protein strands together. As you whisk or otherwise agitate the whites, those protein balls are slammed around, and the impact loosens the bonds. The balled-up proteins begin to unfurl and form new bonds with other proteins, rather than with themselves. This creates a loose network. If you continue to agitate, you begin to introduce air bubbles into the network. The air is captured by the proteins, and the result is foamy or fluffy whites, depending on how far you go.

Beat the whites slightly to loosen them up; use your bar spoon or a small whisk, depending on how many whites you're working with. Label a small squeeze bottle with the date and store the egg whites in the bottle in the fridge. During service, you can keep the whites in a small hotel pan of ice; you really do need to pay attention to proper food handling methods here, since raw eggs of any kind have some risk associated with them (see page 152). They will keep for about 1 week.

HOW TO SHAKE AN EGG-WHITE COCKTAIL

Drinks containing egg whites benefit from an initial shake without ice—called a dry shake—which will develop a thicker, more voluptuous and stable foam. Chad Solomon, former bartender at New York's Pegu Club and partner at the beverage consulting company Cuffs & Buttons, has championed the technique, though bar historians have recently found references to the method going back decades.

Proteins will stretch and unwind more easily, as previously described, if they're given some time to loosen up rather than being rushed into the process. A chef usually whips eggs whites more slowly at first and then turns up the speed once a light foam has formed. The dry shake accomplishes this for the bartender.

The dry shake also just allows more total time for you to shake the whites—once you add ice, you're limited as to how much shaking you can do because you can't risk overdiluting the drink with melting ice. So shake first to get a good foam established, and then continue with ice, which will create even more agitation and foam.

Another way to jump-start a good foam is to prefroth the whites using a small electric whipper, such as the Aerolatte, intended for whipping milk for espresso drinks, but perfect as an adjunct bar tool.

Some bartenders will remove the spring from a spare Hawthorne strainer (see page 219) and toss it in the shaker with the drink for even greater whipping power, though I use Mr. Solomon's dry shake with fantastic results. I also don't have to deal with a steel spring covered in sticky egg-white cocktail when I'm done, so I've got that going for me.

Sealing a Boston Shaker for a Dry Shake

When you're doing a dry shake, you do need to modify your method if you're using a Boston shaker (see page 213). Because there's no ice, your contents aren't cold, and your shaking tins won't contract to make the tight seal you need. With a Boston shaker used in the typical fashion, with the top tin seated in the bottom half at a slight angle (see page 218), you run the risk of egg whites and cocktail leaking out of the sides and onto your shirt, face, the wall behind you, and your guests.

So instead of sealing the Boston shaker in the traditional method, align the two halves perfectly, dead center, and give the top half a solid smack with your fist. Do your dry shake, open, add ice, and then close in the normal way to do your final shake with ice.

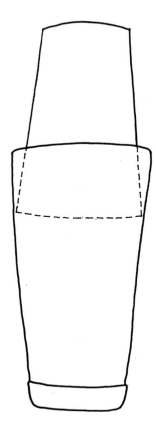

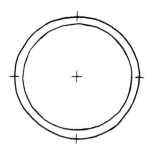

Boston Shaker in Dry Shake Alignment

WHITE LADY

MAKES 1 DRINK The original white lady recipe in Harry Craddock's *Savoy Cocktail Book*, published in 1930, doesn't contain any egg whites. However, almost every recipe you'll find after that inexplicably does. Maybe it's because bartenders learned what I learned: while a white lady made without egg white (a gin sidecar, essentially) is a great drink, one made with egg white is absolutely sublime.

I've taken a few other liberties with this drink, but my favorite has to be the addition of the thyme-infused Cointreau.

1½ oz/45 ml London dry gin

1 oz/30 ml Thyme-Infused Cointreau (page 127)

¾ oz/22.5 ml fresh lemon juice (see page 22)

1 tsp/5 ml 2:1 simple syrup (see page 78)

½ oz/15 ml egg white

Ice cubes

1 orange peel for garnish

CHILLED COCKTAIL GLASS

Combine the gin, Cointreau, lemon juice, simple syrup, and egg white in your cocktail shaker. Shake without ice until the white is frothy (see page 157). Add ice cubes and shake again until chilled.

Strain into the chilled cocktail glass. Twist the orange peel over the drink, discard the peel, and serve.

ICE

SELECTING A SHAPE FOR
PROPER CHILLING AND DILUTION

The quest for flawless ice—crystal-clear cubes, perfectly round spheres, and frosty crushed snowdrifts—has been a huge part of the modern cocktail renaissance. But it isn't the first time people have gone above and beyond for the perfectly chilled drink.

Before the nineteenth century, some people knew the pleasures of ice and some didn't. Ice existed only in the imagination of folks living in hot climates. Northern societies, in contrast, harvested blocks of ice from lakes and ponds in the winter, and kept it frozen through the warm seasons by storing it in deep wells insulated with straw, for use in summer drinks consumed by genteel company in upper-crust drawing rooms.

In one of those drawing rooms, at the home of wealthy Boston lawyer William Tudor, was his ne'er-do-well son Frederic, who turned down his admission to Harvard, preferring instead to hang out at the family estate, hunting and fishing. Perhaps while sipping an iced drink one day, Frederic had an early inspiration: somebody ought to bring this stuff to the tropics.

Beginning in 1806, with an entrepreneurial mania and a few thousand of his father's dollars, Tudor bought ships; packed ice; braved oceans, skeptics, and tropical heat; and eventually established a worldwide ice trade, bringing ice from picturesque New England ponds to the American South, Cuba, Calcutta, and beyond. Tudor's company cut ice from the fabled Walden Pond, causing Henry David Thoreau to write in

his journal, "The sweltering inhabitants of Charleston and New Orleans, of Madras and Bombay and Calcutta, drink at my well. . . . The pure Walden water is mingled with the sacred water of the Ganges."

It's interesting to note that back then, ice had provenance, and the best ice came from the best places. Much as we get all misty-eyed these days over Copper River salmon, Ethiopian Yirgacheffe coffee beans, or ham from the little black-footed pigs of Spain, fancy Londoners in the mid-1800s would serve only crystal-clear ice from Wenham Lake, in Massachusetts.

Today's bar culture may not be *that* obsessive about ice, but we're getting there. For the modern bartender, it's not a matter of what lake the ice comes from, but rather what form it comes in: crushed, cubed, speared, "sphered," and even smoked. Ice means more to the professional bartender these days than simply whether a drink is served straight up or on the rocks. We now talk about dilution and temperature when we talk about ice. And the best cocktails are perfectly diluted, and very, very cold.

Because it's this last property—the one that creates the beautiful frosty glaze on your silver julep cup, the thirst-quenching relief when you take a sip of a cold drink on a hot day, and the brain freeze when you suck down a Slurpee too quickly—that has driven people to do crazier and crazier things since Frederic Tudor started shipping that ice around the world.

HOW ICE BEHAVES

We say that ice is to the bartender as fire is to the chef. In the same way a skilled cook uses heat to prepare food, the professional bartender uses ice to prepare cocktails. And as the chef creates and manipulates heat differently to get different results—think of the difference between a seared steak and a braised pot roast—the bartender uses different forms of ice in different ways to prepare cocktails. And in order to know how to use ice properly, it's important to know what ice is and understand how it behaves.

Ice is the phase of water (H_2O) that occurs at 32°F/0°C. When water begins to freeze, the molecules begin to form a hexagonal crystalline structure. Water molecules always form a hexagon when they approach that temperature, which is why snowflakes always have six sides. Water also comes with another pretty remarkable characteristic, which is that in its frozen form, it (unlike, say, steel) occupies more space and is therefore less dense than its liquid form.

Water in its Liquid State   Water in its Solid State

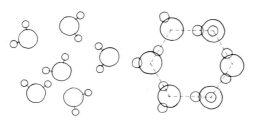

Ice performs two important tasks in cocktails: it chills and it dilutes. It always does both at the same time, though it does so at different rates, depending on the size and shape of the ice, and the method you employ to mix the drink. Some of it happens during mixing, whether you're stirring, shaking, blending, or swizzling. And some happens after you've poured the drink, if the drink is served on the rocks. The challenge for the bartender is using both of those variables in a controlled way, by using a specific form of ice for each type of drink.

WHY ICE CLARITY MATTERS

A typical ice cube from a home freezer is fairly cloudy—parts are clear, parts are milky, and there are probably a few fissures running through the cube. The cloudiness in ice comes from two sources: impurities and air, neither of which we want in our drinks. This might not seem like a big deal when you're dropping the cubes into a Diet Coke or glass of iced tea, but it can make or break a cocktail. Whether your ice is clear or cloudy isn't simply a matter of aesthetics; it's also a matter of performance.

The first reason we are concerned with the purity of the ice we use is that the ice will become an ingredient in your cocktails through the process of dilution. Some of that ice is going to melt, and the water will be mixed with the other ingredients in your drink. So you need ice that tastes only like pristine water, and not like pipes or a freezer.

Air in ice is a problem for other reasons. At normal atmospheric pressure, oxygen and other gases are dissolved in water. As the water freezes, it traps the air, resulting in opaque ice cubes, which aren't very attractive. More air in the ice also equals less density, which means less cooling power and faster melting.

Drop a cube of pure, hard, clear ice into a glass of good whiskey and you'll have a long period of sipping with minimal dilution. Drop the same size cube, but one that's frosted on the inside, and your whiskey will be tasting pretty weak in a shorter amount of time; there's less actual chilling power in the cube.

OBTAINING CLEAR ICE

High-end ice machines are designed to purify the water used in making ice, which is one step toward clarity. But, more important, they also freeze the water slowly, from the bottom up. As the ice crystals slowly form in those bottom layers, they squeeze the air out, sending it up to the next layer of water. That layer freezes, and the air moves up to the next layer. Eventually the whole quantity of water is frozen solid, and all the gases have been pushed to the surface, where they escape. The slow process leaves you with gas-free, crystal-clear ice.

When making ice yourself, whether large-format or smaller cubes, it's nearly impossible to manipulate the direction of the freeze, and I've tried pretty much every method out there. Here's the deal with clear ice:

There are a lot of knuckleheads out there who will tell you that you have to boil the water first, in order to boil off the air. Some even say to boil the water twice, letting it come to room temperature in between. Some say you've got

to freeze the water, let it melt, and then freeze it again in order to obtain clear ice. I've even heard (God help me on this one) that you've got to put the water in the freezer while still boiling, because boiling water freezes faster and clearer than cold water. Let me just share this with you right now, my friend: every one of those methods is 100 percent pure, crystal-clear, ice-cold b.s.

I've tried using an aquarium pump to circulate water in a container in the freezer, but I still had a hard time controlling the direction of the freeze. Oh, and I also had an electrical cord hanging out of my freezer door and an aquarium pump frozen solid in a block of ice at the end of the experiments. I ended up with ice that was kinda clearish . . . in some places.

I've tried filling an Igloo cooler and cramming it into my freezer, so that the water would freeze from the top down. But then I realized that the only thing I had in my freezer was an Igloo cooler and a block of ice that still wasn't perfectly clear. And it took a good day and a half to freeze.

I've set my freezer to a higher temperature, but still below freezing, in order to give the air time to escape as the ice formed more slowly. But then I had a freezer dedicated to cocktail ice, as my ice cream melted and my fish started to smell.

And then I realized something: there's a place down the street that sells 300-lb/136-kg blocks of commercial-grade, crystal-clear ice. Now I grab a few fellow bartenders, load the block into a truck, grab some chainsaws, and

have an ice-block carving party. And I walk away with enough large bricks of ice to fill a chest freezer.

But if you're still hell-bent on making the densest, best-tasting ice at home, just do yourself a favor and pick up some distilled water at the grocery store and freeze that. It's got air in it, there's no way around that. But it's also going to be the purest water you'll find, so just do it and be happy with the results.

STORING ICE

You're always going to be making ice ahead of time since it needs time to freeze, and for the most part, you can make it many days ahead. But ice doesn't keep indefinitely. It easily absorbs odors from other ingredients, so try to keep your freezer as free from old food as possible, and cycle through your ice at least every week. If you don't use it by then, dump it and start fresh. If you really want to be fussy, or if you've spent time fabricating special shapes or sizes, you can seal your ice with a vacuum sealer, which will keep it fresh and clean for months.

TRANSPORTING ICE

If you've gone to the trouble of making high-quality ice—whether that means one hundred 2-in/5-cm cubes or one stunning punch ring —and you need to transport it, line your cooler with dry-ice packs, add your cocktail ice, and then top with more packs. You can get dry ice from a number of sources, including hardware stores, ice cream shops, and grocery stores.

But take care when handling dry ice, which is frozen carbon dioxide. Dry ice clocks in at about -100°F/-73°C, and if you touch it for more than a split second, your cells will freeze, and the result will be like a burn. You also don't want to store dry ice in a perfectly airtight cooler. As the frozen carbon dioxide "sublimates," or vaporizes, it turns into gas, which could cause any airtight container to expand and possibly explode.

HANDLING ICE

There are really three ways to handle ice: with your hands, with a pair of ice tongs, or with an ice scoop. And of course, each technique has its own peculiar tricks.

You'll mainly be handling large chunks of ice with your bare hands—whether pulling a block from the freezer to cut and shape, or putting a sphere or large cube into a glass—so your hands need to be impeccably clean before touching anything that will be going into your guest's drink.

Tongs are used for handling medium-size ice, when a pair of bare hands might seem a little unsightly to the guest, yet an ice scoop might be too small for unwieldy pieces. There are many types of stainless-steel tongs to choose from, and the choice is a matter of preference. I like the tweezer-style tongs with textured tips, as I think they're a little more elegant and maneuverable than standard scallop-tipped kitchen spring tongs. Bamboo tongs are another, mainly stylistic, option. If

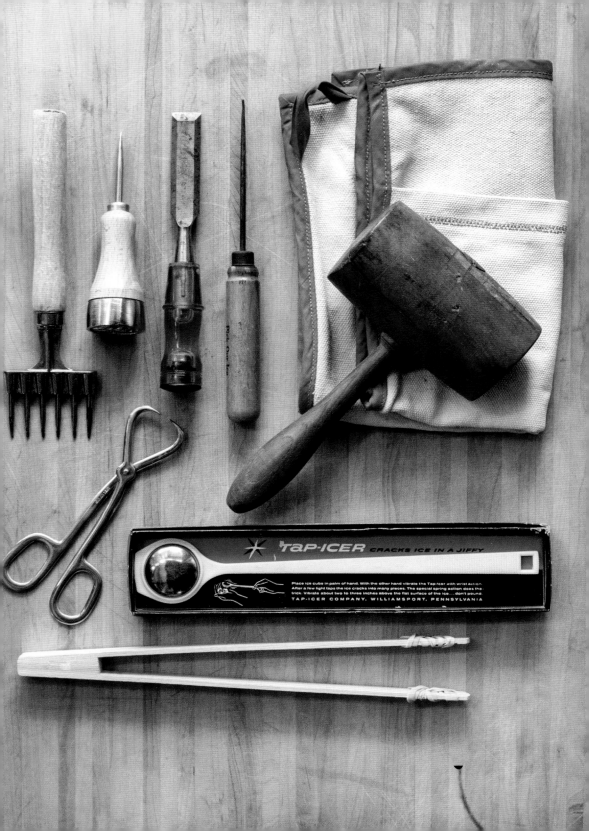

Tap-Icer CRACKS ICE IN A JIFFY

Place ice cube in palm of hand. With the other hand vibrate the Tap-Icer with wrist action. After a few light taps the ice cracks into many pieces. The special spring action does the trick. Vibrate about two to three inches above the flat surface of the ice ... don't pound.

TAP-ICER COMPANY, WILLIAMSPORT, PENNSYLVANIA

I'm using a pair of bamboo tongs, I always wrap a rubber band around each tip to provide a little extra gripping power.

For smaller pieces of ice, such as cubed or crushed ice, I keep a 12-oz/360-ml stainless-steel ice scoop with a solid, contoured handle. Using a glass to scoop ice from a bin is absolutely forbidden, as the risk of even the tiniest shard of glass in your ice supply is one you can't afford to take.

TYPES OF ICE

Here's a description of the basic categories of ice used by bartenders. Some are achievable in a home setting and others really are the province of the pros.

BLOCK ICE

Let's start with large blocks of ice, and in many cases, we mean really large. Bars that make a big commitment to ice programs are buying Clinebell Equipment Company's Carving Block Ice Maker, a serious investment of a machine that produces two 300-lb/136-kg blocks of crystal-clear ice every three or four days. Special pumps and filters remove impurities, but, more important, the water is circulated over a metal cooling plate so the ice is formed from the bottom up in layers, as described earlier.

Clinebell ice makers were originally designed for people who needed very large blocks of ice in order to do ice sculpture. If you've ever been to a culinary school graduation, or perhaps a midnight buffet on a cruise

ship, you've probably seen ice sculptures: soaring eagles, graceful swans, and, of course, tasteful nudes. Whether you get why someone would spend twenty hours in a walk-in freezer creating an ice sculpture or not, you can understand why they need clear ice. Any vein of bubbles or change in density could mean a fracture or crumble that ruins the painstaking hours of work. By contrast, bartenders are rather restrained in their ice sculpting, sticking to large cubes, spears, and, occasionally, dramatically shaped shards.

How to Break Down Block Ice

A large block of ice needs to be broken down into usable pieces. My friends and I have a chainsaw that we've set aside for specifically this purpose. We carve the massive block into more usable 12-by-12-by-24-in/30-by-30-by-60-cm pieces, which are then sealed in plastic bags and stored in a chest freezer.

The first thing I do when breaking down block ice is remove it from its bag or container, and then let it set out at room temperature for 15 to 30 minutes, depending on the size of the block and what temperature the freezer is set to. To warm it up, place it on a lint-free towel laid over a sheet pan. This step is important to bring the ice up to a temperature that will allow cutting without shattering. Ice below 15°F/-9°C is susceptible to shattering.

After a short warm-up, your ice block should be ready to use. Drain the sheet pan of water, and place the ice block atop a fresh towel (to prevent slipping) on the sheet pan.

The key here is to work slowly and let the ice do the work. I use a fine-toothed Japanese crosscut razor woodworking saw for this process. Measuring approximately 6 in/15 cm from one side of the block, cut a guideline with the saw. Once you're certain that you have the right placement, begin to slowly cut through the block.

This process takes some time and some elbow grease, so work deliberately and carefully until you've made your way through the block. I usually place this first slice back in the freezer to prevent melting while I continue to divide the remainder of the block.

Breaking down the pieces further will require more cutting, breaking the slices down until you have a bunch of perfect, large cubes of ice.

LARGE-FORMAT ICE

Large cubes are the best option for serving ice in spirit-driven drinks, as they melt slowly, keeping the cocktail cold with only minimal dilution over a long time. One big, chunky cube is impressive as it sits there chilling a cocktail or measure of whiskey in a rocks glass. Bar programs that make big blocks with a Clinebell ice maker or large molds often carve large made-to-measure cubes for various drinks using the tools and methods described previously, but there are other options for getting large-format cubes.

You can use special molds, such as those from Tovolo; the flexible silicone makes it easy to pop out the cubes. The King Cube model makes 2-in/5-cm cubes, which are actually quite big. Or you can do what I do: Pick up a multicompartment plastic storage box at a hardware store, the lidded type most often used for holding nails and screws. Simply discard the lid, fill with distilled water, and freeze. The model I have at home has 1¾-in/ 4.5-cm cubed compartments. You can store your big, beautiful cubes in a lidded plastic container in the freezer; just reach in and grab to order. (If you're making ice to use in a commercial setting, however, you should stick to food-grade materials.)

CUBES

Large-format ice isn't great for mixing cocktails, however, as one large cube won't provide the same agitation as a few smaller ones. The best standard-size ice cubes for shaking and stirring cocktails are made by Kold-Draft or Hoshizaki ice machines, which produce extra-large 1¼-in/3.2-cm cubes, appreciated by bartenders for their clarity and handsome square shape, as well as their slow-melting property. At home I use Tovolo Perfect Cube silicone ice trays to make my own 1-in/2.5-cm cubes, which I then store in a lidded Lexan plastic container until I'm ready to use them.

Stirring a drink with large cubes requires a longer time to accomplish proper chilling and dilution; in a busy bar setting, that can be a drawback. A combination of large cubes and cracked ice will speed up the process. I often use a ratio of 3:1, whole cubes to cracked cubes.

SPEARS

While an ice spear's main contribution to a drink is its dramatic aesthetics, it does provide a slow-melting chill. It's essentially a long cube, cut to fit the height of a collins glass. Spears are usually carved from big blocks by industrious barbacks, or they may be frozen in special molds.

You can make your own ice spear molds by carefully cutting out the separators between the chambers of a flexible ice cube tray, like the Tovolo, using a sharp razor or X-Acto knife. Simply choose how many cubes tall you'd like your spears to be and cut accordingly. You can also order purpose-made collins cube molds from Cocktail Kingdom online (www.cocktailkingdom.com).

Store spears in a lidded plastic container in the freezer, with the layers separated by sheets of wax paper, and grab to order. Just be careful, though, as spears are more fragile than cubes.

CRACKED ICE

Half to a quarter the size of ice cubes, but nowhere near as fine as crushed ice, cracked ice offers more surface area for rapid cooling and dilution, and gives a sparkling look to your drink. I like to use cracked ice to speed up stir times as well as to serve in highballs—there's something almost romantic about the tinkle of small pieces of ice in a glass as you sip a gin and tonic with a mixture of cracked and cubed ice.

Unfortunately, cracked ice shouldn't be made ahead of time, as one would do with larger specialty ice. In order to minimize exposed surface area and prevent melting, the bartender needs to make cracked ice to order; I find that ice cracked ahead of service always results in either a watery mess, or a mass of cracked shards frozen together in the freezer.

To make cracked ice, start with a cube. Cradle it in your (impeccably clean) hand and strike it sharply with the edge of the hammer end of your bar spoon; two or three blows should give you the consistency you want. I also like using a tool called a Tap Icer from the '50s or '60s that I picked up at an online auction. On the end of its flexible plastic handle is a stainless-steel ball that shatters ice cubes on contact.

An alternative method is to slide some cubes into a small ice scoop, hold the scoop in your palm, and thwack the ice with a muddler. Then you can simply pour the cracked ice from the scoop into the glass. The disadvantage of this method is that the ice is more likely to jump around, since the scoop doesn't always cradle and contain it.

CRUSHED ICE

Crushed ice is as it sounds—highly fractured ice, which means lots of surface area and quick and easy melting. Crushed ice also has a particular aesthetic, both in the way it looks in the glass or cup and in the way it feels, sounds, and releases the liquor held within the myriad tiny pockets as you sip.

For a small quantity of crushed ice, I use what's called a Lewis bag. It's essentially a small canvas sleeve into which you stick some ice cubes and then smash them with a mallet. The canvas wicks away the melting water, so that you're left with crushed ice that's fairly dry. You can reach in with your ice scoop and fill your glass directly.

The canvas needs to stay pristine, of course, so it doesn't "flavor" your ice. But never put a Lewis bag into the washing machine—you don't want to pick up any laundry soap flavors. Instead, run the bag through the dishwasher as needed and let it air-dry.

You can also use an ice-crushing machine. I've used the Waring IC70 model, which works fine with small or cracked cubes as long as you feed them in slowly, but otherwise it has a tendency to jam. The larger, heavy-duty ice crushers, with burly five-horsepower motors, will happily chew through mounds of ice, but they're a bit overkill for a home bar.

The machine that has always worked well for me at home as well as behind the bar is a regular food processor. Fill with ice cubes, pulse, pulse, pulse, and before you know it, you've got beautiful, granular, fluffy crushed ice. Nothing takes advantage of beautifully crushed ice better than a mint julep.

MINT JULEP

MAKES 1 DRINK I like to think of the mint julep as one of the world's first single-serving cocktails and as the predecessor to the cocktail that we now know as the old-fashioned (see page 82). If you look closely, the two formulas are essentially identical: 1 tsp of sugar, 2 oz/60 ml of liquor, some water, and a little something to add a flavorful kick to the drink. In the case of the old-fashioned, that kick comes in the form of bitters. In the case of the mint julep, it comes from fresh spearmint.

```
10 sprigs fresh spearmint
1 tsp/5 ml 2:1 simple syrup
(see page 78)
2 oz/60 ml bourbon
Crushed ice
```

SILVER JULEP CUP

In the bottom of the julep cup, combine about 10 fresh spearmint leaves with the simple syrup. Muddle the mint gently (see page 230) with the disk end of a bar spoon, add the bourbon, and stir to combine.

Working slowly, add crushed ice while stirring the ingredients to chill them and incorporate the ice. Continue packing the cup with crushed ice until the ice forms a mound on top of the drink.

Insert the tip of a chopstick into the ice to make a small hole. Gather together 6 to 8 trimmed sprigs of mint, and insert the bouquet into the hole. Guide a straw into the hole alongside the garnish, and serve.

ICE FOR PUNCH

Punches are made in batches, either to be served one glass at a time from behind a bar, or as a community drink, ladled from a pretty crystal bowl at a party. In either case, you need a lot of ice to cool the large volume of punch. There are two schools of thought when it comes to keeping punch cold—adding ice directly to the punch or chilling it externally. Whichever approach you use is really a matter of service. Which one will provide the coldest, most attractive, and easiest way to serve punch in your situation?

Adding Ice to the Punch

You can add ice to punch decoratively, by making an ice mold, with or without frozen garnishes. To make molded ice for punch, choose a mold that will fit your punch bowl—an ornate Bundt pan or gelatin mold usually is a good size. Slice citrus fruit very thinly and arrange it in an attractive pattern on the inside of the mold. Don't add your water next, or your design will float away. Rather, pack the mold with crushed ice, which will keep everything in place, and then fill with cold water and freeze. An ice mold does require some forethought. It can take up to 12 hours for a ring mold to freeze, so plan ahead.

If your punch isn't on display, say it's behind the bar where your guests won't see it, you can keep it cold without diluting it by filling a 1-qt/960-ml zip-top bag with ice cubes and plunking it right into the punch. Over the course of your evening, the ice will melt, so you can simply unzip the bag, pour out the melted water, and refill with new cubes.

Chilling Punch Externally

To keep punch cold without internal ice, fill a large bowl with cracked ice and then position your punch bowl in the ice. Top off the ice bowl with water, staying below the rim of the punch bowl so you don't risk sloshing into the punch.

MAKING SPHERICAL ICE

A sphere made of any material is a special shape, in that it provides a greater amount of volume for its surface area than any other form. For our applications, this means that a sphere that is equal in volume to a cube has less surface area exposed to the liquid that will be melting the ice—24.069992018164 percent less, to be exact. So, theoretically, a sphere of ice will chill the whiskey that surrounds it while imparting less water to the alcohol. There are a few ways to create this difficult shape in ice.

To shape a sphere from a large-format cube (see page 170), place the cube on a cutting board or on a towel on the counter. With one hand pressing down on the top of the cube, take a serrated bread knife and slowly chip away the bottom four corners of the cube. Flip the cube over and repeat on the opposite surface. What you should be left with is a sort of polyhedron, or a soccer ball–looking piece of ice. Wearing gloves or cradling the ice with a towel, use an ice pick or serrated bread knife to knock off any sharp corners, rotating the ice until you arrive at a uniform shape.

Most bartenders I know then rinse the ice ball under cool running water to further smooth out any rough edges. The ice ball is then dried with a lint-free towel and placed in the freezer until ready to use. While this method is essentially free of extra cost and equipment, it still requires time and expertise on the part of the bartender. Less effective and more expensive options that require less technical ability do, however, exist.

Many companies now make silicone ice ball molds. This is essentially two halves of a sphere, which fit together snugly to form a shell. The water is poured into a hole in the top half of the unit (the hole also catches the overflow as the water begins to expand). The unit is then frozen solid, the silicone halves are peeled from the ice ball, and the ice is ready to be used. My experience using these has resulted in more than a few cracked ice balls, whose deep fissures essentially increase the surface area of the ice ball, negating any benefits in that department.

The third method requires an expensive piece of equipment and seems to be more of a parlor trick than a classic bar technique, but it sure is awesome to watch. The device is called an ice ball maker or ice ball press, and it consists of two heavy copper or aluminum cylinders, which fit one on top of the other and are connected by pins. In the center of the cylinders are hemispherical depressions; if you put the two together, you'd have a spherical void in the center.

You separate the cylinders and place a large cube of ice in the bottom hemispherical depression. Place the top one onto the pins so it slides down to rest on the ice. The heat transfer from the copper to the ice creates instant melting, and as the cube melts, the cylinders move closer together, eventually closing altogether, with only the ball of ice remaining on the inside. You sort of have to see it to believe it; watch one of the many videos online that demonstrate it. It's really cool. The downside to these units is that they tend to be very expensive.

CHAPTER № 9

MEASURING

DEVELOPING BALANCE BETWEEN PRECISION AND EFFICIENCY

A few years ago, I was behind the bar on a slow weeknight, wiping down bottles and telling jokes with the regulars, when I spied a young man coming in the door.

He approached the bar casually, looking around the room to check out the other patrons, and then sat down. When I asked him what he would like, he gestured nonchalantly toward the bottles behind me. "Just give me a couple of fingers of Scotch, please."

"Certainly, sir. May I see your ID, please?"

And with the heavy sigh of an inconvenienced man, he produced a driver's license stating that he was twenty-three years old. But, unfortunately for this gentleman, I had already determined that he wasn't of age and so I asked to see a second piece of identification.

"I, uh, left it in my, uh, car. I'll go get it." And without another word, he snatched the driver's license out of my hands and darted out the door. I went back to what I was doing, with no intention of making the drink he requested.

"Wow, that must have been one shitty fake ID, huh?" asked one of the regulars seated at the bar.

"Oh no, it looked really good, actually. Definitely good enough to fool even my eyes." I said.

"So, then how did you know he wasn't really twenty-one?" asked another one of the regulars.

"It was pretty easy, actually," I said. "Only cowboys in old movies measure their whiskey in fingers."

WHY DO WE MEASURE?

Bartending is not, to the dismay of many, an art form. It is a craft. What's the difference? Well, simply put, art is about creating something beautiful and unique, an object, a one-of-a-kind moment in time. Craft work is about doing the same thing, over and over again, improving slightly each time, fine-tuning, adjusting, and aiming for the unattainable goal of pure perfection. Sounds kind of dreary to some, but to those of us who enjoy that sort of thing, it's a Zen practice.

Cooking could be considered an art form. For the savory cook, a dash of this and a pinch of that is the way to respond to a particular set of ingredients on a particular day when in a particular mood. Making cocktails is more akin to baking: everything is carefully measured before being put through a calculated transformation—in baking, through heat; in cocktails, usually through cold. There is no leaving it on the stove for another half hour, adding a bit more butter, or seasoning to taste with salt and pepper. Baking demands precision, and so do cocktails.

There's also the matter of consistency—being able to duplicate that perfect drink for your guests, over the course of their stay, or over the course of many years. Believe me, your husband appreciates that perfect margarita you make him every summer just as much as the stock broker appreciates the Manhattan

I make him every night at happy hour. And the only way to do that is by carefully measuring every ingredient, every time.

But, as with most things in life, measuring is not as simple as it sounds. Determining how other people have measured their ingredients, and figuring out the best way to quantify the ingredients for your own drinks, can be somewhat puzzling at times.

OLD TERMINOLOGY

A quick once-over of nineteenth- and early-twentieth-century cocktail books turns up a litany of outdated, nonstandardized, bizarre-sounding measurements, which might have simply remained quaint terms, except for the fact that old cocktail books are a fertile source of inspiration for modern bartenders.

Jerry Thomas (author of *The Bar-Tender's Guide*, 1862) was fond of a unit called a wineglass, generally assumed to be 2 oz/60 ml, when not described as a *small wineglass* or *large wineglass*. The term was often shortened to *glass* in many books and then fell out of favor around the turn of the twentieth century, which also marked the appearance of the ubiquitous metal "egg cup"–style measuring device, with a 1½-oz/45-ml measure on one side (a jigger) and a 1-oz/30-ml measure on the other (a pony). Yes. A pony.

The Savoy Cocktail Book (1930), written by the legendary bartender at the Savoy in London, Harry Craddock, is a famous disaster of measurement, often calling for absolute measures and proportional measures in the same recipe. For instance, the recipe for the imperial fizz calls for 1 part rum, 2 parts whiskey, the juice of half a lemon (however much that may be; cocktail books were rarely precise when it came to measures of citrus) and a half tablespoonful of sugar. What it doesn't specify is what size those "parts" are: 1 oz/30 ml, a coffee mug, a hollowed-out coconut, or 1 gl/3.8 L?

Adding to the confusion is the gill, an imperial (U.K.) quantity of measure equaling a quarter of a pint. But whose pint? In imperial measures, a pint is equal to 20 oz/600 ml; in U.S. measures, a pint is only 16 oz/480 ml. So a gill could be 5 or 4 oz/150 or 120 ml, depending on whose pint you start with.

And then of course there's the dram, as in, "I'll have a wee dram of Scotch." A dram is legally defined as ⅛ oz/3.75 ml, and is mostly used in apothecary formulas. Hardly enough for me, and definitely too little for any Scotsman. Fortunately for us, a dram in the context of a bar refers to a reasonable measure of whiskey; in bartending it's never given an official quantity.

MODERN MEASURES

As noted earlier, today we measure cocktails quite precisely, and while some of the poetry or opportunity for improvisation that came with those older terms may be lost, we're probably drinking much better, or at least more consistently made, cocktails for it. Most U.S. drink recipes will use the U.S. measurement system of fluid ounces and related terms. Here are about the only terms you will ever come across these days in cocktail literature in the States:

OUNCE	TEASPOON	DROPS AND DASHES
1	1	Any number of dashes
¾	½	Any number of drops
½		
¼		

You'll see these measurements in any combination that doesn't combine columns, meaning that you'll see 1½ oz/45 ml, but you'll almost never see 1 oz/30 ml plus 1 tsp. So the ingredients list for a brandy milk punch might read like this:

```
2 oz/60 ml whole milk
1¼ oz/37.5 ml brandy
¾ oz/22.5 ml Jamaican rum
½ oz/15 ml 1:1 simple syrup
1 tsp/5 ml 2:1 Demerara syrup
1 dash vanilla extract
```

Notice that "tablespoons" has been left out of most bartenders' terminology, probably because 1 tbsp is equal to ½ oz/15 ml. And since 1 tbsp is equal to 3 tsp, there are 3 tsp in ½ oz/15 ml, which is a very good thing to remember.

I sometimes find it easier to give larger measurements in cups, but not all bartenders think this way:

U.S. FLUID OUNCES	ALSO CALLED
2	¼ cup
4	½ cup
6	¾ cup
8	1 cup
16	1 pt
32	1 qt
64	½ gl
128	1 gl

(Notice that there isn't a ready term for 3, 5, or 7 fluid ounces.)

THE METRIC SYSTEM

Then there's the metric system. In the American system of measurement, the units of measure start with a system of thirds and then switch to eighths—3 tsp are equal to 1 tbsp, but 2 tbsp are equal to 1 fl oz, and 8 fl oz make 1 cup—so it's difficult to scale up and down, not to mention that multiples of 8 can get confusing.

On the other hand, the metric system is based on tenths, or multiples of tenths. It's so much more *logical*. The basic relationships between amounts are easy to understand and adapt. Start with 1 ml. If you multiply it by a thousand (10 x 100), you get 1 L. And it's a cinch to figure out percentages: 65 percent of 1 L is 650 ml. What's 65 percent of 2 cups? At the time of this writing, I'm aware of only three countries on the planet that *don't* use the metric system: Liberia, Myanmar, and the United States. There's so much to say there, I honestly don't know where to begin. If I thought I could pull it off without inspiring a mutiny, I would convert my entire bar staff to metric. It's easier to learn, and it's way more precise.

Perhaps more important than the easy-to-grasp system of tenths, metric measures are broken into much smaller increments than the U.S. system of measurements, allowing the bartender more precision. As we said earlier, since you'll almost never see a cocktail recipe calling for 1 oz/30 ml plus 1 tsp, the most precise measurement you'll ever get, when not measuring everything in tsp, is a ¼ oz/7.5 ml.

In a metric cocktail recipe, you have amounts in increments of 5 ml, which is coincidentally 1 tsp! So you'll see metric recipes calling for 5, 10, 15, 20 . . . up to 30 ml, which is the equivalent of 1 oz. The logic of metric measurement is beautiful, efficient, and precise for bartenders who truly care about the fine details.

HOW MUCH IS A DASH?

A dash in cocktail measurement terms isn't nearly as precise as other amounts, but it's not at all arbitrary, either. A standard dash will typically measure out at 6 to 8 to the tsp, so 1 dash is just shy of 1 ml.

Dashes are mainly used for measuring bitters, and while some bartenders simply invert the bitters bottle and call what comes out a dash, others like to put their bitters and tinctures into eyedroppers or even specially designed bitters bottles, which make dispensing tiny amounts—such as a single drop—more controllable. It's an imprecise science, to be sure, but one we've learned to cope with by tasting our cocktails before we're done building them.

MEASURING TOOLS

As with everything in the world of bartending equipment, there are good tools for the job, and there are better tools for the job. The tools we use for measurement are no exception.

JIGGERS

No tool kit is complete without a set of jiggers. I insist on carrying at least two, but I'm really most comfortable when I've got three on me.

The first should hold both 1- and 2-oz/ 30- and 60-ml measures. The second should hold a ½-oz/15-ml measure on one side, and ¾ oz/22.5 ml on the other. This should get you every possible combination you need, but for speed, I also stock one that has 1½ oz/45 ml on one side and either a full 1-oz/30-ml or a ¾-oz/22.5-ml measure on the other.

But what about the ¼-oz/7.5-ml measure, I can hear you screaming. Well, some newer jiggers are arriving with a line inside of the ½-oz/15-ml measure that indicates where ¼ oz/7.5 ml will fall. If yours doesn't have this nice feature, simply fill your ½-oz/15-ml measure with 1½ tsp of water, and mark a line where the water line lands.

That describes the volume measurements, but what about the style and shape of the jigger? The world is full of jiggers, but they all can be divided into one of two categories: U.S. measures (ounces) or metric measures (milliliters).

Within the U.S.-measurement category, there are two styles: American and Japanese. The American style is shaped like two wide cones connected at the tips to form a waist—the jiggers are short, squat, and iconic. You've seen them.

Japanese-style jiggers are tall and slender. They have an elegant look, but, more important, you can gain greater accuracy with them. Think about it: if you underpour, for example, by a tiny fraction of an inch (or centimeter), that tiny fraction, spread across the wide surface area of the American jigger is more liquid than that tiny fraction multiplied by the smaller surface area of a narrow jigger.

In the metric jigger category, I like the ones made by Bonzer. Nicely machined in heavy-gauge stainless steel, Bonzers are totally cylindrical, with no pinched-in waist, and just a few horizontal grooves for an easier grip. (This is called a thimble style.) These are, of course, great when you're working in metric measurements for your cocktails. The downside is that you'll need a giant set if you want to accommodate every permutation of the scale.

A good compromise—if you consider compromise a good thing—are the clear jiggers made by OXO. They're essentially small measuring cups that are designed for reading from overhead (rather than having to bring the jigger to eye level). These OXO cups are marked in metric measures as well as U.S. amounts, which I appreciate.

Reading the U.S. measures accurately from overhead is tough, however, especially in a dark bar when measuring clear liquids. The jiggers are also oddly calibrated, and on the U.S. measure side, they're not great (there's no ¾-oz measure, for example). But they do offer you the choice between U.S. and metric—a good option for people who don't want to invest in a complete set of metric jiggers.

The other tools you'll use to measure are regular kitchen measuring spoons, and in some cases, your bar spoon, the bowl of which is, in theory, the equivalent of 1 tsp. But because not all bar spoons are equal, you should always have good stainless-steel kitchen 1-tsp and ½-tsp measures in your kit.

HOW TO MEASURE LIQUOR PROPERLY USING JIGGERS

Hold your jigger level between the thumb and forefinger in your nondominant hand, right next to your mixing glass or shaker. Slowly pour in the liquor so that it fills the jigger, giving you a fully rounded meniscus. Then carefully tip the jigger over the lip of your mixing vessel to add the liquor to it.

HOW TO POUR FROM A BOTTLE

I received my degree in interior architecture from the University of Oregon in 1998. The primary focus of my study, as is the case in any interiors department, was how humans interact with the built environment. Two of the components of the discipline are anthropometrics and ergonomics.

Anthropometry is, literally, the "measurement of man" in Greek. It is the study of the human body's dimensions. People who, say, design clothing for a living have the tough job of summing us all up in terms of large, medium, or small, despite the fact that each and every one of us is proportionally unique.

Ergonomics, on the other hand, is the science of reconciling that fact with the reality of living in a static built environment. If you've ever taken a minute to think about the distance from the seat of your car to the gas pedal, that's ergonomics. Toilet paper dispensers are at the same height, door handles are always where we expect them to be, laptops are a specific width, and stairs are generally of a certain tread width and riser height. That's all ergonomics.

Since I did start tending bar while in school, I have always been very conscious of my large frame behind the bar. I walk into a bar and immediately note where the liquor is kept, what height the sinks are, how high the bar top is, and the distance from the ice well to the back bar counter. Nearly everything about tending bar is physical. Couple that with the fact that you're lifting and rotating a 2-lb/910-g bottle of booze every few seconds. If you've ever had carpal tunnel, as I did when I spent nine hours a day drafting with a mouse, then you know what excruciating pain awaits you when the body and the built environment don't work well together.

The typical grasp you'll see bartenders use when reaching for a bottle is an overhanded grab, meaning that with palm facing inward, the bottle is held either at the neck, middle, or base and rotated well over 45 degrees in order to pour the contents—the problem here being that at this angle, the wrist can only rotate 45 degrees without injury. So, in essence, every degree past the 45-degree mark is going to require additional strain on the wrist, elbow, and shoulder.

Making this motion hundreds of times a night over the course of years behind the bar has given some bartenders injuries that preclude them from working or force them to wear a brace or use their nondominant hand.

But there's a better way to hold a bottle of liquor that is gentler on the wrist and results in less possibility of injury, and that's the underhanded pour. An underhanded pour uses the full 90-degree range of the wrist, puts less stress on the arm's joints, is a more elegant hold, and is even more precise when measuring.

Start by holding your dominant hand with the palm open and facing up toward the ceiling. Or, if you're bartending in the great wide open, the sky. Whatever. Now slip the neck of the bottle between the middle and ring finger, and use your thumb to pinch the seal of the pour spout where it meets the bottle neck.

Lifting the bottle slowly, and curling your index finger around the neck as you do so, begin to turn your wrist inward to pour.

Soon, the ring finger will naturally be supporting most of the bottle's weight while the index and middle fingers continue to curl around the neck and the thumb presses downward, supporting the turn.

Once you complete the pour, curl your middle finger back in toward the palm; your thumb and forefinger are left pinching the bottle neck, which is ready to be placed back in its place. It may seem awkward at first, but with some practice it becomes a gentler, more natural way to hold a bottle.

SPEED AND FREEDOM

It's one thing if you're making a cocktail for one or two people; it's another when you're in a busy professional situation. How do you balance precise and controlled measurement with moving a lot of drinks across the bar?

Obviously, part of that answer is by experience and acquired skill. Most bartenders outfit their liquor bottles with a speed pourer, a spout that allows a controlled stream, making it a lot easier to swiftly and smoothly deliver the right amount of spirit to the jigger. Speed pourers also keep your bar neater, avoiding drips and open bottle necks.

At my bars, all of my bartenders are taught to measure, but they deliver the liquor using speed pourers. The model most widely used by professionals is the Spill-Stop model number 285-50. They're available pretty much everywhere.

There's a step beyond that, however, which is actual free pouring. Some chain restaurants require their bartenders to free pour because they feel it adds a degree of showmanship, which they like. Those bartenders undergo intense training in order to develop the feel for the pour, and there are a lot of quality-control checkups.

You can teach yourself to free pour at home, as I did when I was learning how to mix drinks. Simply fill an empty liquor bottle with water and fit the bottle with a Spill-Stop pour spout. Get your 1-oz/30-ml jigger ready, stand over the sink, and prepare to count.

There are two keys to great accuracy when it comes to free pouring. The first strategy to be mindful of is the counting system you choose. Holding the jigger in your non-dominant hand, quickly invert the bottle so that it is straight up and down, and pour from the bottle of water into the jigger while counting to 4. The number 4 is important, as it is easily divided and multiplied. By learning how to pour 1 oz/30 ml while counting to 4, you can easily pour all of the common measurements using this system:

- ¼ oz/7.5 ml by counting to 1
- ½ oz/15 ml by counting to 2
- ¾ oz/22.5 ml by counting to 3
- 1 oz/30 ml by counting to 4
- 1½ oz/45 ml by counting to 6
- 2 oz/60 ml by counting to 8

When the water has nearly filled the jigger, snap the bottle sharply in a downward motion. This will force a small air bubble into the pour spout and momentarily stop the flow of liquid. Quickly turn the bottle 90 degrees, and with any luck you should have a neat, full jigger.

See how easy that is? Well, it's easy once you make a point of practicing every single day (that's the second key to greater accuracy mentioned earlier—practice). Muscle memory is a powerful thing in bartending, and this is a perfect example of that. Repeat your test with the bottle of water and the jigger over and over again until you can do it without need for the jigger.

Now you can test yourself. Get an empty glass or mixing tin, and pour yourself 1 oz/30 ml by counting to 4. We'll call this "pouring blind." Now empty the contents of the glass into the jigger to test your results. Adjust your count as necessary.

You can also pick up an Exacto-Pour testing set if you really want to get precise about counting. The testing sets are essentially graduated test tubes hidden within a small box. You pick your pours and then turn the unit around to see how precise you are.

The debates between the jiggering camp and the free-pouring camp can get acrimonious, and there are definitely virtues and challenges to each. My feeling is that measuring is the simplest, most reliable way to go in any situation where you have multiple people making drinks—as in a professional bar.

SPEED POURING VERSUS FREE POURING: THE TWO CAMPS OF MEASURING

When I took over the bar at Clyde Common in 2009, there was no real system in place for measuring the ingredients that went into the cocktails. I mean, there was this little shot glass the bartenders were supposed to be eyeballing their pours with, but as you can imagine, it was imprecise and, at its best, sloppy. The minute I set foot in the place I knew I was going to have to change this "system" to my preferred system of measurement.

So I braced myself for some resistance from the staff. And resistance I received. The most obstinate member of my newly inherited staff was a young man named Justin Pike. He was, and still is, an incredible bartender. And, like most incredible bartenders, he didn't see the point in changing anything he did behind the bar, and he definitely didn't want to be told what to do.

But I knew something about Justin that he didn't yet know about himself: that another quality of a great bartender is their ability to change. And slowly, over the course of the next several months, Justin learned and adapted, and grew, reluctantly, to appreciate the new system we'd built together. And then one day he approached me for my recommendations of bars to visit while on vacation in Seattle.

One of the best bartenders I've ever seen is Murray Stenson, up in Seattle. You'll find a lot of people saying the same about him, which means there's probably something to it. The thing about Murray is how everyone takes something different away from their time spent at his bar. Some folks admire the guy for being a veritable database of cocktails. Some look up to him for his ability to make incredible drinks, or for his extensive knowledge of Scotch whisky. I personally marvel at his ability to remain unflustered with a hundred people shouting at him on a packed Friday. I'm not good at that, and I wish I could be more like him in that regard.

So when Justin asked me whose bar to sit at in Seattle, I immediately thought of Murray and sent him to the Zig Zag Café, where Murray was working at the time. Seated right in front of Murray's station, Justin immediately picked up on something that I'd forgotten about, something that might have made me choose another bar for this particular member of my staff to sit at had I thought of it: Murray doesn't measure. At all. No jiggers, and half the time he's got no speed pourers on the bottle; he's just pouring from the open neck. When I asked him about it for this book, he had this to say:

"I'm not as contrary on jigger use as you might believe. I spent my first fifteen years of bartending using a jigger, but at my last two jobs I was jiggerless. I've had good and bad drinks that were jiggered and from free pours; I think it depends on the bartender."

A very good point, but not the sort of thing I was trying to instill in a young staff member. So when Justin noticed that Murray was free pouring, with my kind words about Murray still ringing in his ears, the conflict of our two opposing camps on measuring became almost too much to bear. And he had to ask the question, "So, Murray, why don't you use jiggers to measure your drinks?" And Murray stopped what he was looking, looked Justin dead in the eye, and uttered the words that nearly set all my hard work over the previous months back to square one:

"Because jiggers are for sissies!"

Justin is now one of the most celebrated bartenders in Los Angeles, and he tells me that he and his staff still measure every drink, so I guess I must have had some sort of impact on him after all.

WHY METRIC MAKES MORE SENSE

In Ian Fleming's 1953 James Bond novel *Casino Royale*, Bond orders what would become his iconic drink of choice: the vesper. He dictates the recipe to the bartender as follows: "Three measures of Gordon's, one of vodka, half a measure of Kina Lillet. Shake it very well until it's ice-cold, then add a large thin slice of lemon peel."

My issue with this drink is that it's enormous. Huge. Barely drinkable, except by Mr. Bond, who declares, "I never have more than one drink before dinner. But I do like that one to be large and very strong and very cold and very well made. I hate small portions of anything, particularly when they taste bad."

Good thing for Bond, because if we take each "measure" to mean 1 oz/30 ml, then our vesper recipe is as follows:

3 oz/90 ml Gordon's gin

1 oz/30 ml vodka

½ oz/15 ml Lillet *blanc*

A whopping 4½-oz/135-ml drink, and that's *before* we shake to dilute it. The more troubling notion for me to wrap my head around is what sort of glass the bartender would have put this in back in 1953.

The 1990s was the decade of the Outrageously Oversized Martini Glass, and we were serving enormous, colorful, boozy, sugary concoctions to our guests in glassware the size of fishbowls. But prior to the '90s, glassware was most often of a

reasonable size, and martini glasses were typically 4 to 6 oz/120 to 180 ml. Fortunately, we've returned to more sustainable proportions in the past ten years.

But where does that leave the vesper? If we simply halve the recipe, we end up with this:

1½ oz/45 ml Gordon's gin

½ oz/15 ml vodka

¼ oz/7.5 ml Lillet *blanc*

A 2¼-oz/67.5-ml drink. Much more reasonable, but hardly a decent-size drink, in my opinion. I would like to land somewhere in between, say two-thirds the size of the original drink, but that's going to give us some very strange measurements:

2¼ oz/67.5 ml Gordon's gin

¾ oz/22.5 ml vodka

⅜ oz/11 ml Lillet *blanc*

Fine, but good luck finding a ⅜-oz/11-ml jigger.

A better and simpler solution would be to use metric measurements. On the next page is what two-thirds of the original recipe would look like in metric, as a 90-ml/3-oz drink— a much more respectable serving, especially for someone who holds a license to kill.

VESPER

MAKES 1 DRINK

60 ml Gordon's gin

20 ml vodka

10 ml Lillet *blanc*

Ice cubes

1 large lemon peel for garnish

CHILLED COCKTAIL GLASS

Combine the gin, vodka, and Lillet in a cocktail shaker filled with ice cubes and shake for 12 to 15 seconds. Strain into the chilled cocktail glass. Twist the peel over the surface of the cocktail and drop in the drink.

BATCHING DRINKS

The ultimate in measuring is knowing how to scale up a recipe from a single serving to a large batch for serving multiple guests. If you're multiplying by 100, that's simple enough; you'll just multiply each ingredient's amount by 100, and you're done.

But more often, you'll need to scale a recipe up for a specific size of vessel. Whether you want a 5-gal/19-L bucket of margaritas for a party, or a fifth (750 ml) of Manhattans as a Christmas gift for the boss, there is a technique for filling that container.

For this example, we'll use one of my favorite classic cocktails, the Improved Holland Cocktail. This drink is a great illustration of complex scaling, due to the three different types of measuring units involved in making it.

2 OZ/60 ML genever gin

1 TSP/30 ML 2:1 simple syrup

½ TSP/15 ML maraschino liqueur

2 DASHES Angostura bitters

1 DASH absinthe

The first thing we need to do is get all of those crazy units (ounces, teaspoons, dashes) into a common unit size. We could convert everything over to metric, or we could use a dash as a common denominator, but to make life easier on ourselves (without having to measure out 20,000 dashes of gin), we're going to convert everything to ounces. Bearing in mind that since there are more or less 6 dashes in 1 tsp, 1 dash is equal to 0.027 oz/0.8 ml: (Note: you can apply the same conversion process and convert everything to milliliters; it's simply a matter of getting everything in the same unit.)

2 OZ genever gin

0.167 OZ 2:1 simple syrup

0.083 OZ maraschino liqueur

0.055 OZ Angostura bitters

0.027 OZ absinthe

Converting all of these measurements into one common unit will let me know the exact size, in ounces, of that cocktail. Adding the above measurements up gives me 2.332 oz of total volume.

I want to make a 750-ml bottle of Improved Holland Cocktail for a party a friend is hosting tonight. A 750-ml bottle equals 25.360 oz, so I need to know how many times my 2.332-oz drink will go into 25.360 oz/750 ml.

Since 25.360 oz divided by 2.332 oz equals 10.874, by multiplying every ingredient by 10.874, I will hopefully arrive at around 25.360 oz/750 ml—a full bottle of Improved Holland Cocktails:

genever gin: **2 OZ × 10.874 = 21.758 OZ**

2:1 simple syrup: **0.167 OZ × 10.874 = 1.815 OZ**

maraschino liqueur:
0.083 OZ × 10.874 = 0.902 OZ

Angostura bitters:
0.055 OZ × 10.874 = 0.598 OZ

absinthe: **0.027 OZ × 10.874 = 0.299 OZ**

I'll probably take some small liberties and round out a few of those measurements into normal amounts:

21¾ OZ genever gin

1¾ OZ 2:1 simple syrup

1 OZ maraschino liqueur

½ OZ Angostura bitters

¼ OZ absinthe

If we add all those together, we arrive at 25.25 oz of cocktail for our 25.36-oz/750-ml bottle. Close enough.

Liquid Measurements

U.S.	METRIC
¼ teaspoon	1.25 milliliters
½ teaspoon	2.5 milliliters
1 teaspoon	5 milliliters
½ fluid ounce (3 teaspoons)	15 milliliters
1 fluid ounce (2 tablespoons)	30 milliliters
2 fluid ounces	60 milliliters
⅓ cup	80 milliliters
½ cup	120 milliliters
1 cup	240 milliliters

STIRRING & SHAKING

ASSEMBLING AND INTEGRATING A COCKTAIL'S COMPONENTS

Stop me if you've heard this one: A guy walks into a bar and orders a martini. The bartender fills a cocktail shaker with ice, adds vermouth and gin, and then shakes the drink as hard as he can. The guy drinks his foamy, slushy cocktail, pays, and leaves. He never comes back.

Okay, how about this one? A guy walks into a bar and orders a Manhattan. The bartender fills a cocktail shaker with ice, adds vermouth and whiskey, and then swirls the shaker with a limp wrist for a couple of seconds. The guy drinks his warm Manhattan, pays, and leaves. He never returns.

If you're not laughing at either of those jokes, then maybe you already know what I know: These two scenarios are played out every day, all over the world, by bartenders who don't know how—or when—to properly shake or stir a cocktail. And it's really too bad, you know, because it's not all that complicated. It just takes, like everything else in bartending, a little attention to detail and technique.

So here are the basic rules that professionals use when it comes to shaking or stirring cocktails: We want any drink composed entirely of spirits—such as Manhattans and martinis—to be crystal clear and Arctic cold. They should be biting, bracing, and free of air bubbles and ice chips. And so those types of drinks are always stirred, because stirring is a gentler process than shaking.

Any drink that contains juice, cream, or egg whites is always shaken, because we want those drinks to be well combined, full of tiny air bubbles, cold, and more diluted than spirit-driven drinks. It's really as easy as that: clear equals stirred, cloudy equals shaken.

But there's more to shaking and stirring than simply knowing when to apply each method, and that's knowing how to execute them perfectly. That is what this chapter is all about.

CHILLING AND DILUTION

Bartending is kind of a weird field in some ways. There aren't many other jobs where you encounter as much superstition as you do in bartending. And within our field, there are no subjects more laden with myth than shaking or stirring, and that's unfortunate because if anything can be explained through science, it's the chilling and dilution of a cocktail. Science even has a word for it: thermodynamics.

When ice (which is typically at around 32°F/0°C when sitting at room temperature in an ice bin, or 5°F/-15°C straight out of the freezer) is combined with a liquid (let's assume around 70°F/21°C for our cocktail), the cocktail cools down, and the ice warms up. Simple enough.

When we agitate a cocktail through shaking or stirring, we're greatly increasing the surface area of the liquid that comes in contact with the ice. It's part of the reason why we shake or stir in the first place and explains why shaking chills and dilutes a cocktail much more quickly than stirring does; shaking is simply a more aggressive process that puts a greater amount of the liquid's surface area in contact with the ice.

It takes a fair amount of energy to melt ice. What is called the heat of fusion—meaning how much energy is absorbed by the ice as 1 gram melts—comes to just under 80 calories per gram. Almost all of that energy is

going to come from the heat in the liquid, which, as we said before, is at around 70°F/21°C. As the warmer cocktail comes in contact with the colder ice, the surface of the ice warms up to the melting point, 32°F/0°C. The ice melts; the cocktail becomes cooler.

Now, chilling and dilution are inextricable, which is to say that no matter how cold your ice is, it's never going to chill your cocktail until its surface warms up to 32°F/0°C, which might be a little counterintuitive, but it's true: ice kept in an insulated bin will chill a cocktail faster than ice kept below freezing (in a freezer).

As you continue to shake, the ice melts until the whole system reaches equilibrium, and the ice and the cocktail are the same temperature. Since our cocktails contain alcohol, the equilibrium point tends to be between 23 and 14°F /-5 and -10°C, because the freezing point of alcohol is considerably lower than that of water. Much the way ice with salt added to it (for the purpose of making ice cream) has a lower freezing point, drinks containing alcohol are able to be chilled to temperatures lower than 32°F/0°C.

Once this equilibrium point is met, that's it. No further dilution takes place, and the drink is finished. This happens regardless of whether you shake hard, or shake very hard, in the span of 12 to 15 seconds. After that, nothing more is going to happen. It's also true that the size of the ice isn't a major factor in chilling, within reason (finely cracked or crushed ice has too much surface area and too little volume). So whether you're using 1¼-in/3.2-cm or ½-in/12-mm cubes, there is absolutely no difference in terms of chilling and dilution. None.

Why bother with bigger, colder ice, then? If the temperature and dilution are exactly the same no matter what we use in our cocktails, why should we bother with what we've been told is bigger, better, colder ice? Well, because none of this takes into account texture, which is of course the difference between a good cocktail and a great cocktail, particularly in juice-forward cocktails and definitely in drinks that contain dairy. All of that violent shaking produces very fine air bubbles, which are one of the hallmarks of a great drink. And larger ice cubes produce the smallest air bubbles, giving you a finer texture.

The whole point of this is to let you know that you should never let people bully you into thinking that you need an expensive ice machine in order to make world-class cocktails. You don't.

You don't ever want to add ice and begin stirring unless you know you won't be interrupted in the process. Adding ice, pouring in your spirits, and then getting called away to sign for the bar linen delivery or take a phone call is a great way to ruin a drink; the ice will melt too much, or at least more than you can accurately perceive.

To avoid this situation, we use a technique called building dry, which simply means adding the ice only after all other components are in the mixing glass and you are ready to mix.

Times and Measurements for Ideal Dilution

	SHAKING	STIRRING
Type of ice needed	Cubes	Cubes plus a small amount of cracked ice (3:1 ratio cubes to cracked)
Fill line	Completely full	Three-quarters full
Ideal time	12 to 15 seconds	30 to 45 seconds
Ideal temperature	23 to 19°F/ -5 to -7° C	32 to 23°F/ 0 to -5° C
Ideal percent of dilution	25 to 40%	20 to 25%

STIRRING

Stirring seems pretty simple, right? We stir liquids all the time: we stir cream and sugar into our coffee, stir some ingredients together to make soup, stir the bubble bath stuff into the tub, whatever. But when stirring a cocktail, we're trying do something more than just mix things together in a glass. Here are our goals again:

- A final product in which everything is thoroughly combined

- A crystal-clear drink, free of bubbles or ice shards

- A properly diluted cocktail—just enough to take the sting off the alcohol

- An Arctic, ice-cold cocktail

Achieving all that just by moving a spoon around a glass requires knowing a thing or two.

THE SPOON

A bar spoon is a long, slender metal spoon specifically designed for cocktails. You know the type; you've probably encountered a cheap stamped stainless-steel version with an inexplicable red-plastic tip at some point in your adventures. Most have a twisted stem, and the good ones often sport a functional shape on each end—the bowl of the spoon itself on one end and another sort of tool on the other, such as a muddler or a fork.

When looking for a bar spoon, the first thing you want to do is skip the liquor stores and restaurant supply shops; most of them carry only those cheap, red-plastic-tipped specimens you see everywhere. Spend a few extra minutes scouring the Internet or specialty shops, and a few extra dollars on something that will get the job done in a more elegant and professional fashion.

The first thing you want to do when evaluating a bar spoon is to gauge the heft, how the weight and balance feel as you hold it. The spoon should fit comfortably in your hand, and the amount and shape of the coils on the stem should provide you a good purchase on the spoon. I steer clear of those sexy spoons without coils, as they tend to slip around in the grip of wet fingers, which you're often going to have behind the bar.

The spoon shouldn't be too heavy, as it wants to dance between the fingers and not clank around awkwardly in the glass. The balance from top to bottom should be evenly weighted; a bowl-heavy spoon is lazy and difficult to control, and a top-heavy one is hyperactive and spastic in the glass.

In addition to the bowl on one end, a bar spoon should have something useful on the opposite end. I look for a spoon with either a disk or hammer end. The disk end is simply that—a flat disk, like a coin, that can be used to muddle herbs (more on that in chapter 11). A hammer end is chunkier, with a flat disk face but also enough mass and weight to double as both a muddler for herbs and a tool for cracking ice cubes with a little less effort than the disk-ended muddlers.

I also always stock a Japanese spoon with a trident fork on the opposite end from the bowl. This provides an excellent tool for spearing olives and cherries, so I won't need tongs (or be forced to grab them awkwardly with bare fingers). However, nine times out of ten I reach for my hammer-end spoon, as the extra weight provides the balance I'm looking for when stirring.

BARTENDER'S CHOICE: BAR SPOON

My favorite spoon is made by Swissmar. It measures 10¾ in/27.5 cm long and is made of stainless steel. The coil is perfectly spun for my larger hands (those with smaller hands might find this spoon a tad overbearing). The hammer end is solid and heavy, with a textured disk face for muddling and a solid base for cracking ice. My only criticism is that the ice-cracking surface could be sharper, and the tiny serrated teeth on the spoon bowl are unnecessary.

If I'm reaching for a trident-end spoon, it's always the Japanese tight-coil 31.5-cm trident-end bar spoon (about 12½ in) from Cocktail Kingdom. It's long, balanced, and elegant, and the tight coil feels great in the hand.

STORING BAR SPOONS DURING SERVICE

Bar spoons get a good workout during service. But maneuvering from stirring a Manhattan to scooping out a cherry packed in syrup to stirring a martini is going to require constant rinsing under the sink if you don't want the remnants of everything that spoon has touched showing up in your next drink. To make rinsing a little simpler, we keep our spoons in a 16-oz/480-ml mixing glass filled with warm water. Before service, we add two drops of bleach—conveniently kept in an eyedropper and clearly labeled—to ensure a sanitary solution.

MIXING GLASSES

For some reason, stirred cocktails are almost always prepared in a glass vessel rather than a metal container. The reason certainly wouldn't be thermodynamic, as metal is better for chilling. My guess is that when properly stirred, a cocktail looks appealing to the guest, dancing around in the glass with an occasional flash of silver or gold.

My day-to-day mixing glass at my bar is a 16-oz/480-ml glass, available pretty much anywhere. But if you want to go beyond this most basic standard, you'll find an array of vessels to choose from. They can be as large as 34 oz/1 L, or more, and come in a variety of shapes. You'll find sloped-sided, straight-sided, and even stemmed and tulip-shaped mixing glasses. Just be sure your glass is a little bottom heavy so that you don't have to worry about tipping in action.

Your choice of size will depend on what your cocktail habits are—a very large glass may make sense only if you plan to mix multiple cocktails at one time. And you definitely need to consider how your glass will fit your bar spoon—no reaching your hand down

into the mixing glass because your spoon is too short—as well as your strainer. Any beauty that you may create by mixing a cocktail in a stunning cut-crystal glass will soon vanish if you slosh the drink over the bar as you strain. (See more on strainers on page 208.)

BARTENDER'S CHOICE: MIXING GLASS

When I'm entertaining at home, I tend to choose one of two options, depending on the size of the group. The first option is a special mixing glass from my collection. The seamless Yarai mixing glass is the one most often found in craft cocktail bars these days, but others such as the Japanese paddle mixing glass and stemmed mixing glass are beautiful and elegant as well. You can find all of these online at my favorite online retailer, Cocktail Kingdom.

A fun option for larger groups can be found in thrift and vintage stores everywhere, as well as at online auction sites: a large glass pitcher, often decorated with goofy 1950s artwork depicting all manner of martinis, Manhattans, and other cocktails and usually adorned with terrible recipes that should never be replicated. They're fun, they're cheap, and they're plentiful.

PROPER STIRRING TECHNIQUE

When I first started bartending, there was one method of stirring: You built the drink in the mixing glass, added the ice, and then violently plunged the spoon up and down into the mix with one hand, while the other hand cupped the opening of the mixing vessel to keep its precious ingredients from spilling out. Any such escapees were splashed unhygienically against the palm of your hand and back into the mix. Since it's still pretty ubiquitous in this country, we're going to refer to it as the American stir.

When I first experienced European bartending, I witnessed a slightly more elegant but almost equally confusing technique. Bartenders there, particularly in the United Kingdom, grasped the spoon by the bowl end using the thumb and forefinger, and stirred the contents by tracing the round disk end around the inside of the round mixing glass. Less violent, to be sure, but hardly a solution with finesse, as the spoon's inverted state and the bartender's grip on the bowl brought to the table the question of hygiene once again. We're going to call this the U.K. stir.

But in the mid-2000s, videos and stories began to emerge online about Japanese bartenders, who grasped the spoon by the middle and effortlessly, almost magically, twirled the spoon around the glass in silence. Their fingers, held perpendicular to the spoon as it spun, seemed not even to move as the contents were thoughtfully and precisely twisted into a vortex in the glass. The Japanese stir is the technique that most trained bartenders around the world have now adopted. It takes some practice, but the results separate the professionals from the amateurs.

How to Perform the Japanese Stir

Build your drink in the mixing glass and add enough ice to fill the glass only three-quarters full. Lightly grasp the spoon in the middle, using your thumb and forefinger. The concave bowl of the spoon should be facing the interior of the glass, and the convex back of the spoon should be nestled in between the ice and the wall of the glass interior.

Using your pinch on the spoon as a pivot only, begin to push and pull the spoon away from and toward your body, using your ring and middle fingers. Doing this should naturally guide the spoon around the interior of the glass in a circular motion, as you push and pull the spoon away and toward you.

With some practice this motion will become effortless, and you can begin to lift the spoon and sink it into the contents of the glass, achieving perfect mixing.

STRAINING A STIRRED DRINK

So we've got our spoon to stir our cocktail with, a glass vessel to stir it in, and now we need a tool to allow us to get that drink off the ice and into the serving glass. That piece of equipment is called a strainer, of which there are two styles: julep and Hawthorne.

Originating in the days before plastic straws, the julep strainer was originally designed as a large, slotted, spoonlike implement, which the drinker placed over the top of an iced drink (such as a mint julep) to hold the ice back away from the teeth. As spirit-driven "cocktails" grew in popularity, bartenders began to use the spoonlike strainer as a tool

to strain stirred drinks. The julep strainer is one of the many cocktail tools in which form and function combine to create a truly beautiful object. Use the julep strainer to strain stirred drinks.

HOW TO STRAIN WITH A JULEP STRAINER

To strain a stirred drink with a julep strainer, place the strainer over your mixing glass, concave-side facing down, convex-side facing up. Hold the strainer in place with the forefinger of your dominant hand. Lift the mixing glass with that same hand and pour.

BARTENDER'S CHOICE: JULEP STRAINER

The variations in julep strainers are mostly a matter of the material and the craftsmanship—the basic shape of all julep strainers is the same. My favorite is Cocktail Kingdom's proprietary silver-plated model.

MARTINI

MAKES 1 DRINK The martini is the great-grandfather of all stirred cocktails. At my bar we prefer a 5:1 gin-to-vermouth ratio, which I've found to be most pleasing to the greatest number of martini drinkers.

2½ oz/75 ml London dry gin

½ oz/15 ml dry vermouth

Ice cubes

1 lemon twist or olive for garnish

COUPE OR COCKTAIL GLASS

Combine the gin and vermouth in a mixing glass and stir with ice cubes. Strain into the coupe glass. Twist the peel over the surface of the cocktail and drop in the drink, or garnish with the olive, to serve.

SHAKING

Unlike stirred drinks, where your goal is clarity and an absence of any fizz or foam, shaken drinks want to be light, almost fluffy, with a bracing chill and lots of tiny air bubbles to dance on the tongue. When shaking, here are the goals:

- A final product in which everything is thoroughly combined

- An aerated cocktail, full of tiny bubbles

- A properly diluted cocktail, enough to take the sting off the alcohol and the weight off of the other ingredients

- A perfectly uniform drink, free of ice shards

- An Arctic-cold cocktail

While the best bartenders in the world make it look easy, achieving all of this requires a bit of multitasking and some proper tools.

THE SHAKER

You have two main options in cocktail shakers: the Boston shaker and the cobbler shaker. I probably shake 95 percent of my drinks in a Boston shaker, as it's best for high-volume bar programs. But it's good to know how to handle both types. Shaking a cocktail is a highly visible gesture; and for the guest, watching the process is an important part of the sweet ritual of drinking a well-made cocktail. So you do not want a leaky shaker or one you can't swiftly and smoothly handle.

The Cobbler Shaker

The cobbler shaker is the one most people think of when they think of a cocktail shaker. It's got three parts: a cup, a lid, and a cap. Most are garbage. The metal they're made from is too thin, and they freeze shut once loaded with ice. Believe me, I've tried these shakers, which you often find at fancy culinary shops, and I've thrown them away more often than I've been able to get them open.

There are high-quality cobbler shakers, however, the best being thick-walled shakers from Japan. WMF, Rösle, and OXO also make decent models. All have built-in strainers under the cap, eliminating the need for a separate strainer, but the small opening of the strainer–pour spout means it takes longer to pour your drink, which can slow you down on a busy night.

I like the 500-ml heavy-gauge stainless-steel model from Japan, sold by Cocktail Kingdom. It's perfectly engineered to open and close without trouble, and the heavy-gauge stainless means it's not going to freeze shut.

The Boston Shaker

The professional's choice of cocktail shakers is the Boston shaker, which consists of two containers, one of which fits into the other. There are two common configurations: The first consists of a mixing glass that fits into a large steel tin; the second is two stainless-steel tins—one large, one small.

Since this is really the simplest style of shaker, there isn't much of a difference in quality across the many brands available. Simply look for medium-gauge stainless steel, and ensure that the two parts fit together smoothly and snugly. The deeper the overlap when the two parts are seated, the better, so make this your foremost consideration. It's going to make life a lot easier when it comes time to get the damn thing open (see page 218).

The Parisian Shaker

The third option in shakers, which is less common, is the Parisian shaker. It's typically made of stainless steel, although if you're very lucky, you may find some vintage silver-plated models out there. The earliest designs seem to date from the 1870s; the German manufacturer WMF started making theirs in 1910 and continue to do so today. You could say the Parisian is a hybrid—in shape it resembles a cobbler, but the combined volume of the two pieces is more like that of a Boston shaker, and there is no built-in strainer.

You'll find some pretty impostors out there, but I stick with the classic made by WMF. This is a heavy-gauge stainless-steel shaker, built to withstand years of abuse. In fact, I find that they take on a nice patina after several years of shaking and scratching the surface.

LEARNING TO SHAKE

What happens inside the shaker you choose is going to make or break your drink. In order to achieve the correct texture and temperature for your cocktail, you need to shake the drink correctly—which means the right grip, and the right motion. Serious shaking isn't merely a matter of style, but once again one of physics.

When I train bartenders to shake a cocktail, I have them start out by shaking a tin full of rice, much the same way that a chef in training learns to flip food in the sauté pan by flipping a pan full of rice for a few tedious hours.

Rice is a perfect training material because it's cheap and not as messy as a liquid, and more important, you can easily feel and hear the motion of the contents. And if you're using a glass mixing cup, you can see the contents as well. It's important to note here that the best bartenders in the world use all of their available senses when working behind the bar, shaking being one of the best examples of that fact.

How to Shake a Cocktail

First, build your drink dry, combining all of your ingredients in the shaker except for the ice. Then add enough ice to completely fill the shaker, position the shaking tin on top, and give it a rap with the heel of your palm to seal.

Most shakers are symmetrical, but the top of a Boston shaker should be cocked to one side. I keep the straight side closest to my body. Grip the base of the bottom cup with the middle and index fingers of one hand, cradling the rest of the cup with your thumb and remaining fingers.

Grasp the top cup, which is also called the shaking cup, with your other hand, holding your thumb on the top of the shaking cup, to keep it secured. The top of the shaker should be facing you, and the bottom should be facing away from you.

The most common mistake you'll see inexperienced bartenders make is shaking it up and down, vertically. Do that with rice, and you'll notice that the contents don't really travel very far inside the shaker, and definitely not with the force you want.

Hold the shaker so that it's parallel to the floor, and—while grasping securely—launch it forward so that you can feel and hear the contents leaving the end closest to your body and hurling against the front of the tin. Right at that moment, as the contents of the shaker are about to hit in the far end of the shaker, you need to snap your wrists back toward your body to send them smashing into the far end of the shaker, and back toward you.

When you do this correctly, you'll hear a clean pop. Launching the shaker forward and pulling it right back with a clean snapping motion is the proper way to shake a cocktail. It's all in the wrists, and should be smooth and effortless. If you're working up a sweat or feel like you're about to tear your rotator cuff, you're doing it wrong.

How Long to Shake

Shaking creates the action that will mix the contents and agitate the ice so that it melts correctly, but how long is long enough?

Quite simply, larger, colder ice should be shaken for a longer time than smaller, wetter ice. Depending on the size and temperature of your ice, use a range of 10 to 18 seconds for your shake.

SHAKING DON'TS AND DO'S

DON'T	DO
shake a cocktail in the direction of your guest. It will happen to every bartender at least once—you lose your grip and send the shaker flying.	turn 45 degrees to one side and shake. Any major catastrophes will be avoided; drops from your wet hands or the contents of the shaker will not be splattered all over your guest.
attempt to get away with filling the shaker only partway with ice.	fill the shaker completely with ice, maximizing chill and minimizing sloshing.

Opening the Shaker

Regardless of which Boston shaker setup you choose, getting the shaker parts connected and unconnected is a big part of the job and not always an easy feat. When you load your shaker with cold liquids and ice, the metal chills and contracts, and the air chills and contracts, essentially creating a vacuum seal. That's a good thing, because the vigorous shaking that's about to take place is going to test the limits of any seal.

But it's a bad thing when it comes time to pour your drink, unless you know how to make the two parts of the shaker release. I spent many years as a young bartender holding my breath as I yanked at the Boston shaker, banged it against the edge of the bar, or even rinsed it under hot water to try to get the cups to unstick. Finally, I learned a

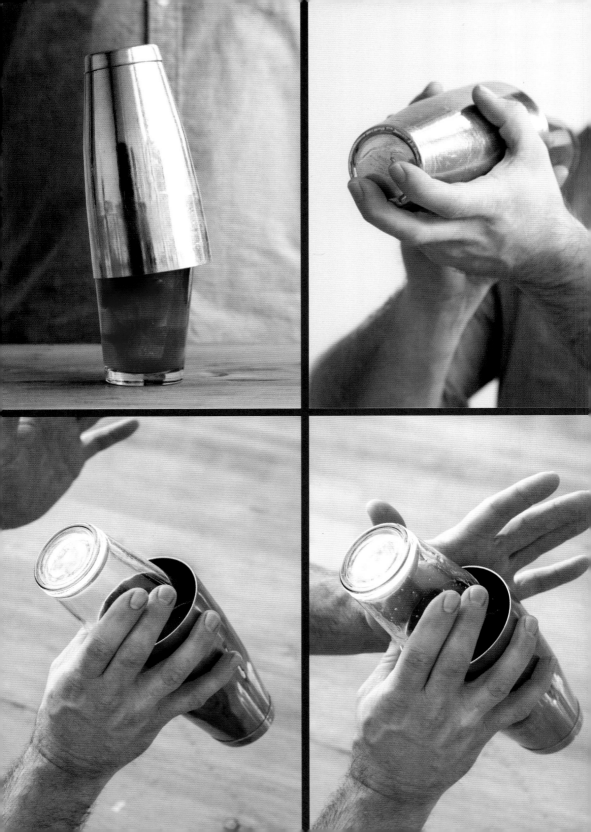

foolproof trick, and I've never had a problem since. But I still see bartenders making my early mistakes and so I offer a piece of professional advice below.

How to Seal and Open a Boston Shaker

If you're going to go the professional route and work with a Boston shaker, you're going to have to know how to open it properly, using only your hands. Banging the shaker against the edge of the bar is not only unsightly and disruptive, but also extremely dangerous if you've chosen to use a mixing glass in conjunction with the shaker tin.

First, pay attention to how you join the two tins (or tin and glass). When you seat the two pieces, the top one will naturally want to cock to the side, which leaves one straight cup.

Now invert the shaker and look straight down through the long axis. You will see the two circles formed by the rim of each cup. At one spot, they will be touching each other—that's your six o'clock. Directly opposite will be your twelve o'clock, and that's where the gap between the circles is largest.

You could hit the shaker near six or twelve o'clock a hundred times, and it won't open even once. On either side is three o'clock and nine o'clock. To release the cups, smack the heel of your hand smartly against the lower cup at either the three or nine o'clock position, depending on your dominant hand. The shaker will pop right open.

The Boston Shaker

Straining Twice for Texture

The strainer you use with a shaken cocktail is the Hawthorne strainer, which is a tool that you'll find only behind a bar; there's no real counterpart in the battery of kitchen equipment. A Hawthorne consists of a small slotted plate with a couple of tabs, which help it to span the opening of your mixing tin (or glass) when placed on top. The Hawthorne also has a spring around the underside, which is what strains out ice and other large solids.

Over the course of an evening, bits of fruit pulp, mint, egg whites, etc., will remain trapped in the coils of the strainer, which would be unsightly in a crystal-clear, single-strained drink. So we'll be double-straining all of the drinks made with Hawthorne strainers—through the Hawthorne and then through a fine-mesh strainer.

My favorite Hawthorne strainer is made by OXO, and like many of OXO's products, it is a good value for the money. It costs very little and is nicely made, feels good in the hand, and is easy to manipulate because its handle is noticeably shorter than the handles of most other Hawthorne strainers.

When you strain a stirred, spirit-driven cocktail, you're essentially straining a pure liquid with your julep strainer, and all it needs to do is hold back ice cubes, so there is no need to double-strain. But a shaken cocktail is likely to have more small solids—perhaps from fruit juices—and it also may contain tiny shards of ice, a result of the vigorous shaking.

You don't want any of that in your final drink, as a shaken cocktail should have a pristine, uniform texture and no further dilution from tiny shards of ice. So I double-strain all my shaken cocktails. Double-straining is simple—just outfit your nondominant hand with a small fine-mesh strainer and pour from your Hawthorne through the mesh strainer into the glass. You may be surprised to see how much gets past the Hawthorne.

Fine-Mesh Strainer

My favorite tool for double-straining is the Norpro Krona 4-in/10-cm stainless-steel deluxe double-mesh strainer. It's well made with very fine-gauge mesh, and the handle has some heft to it, which gives it some balance. It's also attractive to look at, with its contoured handle and chrome plating, as it rests on your bar.

SIDECAR

MAKES 1 DRINK The first drink I really got to know was the sidecar. A tart, bracing blend of cognac, Cointreau, and fresh lemon juice, a perfectly made sidecar is the ultimate expression of a shaken cocktail. Most recipes you'll see out there call for a sugared rim; I skip it and choose to balance the drink in the glass instead.

1½ oz/45 ml cognac

¾ oz/22.5 ml Cointreau

¾ oz/22.5 ml fresh lemon juice
(see page 22)

1 tsp/5 ml 2:1 simple syrup
(see page 78)

Ice cubes

1 orange peel for garnish

COCKTAIL GLASS

Combine the cognac, Cointreau, lemon juice, and simple syrup in a mixing glass and shake with ice cubes. Double-strain into the cocktail glass. Twist the peel over the surface of the cocktail and drop in the drink.

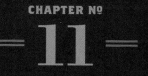
OTHER MIXING METHODS

TECHNIQUES TO MATCH MANY STYLES OF COCKTAIL

There's another technique for mixing drinks that you'll see performed from time to time. Granted, you won't see this one at any of my bars; nor will you see it at any of the many places around the world that serve a well-made cocktail these days. But you will see it in a chain restaurant bar. You'll also see it at the airport, but only when traffic in the concourse is slow. You'll definitely see it in sports bars, and just about any place on the beach. Gary Regan dubbed it "the Seattle muddle" in his book *The Joy of Mixology*, but it's long left that city's limits and spread to the far corners of the globe. And here's how it goes:

The bartender fills a mixing glass with various chunks of spoiled fruit from the garnish tray, maybe a packet of sugar or some mint, seemingly whatever's lying around. Finally, ice is added and the whole shebang is covered up with the palm of one hand, and a wooden muddler is taken up in the other. And then the magic begins. The muddler is thrust into the gap between the thumb and fore-finger, and with a violent thrashing, the ingredients are pulverized with the ice in the mixing glass. Harder and harder the bartender mashes and churns, as the wet ingredients are splashed all over the palm of his or her hand and back into the drink. Bitter peels are obliterated, herbs are turned into paste, and ice is crushed into wet, hand-flavored crystals.

The alcohol and any other incidental mixers are then added, the whole mess is likely to be shaken limply for a second or two, and the drink—or whatever you want to call it—is served to the poor, unsuspecting guest.

There are, of course, many better methods out there for mixing cocktails. And while 90 percent of the time you'll be using the two described in the previous chapter, stirring and shaking, there are a few other methods that should be understood by the well-rounded bartender. Just know that the scenario just described is definitely not one of them.

BUILDING IN THE GLASS

The simplest, most elementary mixing method is common, important, and exactly as easy it sounds. You "build" the drink right in the serving glass, as opposed to creating it in a mixing glass, shaker, blender, or other vessel. You'll typically use this for highballs or cocktails with just a spirit and a mixer; but it also applies to drinks such as Caipirinhas, Mojitos, and some swizzled drinks (see page 226).

To build in the glass, add your liquor to a chilled serving glass, and then add ice. Finish by topping off with your mixer: water, tonic, soda, fruit juice, or whatever. Adding the mixer last allows you to achieve the correct volume and strength of drink for your glass size.

ROLLING

The idea behind rolling is to mix the ingredients together without introducing any air or froth. Tomato juice is particularly susceptible to frothing, so we always roll a Bloody Mary rather than shake it, in order to combine all those powerful ingredients.

How to Roll a Cocktail

After building your drink in a mixing glass, cap the glass with a mixing tin and, holding the shaker horizontally in the palm of your hand, rotate your wrist so that the shaker moves in a lazy circle. You can feel the contents rolling over on themselves without becoming overly aerated.

SWIZZLING

Ask the man on the street what a swizzle stick is, and he'll describe a long, colorful plastic stick with something ridiculous on the handle end—a flamingo, a monkey, or maybe a mildly offensive island native in a grass skirt. You stick it in a cocktail and stir, and then lay it on the counter, to be thrown away. But that's not swizzling.

True swizzling is a method used to mix a very specific type of drink—a crushed-ice drink, usually Caribbean, sometimes tiki—and it requires a specific tool. The authentic swizzle stick was born in Martinique, and is made from the *Quararibea turbinata*, commonly known as the swizzlestick tree, an aromatic tree that grows on most of the Caribbean islands. The tree forms slim branches, which end in multiple fingers. When trimmed, the fingers look like spokes at the end of the long stick. In Martinique, this is called a *lele*.

How to Swizzle

Generally, swizzled drinks are built in the glass first. I like to start with a collins glass that I've chilled in the freezer. Combine all of the ingredients in the glass, and then fill the glass with crushed ice. Insert the swizzle stick into the glass, and hold the stick between both palms. Rubbing your palms back and forth rapidly to spin the stick, slowly begin to move the stick up and down within the glass. You're mixing and aerating the drink, but you're also churning the crushed ice so that it super-chills the inside of the glass, which creates a beautiful frost on the exterior.

QUEEN'S PARK SWIZZLE

MAKES 1 DRINK Long before anyone came up with those overly alcoholic, sugary concoctions for chugging down in dance clubs and college bars, like the Long Island iced tea, there was another tall, boozy drink, which was served and sipped at the bar in the Queen's Park Hotel, in Trinidad. Composed mostly of rum, with a few other ingredients and a lot of crushed ice to temper the heat of the alcohol, the Queen's Park swizzle is a classic booze-laden sipper.

3 oz/90 ml Demerara rum

¾ oz/22.5 ml fresh lime juice, plus the spent lime half

½ oz/15 ml 2:1 Demerara syrup (see page 78)

Crushed ice

3 dashes Angostura bitters

1 bunch fresh spearmint

CHILLED COLLINS GLASS

Combine the rum, lime juice, Demerara syrup, and the spent lime half in the chilled collins glass. Fill the glass with crushed ice and swizzle until the glass becomes well frosted. Finish with the bitters, and garnish with a large bouquet of spearmint (see page 260). Serve with a straw.

BLENDING

The cocktailian world has a love-hate relationship with blended drinks these days. There are few people out there who don't truly enjoy a good slushy drink on a hot day, and those who say they don't are probably lying to you anyway. Fancy cocktail bartenders sneer and scoff at the idea of having to serve blended drinks, although most of them have never actually had to do so.

I, on the other hand, have worked in my fair share of Mexican restaurants and, as a result, I became very friendly with the blender station. And you know what? Sure, it's kind of annoying sometimes. A blender is loud, it's fairly cumbersome, and it takes a certain amount of finesse to be able to make a blended drink properly. Plus, you can make only one type of drink at a time, so if you've got three blended margaritas, two piña coladas, and a blended daiquiri on the same ticket, you're kinda screwed.

But it would be foolish to write a book on bar technique and not include this venerable system of making delicious drinks, so I present to you the proper way to blend a drink. With the way drinking trends wax and wane, we might all be drinking blended drinks again very soon.

How to Make a Blended Drink

There are two factors to a successful blended drink: First, the drink should have a completely uniform, silky-smooth texture. This is the one time you're going to be allowed to drink out of a wide (also known as a turbo)

straw, so the drink needs to be free of ice chunks and able to flow smoothly. The next important dynamic in a blended drink is its thickness: The drink should never be so thin that it sloshes around in the glass; nor should it be so thick that the ice can be separated from the rest of the cocktail when sucked down through a straw, leaving behind a pile of snowy ice in the glass.

Your main weapon in this balancing act is the type of ice you use, and for blended drinks I use only crushed or finely cracked ice. Yes, the point of the blender is to pulverize ingredients with its sharp metal blades, but if you start with whole cubes and keep your fingers crossed in the hopes that you've used exactly the right amount of ice and that it will reach the proper fine consistency, you're probably in for some disappointment. Assuming your blender can handle whole cubes in the first place.

In a bar situation, you might have crushed ice on hand, but at home, you can use the food processor to crush your ice (see page 176). Unfortunately, you can't make the actual blended drink in the food processor because of the hole in the center of the bowl; liquid will leak out and you'll have a mess all over your counter. Seriously, don't bother trying to make blended drinks in a food processor.

Add your drink ingredients to the blender, start it on the lowest possible speed, and then slowly add your crushed or finely cracked ice and blend. (Put the lid on, yes.) I'd love to give you an exact quantity of ice to use in a blended drink, but so much depends on the other ingredients. I do it slowly, by feel, and by watching the shape of the contents in the blender. The perfect amount of ice will produce a central vortex, with distinct curves of drink flowing into it, almost like pillows of drink folding into each other. When there's not enough ice, the contents just slosh around; and when you've got too much ice, the mix will look thick and flat in the blender, with no curves forming at all.

THE BLENDER OF DESIRE

In the world of cars, there are really nice cars, and then there are Italian sports cars. In the bar world, there are good blenders, and then there's the Vitamix. If given the choice between these two, I might pick the car, but I'm still pretty crazy about my Vitamix. I use it for everything from blending drinks to making syrups from fibrous ingredients (see page 97), and after ten years, it still performs like a champ. I may have mistakenly compared it to a finely tuned Italian sports

car; it's really built more like a tank. And what I love as much as the performance is the story.

Vitamix is made by an American family business that's been at the same thing for four generations now; their headquarters are outside Cleveland, Ohio. The current CEO is the great-granddaughter of founder W. G. "Papa" Barnard.

Barnard started by selling appliances door-to-door, but more notably, he was the first to create an infomercial for TV, in the late 1940s. Given how ubiquitous infomercials are now, I'm not sure why I think this is cool, but I do. The best part is that Barnard hadn't really anticipated the response to the commercial and wasn't quite ready to handle the hundreds of calls that came flooding in after his (highly effective) pitch. Barnard spent the next many hours crouched on his hotel-room bed, phone in one hand, pencil in the other, taking down order after order on a notepad. That flow of orders doesn't seem to have slowed down.

I don't mess around with the bar-specific line that Vitamix makes, as they seem to be geared more toward smoothie shops than toward the professional bartender. Instead I use what the kitchen uses, the Professional Series 200 variable-speed blender. I've never been happier.

PIÑA COLADA

MAKES 1 DRINK The piña colada is likely the most famous, and in some quarters maybe even the most reviled, blended drink. The drink—rum, fresh pineapple juice, and coconut cream—was popularized in 1954 at a jet-setters' destination, the Beachcomber Bar of the Caribe Hilton in San Juan, Puerto Rico.

Who actually "invented" the drink is in dispute. Most sources, including Hilton press releases, credit bartender Ramón "Monchito" Marrero Pérez, but another Hilton bartender, Ricardo Gracia, has claimed over the years that he invented it. *Invention* is a tricky term in the food and drink world, because it's almost never possible to pin down a time and place where three ingredients were mixed together for the first time. The *New York Times* mentioned on April 16, 1950, that "Drinks in the West Indies range from Martinique's famous rum punch to Cuba's piña colada (rum, pineapple, and coconut milk)," so clearly the drink predates Marrero's creation.

Two technological developments secured the status of the drink as a worldwide favorite—the invention of a method for extracting coconut cream from coconut meat, and the invention of the blender. Early versions of the drink were made with coconut cream obtained the way generations of tropical cooks had done it: Crack the coconut, pry out the meat, shave off the brown skin, chop or grate the meat, soak it in water, squeeze out the liquid, and then wait for the fat—the cream—to rise to the top so the cook could skim it. A labor-intensive process to be sure. The University of Puerto Rico's agricultural department awarded a grant to a professor who succeeded in creating a mechanized process in 1949, and ultimately the Coco López company was born; its success became intertwined with the piña colada.

A decade or so before the professor made his discovery, Fred Waring perfected his Waring mixer. Waring, who was also a famous big-band leader, had purchased the design from the inventors and improved upon it. The blender became popular throughout the bar and restaurant world as well as among consumers. The piña colada received one more boost to its popularity, a musical earworm that came out in 1979, but we'd rather just leave that one alone.

When I make this drink at home, I like to break out a special tool just for the occasion: my vintage 1950s-era Waring blender. Its beehive shape and ribbed glass blender cup just look so damn good with a frosty piña colada whizzing around inside.

2 oz/60 ml aged rum
1 oz/30 ml fresh pineapple juice
1½ oz/45 ml cream of coconut
8 oz/240 ml crushed ice
1 pineapple spear for garnish

WINEGLASS

Combine the rum, pineapple juice, cream of coconut, and crushed ice in a blender and blend until smooth. Serve in the wineglass and garnish with the pineapple spear.

MUDDLING

With the resurgence of drinks such as the Mojito and the Caipirinha over the past fifteen years, we've seen muddling rise from near obscurity to become part of the public consciousness. Muddled drinks are somehow seen as "fresher" by drinkers, and I'm regularly asked to "muddle" my margaritas and gimlets. These customers don't know why they prefer their fruit pressed with a wooden stick over having it freshly squeezed by a juicer; they just know they've seen it done before and that's the way they'd like it.

Muddling is nothing more than a quick-and-dirty method for making some of the ingredients we've discussed in previous chapters: fruit juice, fruit puree, and compound syrups. That, in a nutshell, pretty much sums up what muddling accomplishes behind the bar, and little more. You're trying to extract the flavor from whatever you're muddling—fruit, herb, or vegetable—but without the bother of getting out the kitchen tools and doing it *à la minute*, which is professional kitchen language for "to order."

The benefit of muddling versus making these ingredients is that it's faster if you're making only one or two drinks: there's no need for 4 cups/960 ml of tarragon syrup if you're making only a couple of tarragon drinks. The disadvantage of muddling is that it's less accurate; it's difficult to control the amount, intensity, and consistency from day to day, or from drink to drink. Four raspberries might give up 1 oz/30 ml of their precious juice one time and ¾ oz/22.5 ml the next.

In some cases you'll leave the solids in the drink after muddling, to become an integral part of the cocktail. In a Caipirinha, for example, the muddled limes stay in the glass, to some extent for aesthetics, but also so they can continue contributing their flavor. In other drinks, you'll double-strain to remove all the solids, such as the tiny seeds from a raspberry. Depending on what you're mudding, you'll use one of two muddling methods, and a special tool for each.

How to Muddle Herbs

Muddling herbs is a delicate process, and for this you'll use the disk end of your bar spoon (see page 203). We want to press the herbs gently into simple syrup until the fragrant oils are released. You don't want to grind and mash the herbs because you'll bruise them and release their chlorophyll, which will oxidize quickly and become bitter and swamp flavored.

Pick the leaves off the stems (large stems are unsightly and usually don't contribute much flavor), and pile them in your glass, along with your simple syrup or sugar. Using the hammer or disk end of your bar spoon, press the leaves, moving them around in the mixing vessel so they fold over, and press again. Continue pressing and folding just until you smell the herbs, and then stop. Once you catch that whiff of fresh herb, you're done.

MOJITO

MAKES 1 DRINK Sure, since the Mojito became the most popular drink ever, once again, it's also become popular for bartenders and self-described cocktail geeks to complain about it: It's pedestrian, it's the new cosmopolitan, it takes too long to make.

But I remember a time when we were all just beginning to rediscover the Mojito. And despite the fact that I've made literally thousands of them during the course of my career, I still have fond memories of those summers when we'd all gather in the kitchen while we waited for the grill to heat up and discovered the drink together, a new generation of Mojito lovers. It's an amazing drink when it's made right, and that's all you really need to know.

1 bunch fresh spearmint

½ oz/15 ml 2:1 simple syrup
(see page 78)

2 oz/60 ml white rum

1 oz/30 ml fresh lime juice (see page 22),
plus the spent lime half

Crushed ice

2 oz/60 ml chilled soda water

CHILLED PINT GLASS

Put 12 or so large spearmint leaves in the bottom of the chilled pint glass and add the simple syrup. Muddle the spearmint gently to release the oils. Add the rum, lime juice, and the spent lime half.

Fill the glass with crushed ice and finish with the soda water. Serve with a straw.

MUDDLERS FOR FRUIT

Fruit, unlike herbs, benefits from the use of an actual muddler. You'll sometimes see muddlers next to the register at liquor stores—they look like miniature baseball bats. Stay away. They don't perform the way you need them to, and usually they're finished with either paint or varnish, which can flake off in your drink.

Instead, seek out a natural wood muddler with no finish or stain. These can be treated with food-grade mineral oil to help preserve and protect the natural beauty of the wood. If you're muddling fruit that stains, such as dark berries or cherries, think about using a heavy-duty food-grade plastic muddler, made from the same material as a cutting board. They're easy to pop into the dishwasher and won't show the results of all your past work. I keep one of each type of muddler on hand at all times.

Whichever style you use, it needs some weight, so the tool can do as much of the work as possible for you. Having a large end and a small end gives you the flexibility to muddle in different size glasses. And a good muddler will be long enough so that it stands taller than your mixing vessel; you shouldn't need to reach your fingers into the glass in order to crush your ingredients.

When it comes to wooden muddlers, I want some agility in there and not just a big billy club to beat the ingredients into submission with. My favorite wooden muddlers are made by our friend David Nepove at Mister Mojito (www.mistermojito.com). He's got a variety of really cool designs, many of which I own. But my all-time favorite of his is the very simple and elegant Master Muddler, which is essentially a long tapered dowel that looks a lot like half of a French rolling pin.

Mister Mojito also makes a contoured food-grade plastic muddler, but my personal favorite is the Bad Ass Muddler made by Cocktail Kingdom (www.cocktailkingdom.com). It's heavy and sturdy enough to handle being washed in the dishwasher. And it's black, which means it's never going to show stains, no matter how many raspberries or cherries I end up muddling with it over the years.

How to Muddle Fruit

Most often, you'll be muddling citrus, lime in particular, though other citrus fruit certainly comes into play, depending on the drink you're making. Other fruit that's often muddled includes berries, peaches, pineapples, grapes, and, hell, even cherry tomatoes.

Cut your citrus into quarters; if you're using something large, such as an orange or grapefruit, go ahead and cut it into eighths. Put the citrus in your glass, preferably peel-side up, and then add the sugar. Work the citrus by pressing and twisting it with the muddler, grinding the sugar into the peel. The sugar acts as an abrasive and helps liberate the citrus oils and juice. As the juice is released, it will form a syrup with the sugar. Press and twist until you see a nice syrup forming and you smell the fragrance of the citrus zest. A good bartender uses every sense, and your sense of smell is one of the most critical tools.

CAIPIRINHA

MAKES 1 DRINK Cachaça is one of the most rustic spirits in the world. The national liquor of Brazil, cachaça is made from the juice of fresh-pressed sugarcane, which is then fermented and distilled. Unlike rum, which is usually made from molasses, cachaça retains the fresh, grassy, vegetal flavors of the cane juice.

It would be tough for cachaça to claim its position as the third-most-consumed spirit in the world if it weren't for the simple, peasant-like preparation of a drink known as a Caipirinha. With nothing more than a little sugar and lime to ameliorate the rough edges found in many cachaças, this is one drink that's more than the sum of its parts.

½ lime, quartered lengthwise, and white membrane removed

Heaping 2 tsp sugar

2 oz/60 ml cachaça

Crushed or cracked ice

CHILLED OLD-FASHIONED GLASS

Combine the 4 lime wedges and sugar in the bottom of the old-fashioned glass. Muddle the lime wedges with the sugar to release their juices and grind their oils from the peel. Add the cachaça.

Fill the glass with crushed or cracked ice and serve.

"MIXING" ABSINTHE

Absinthe is an anise-flavored spirit developed in the mid-1700s in Switzerland and in the French Jura Mountains; it gained huge popularity in French café society during the Belle Époque. But absinthe contained a small amount of thujone, which was thought (incorrectly) to be hallucinogenic. So in 1915 absinthe was banned in the United States and much of Europe, including France.

Almost a century went by before the regulations controlling absinthe were reinterpreted to allow its sale and consumption in the States. Provided that the absinthe contains less than 10 parts per million of thujone (a compound in wormwood), absinthe is okay. And, thanks to some analysis of pre-ban absinthes, we know that's all the thujone traditional absinthe contained anyway.

So drinkers are now discovering the proper way to enjoy absinthe, which involves a slow drip of water over a sugar cube, to add a touch a sweetness and a dilution of between three and five times the volume of the spirit, depending on the proof and personal taste. Most absinthe nowadays is served and diluted with a small carafe of water, but in the grand cafés, they would use elaborate absinthe fountains, which were fancy urns with multiple spigots that would dispense the water in slow drips.

To Serve Absinthe

Fill your glass with about 1¼ oz/37.5 ml of absinthe. Authentic absinthe glasses will often have a bulb at the bottom, which holds the right amount. Set your absinthe spoon— a slotted, flat, trowel-like utensil—usually beautifully ornamented, like the glasses— across the top of the glass and set a plain sugar cube on that.

Slowly drip between 4 and 6 oz/120 to 180 ml of cool water over the sugar cube, pausing to let it become saturated, and then continuing to drip water into the glass. You want to take your time with this, rather than simply pouring the full volume of water all at once, because slowly dissolving the sugar and coaxing out the oils held in suspension in the absinthe is part of the ritual. As the water hits the spirit, it forms an emulsion with those oils, creating a lazy curl of milkiness, known as a louche.

Some references to serving absinthe mention soaking the sugar cube in the absinthe, igniting it, and then adding it to the glass. Don't *ever* do that. The practice came about because of some highly inferior spirits that were produced in the Czech Republic in the '90s. Called absinth (no final *e*), they were mostly just neutral spirits flavored with herbal and other oils and were more like mouthwash than true absinthe. These fake absinthes didn't louche, so drinkers concocted another type of serving ritual. It's best left out of the modern bar, so skip the fire and stick to the drip method described above.

FLAMING DRINKS

A big part of bartending is theater: It's a show, and there's nothing more theatrical or showy than some clown playing with fire, which is why the cocktail repertoire contains a few famous incendiary drinks. The flame throwing in these cocktails does conveniently come with functionality, however; it's the way we use fire to transform ingredients and develop and deepen flavors.

Mixing alcohol (whether it's inside a glass or inside your belly) and an open flame can spell extreme danger, and should give the phrase *Drink responsibly* a whole new meaning.

FIRE TO BURN ALCOHOL AND BALANCE A DRINK

The blue blazer was supposedly invented by San Francisco bartender and author Jerry Thomas back in the late nineteenth century, purportedly at the request of a grizzled gold prospector, who wanted to be impressed. The drink consists of high-proof Scotch whisky, water, sugar, and lemon peel. Nothing impressive about the ingredients; the same ones go into the world's least exciting hot cocktail, the whiskey skin. It's the mixing method that is somewhat jaw-dropping. You'll need to find cask-strength Scotch whisky for this, between 100 and 140 proof. Anything less doesn't ignite below a room temperature of about 75°F/24°C.

To make a blue blazer, you need two heat-proof mugs with handles, preferably large tankards. It's a good idea to prewarm the mugs by filling them with boiling water and letting them sit for a few minutes. When warm, empty the mugs and add boiling water and a little sugar to one, whiskey to the other, and light the whiskey on fire. You then pour the flaming whiskey into the water-filled mug, and quickly pour that mixture back into the first mug. Repeat this several times, each time moving your mugs farther apart, so that the burning liquid makes an arc of blue flame between the two. After several pours, extinguish both mugs by covering one with the bottom of the other. Pour the hot mixture into a fresh mug or a tempered wineglass and garnish with a generous length of lemon peel. Serve, and take a bow.

The things you need to remember during this process are:

- Long fireplace matches are really the safest way to light this thing, or any flaming drink, really, as it keeps your fingers as far away from an open flame as possible.

- Flaming alcohol can easily ignite anything combustible, including eyebrows, beards, and the long blonde hair of the very guest you're showing off for. Pay attention.

- You really need to use heavy metal mugs with handles that are big enough to keep your knuckles away from the contents. The mugs can get very hot, though, and it's not okay to drop them on the floor, going "Jeez, that's hot."

- If you want to be especially careful, wearing oven mitts doesn't look particularly cool, but they will protect your forearms from fiery liquid.

- You should hone your pouring skills by simply using plain old water before you try this.

Our friends at Cocktail Kingdom make some pretty awesome silver-plated blue blazer mugs, if you feel like investing. Or you can scour the thrift stores, estate sales, and online auctions for silver mugs. They usually look like big beer tankards.

BLUE BLAZER

By Jerry Thomas

MAKES 1 DRINK Personally, I've never found the combination of Scotch and hot water all that interesting or appealing, but a whole new generation of bartenders has rediscovered this cocktail, so there's got to be something to it. Here is Jerry Thomas's original recipe.

2 oz/60 ml boiling water
1 tsp sugar
2 oz/60 ml cask-strength (100- to 140-proof) Scotch whisky
1 lemon twist for garnish

2 BLUE BLAZER MUGS

6-OZ/180-ML TEMPERED WINEGLASS

Prewarm your blue blazer mugs with boiling water for several minutes. Empty the mugs.

Mix the 2 oz/60 ml boiling water and sugar in one mug, and put the whisky in the other. Carefully ignite the whisky, and while it is flaming, pour the whisky into the water. Mix the ingredients by pouring them back and forth from one mug to the other several times. Serve in the wineglass and garnish with the lemon twist.

FIRE FOR TOASTING

The café brûlot doesn't have the blue blazer's Jerry Thomas pedigree, but it is equally dramatic and dangerous. As its name implies, this is a coffee drink. It was invented in New Orleans and is still served in traditional restaurants such as Galatoire's and Antoine's. Café brûlot is really more of a maître-d'-at-tableside drink for restaurant patrons, rather than a bartender's drink. Waiters make it in the same way they might prepare other flaming classics, such as crêpes Suzette or steak Diane. My brother-in-law Joseph Brooke is quite the celebrity bartender down in Los Angeles, and he happens to be the brûlot expert in our family. So I asked him for his advice on this one.

To make a café brûlot, you first need to drag my sister all over Los Angeles County looking at estate sales in order to procure a brûlot cauldron, which is a rounded metal chafing dish that sits over a sterno flame. You add whole spices (usually cinnamon and cloves, but sometimes cardamom as well), sugar, brandy, and an orange liqueur, such as Grand Marnier. Those ingredients are combined in the bowl, left to macerate for 10 to 15 minutes, and then heated with the sterno.

Meanwhile, you and an in-law peel an orange and a lemon, each in one long, continuous spiral, also known as a horse's neck (see page 262), while you argue about who makes the better peel. Leave as much pith as possible intact on the peel, as it will help provide some structural support for later. You also want to make the peel's edges as smooth and even as possible, as too sharp of an angle could result in the peel breaking or sending splatters of hot booze flying in undesirable directions as you luge the flaming liquid down the peel. Next, stud the orange peel every 1 in/2.5 cm or so with whole cloves, straight down the middle like the dividing lane in a road. Leave the lemon peel unstudded and put it in the cauldron.

Now comes the fun part: While my sister yells at you to not burn the house down, ignite the hot liquor in the bowl with a long fireplace match, and stir it around with a small ladle to mix. Then, holding the orange peel with the longest tongs you can find, you ladle spoonfuls of the burning alcohol over the peel, so that the alcohol courses down its length. In theory, this toasts the oils in the peel, adding more flavor to the drink.

After a minute or so of this (anything longer is quite frankly too hot to hold, and in Joe's case, it means that he's just showing off for the crowd again), you pour strong black coffee into the mix, which will put out the flames. Finally, you ladle the coffee into demitasse cups and serve. Major bonus points if you have—as Joe does—a brûlot ladle, which contains a small strainer to filter out the bits of spice and peel as you ladle the drink into the cups.

CAFÉ BRÛLOT

MAKES 4 TO 6 DRINKS

1 orange, peeled in a single, long, continuous spiral
9 whole cloves
1 lemon, peeled in a single, long continuous spiral
1½ tbsp sugar
1 long cinnamon stick
3 oz/90 ml cognac
2 oz/60 ml Grand Marnier
24 oz/720 ml hot freshly brewed strong coffee

BRÛLOT DEMITASSE CUPS

Stud the orange peel with the cloves, placing them about 1 in/2.5 cm apart, and set aside. In a brûlot cauldron, combine the lemon peel, sugar, cinnamon stick, cognac, and Grand Marnier. Light the burner and adjust the flame so it's low. Cook for 2 to 3 minutes, stirring with a ladle to dissolve the sugar and warm the ingredients.

When the mixture is warm, carefully ignite with a match. While the mixture is flaming, hold the spiraled orange peel with very long tongs over the cauldron, ladle the flaming mixture down the peel into the bowl several times, and then drop the peel into the cauldron.

Add the hot coffee, stir to combine, and ladle the café brûlot into brûlot or demitasse cups, being careful to leave the spices and citrus peels behind in the cauldron. Serve immediately.

FIRE AS CARAMELIZATION TOOL

There's one more drink, newer than either the café brûlot or the blue blazer, that's something of a legend here in the Pacific Northwest. You almost never hear calls for it outside of Oregon, but within the state line it's the most well-known of the drinks that have originated here, and that's the Spanish coffee.

I can walk from my apartment to where the drink was first invented in the 1970s, Huber's Cafe, arguably the oldest restaurant in Portland. Underneath the barrel-vaulted stained-glass ceiling in the bar room, bartenders and waiters make hundreds of their famed concoction every night. The process is a joy to watch from a technique perspective, and I sometimes find myself seated at the bar on winter afternoons on my days off, writing and lazily watching in wonder as these masters of their single-drink craft make one after another.

It begins with a 6-oz/180-ml tempered wine-glass, which is moistened with a lime wedge and banded in sugar (see page 269). Next, 151-proof rum and Triple Sec are poured in a long arc in the txakoli (a Spanish wine) tradition, with the glass held low and the bottle held high above the head. And then the mixture is set alight. Twirling the stem between the fingers, the bartender angles the glass to point the fire toward the sugared rim, twirling and swirling until the sugar begins to bubble and caramelize.

Kahlúa is then added in a long stream, and the glass is topped off with strong black coffee to extinguish any remaining flame. A layer of cold whipped cream is floated on the surface, and then the whole mixture is finished with freshly grated nutmeg. It's strong, bright, acidic, and perfect for the weather we enjoy so much up around these parts.

SPANISH COFFEE

MAKES 1 DRINK

Sugar for rimming the glass

1 lime wedge

¾ oz/22.5 ml 151-proof rum

½ oz/15 m l Triple Sec

1½ oz/45 ml Kahlúa

3 oz/90 ml hot freshly brewed coffee

Lightly whipped cream (see page 148) for garnish

Freshly grated nutmeg for garnish

6-OZ/180-ML TEMPERED WINEGLASS

Put some sugar in a shallow bowl. Make a slit in the lime wedge, and moisten the rim of the wineglass with it. Make a band of sugar around the rim (see page 269). Fill the glass with the rum and Triple Sec, and light with a match.

Holding the glass at an angle, heat the sugar using the flame until the sugar begins to bubble and caramelize, about 1 minute.

Add the Kahlúa and coffee, and finish with whipped cream and freshly grated nutmeg to serve.

GARNISHING

**FINISHING THE COCKTAIL
VISUALLY AND AROMATICALLY**

Of all the topics in bartending that arouse spirited debate (ugh, no pun intended, I swear), there are few more controversial than the garnish conversation. Guests love a beautifully garnished cocktail, while modern young mixologists, often conditioned to respond to their guests' joy with disdain, have begun to spend less and less energy on finishing the drink. Although I applaud the modernist, minimal approach in the right situations, there is a time and a place for everything. And when it comes to garnishing, the time is often, and the place is in your drink.

And in your mouth, and in your nose, and in your eyes as well. I've been looking for a way to avoid the old cooking adage "We eat with our eyes first" while organizing this material, but I don't know if there's any way around it. Cocktails are something that are, most often, handed to us by someone else. I don't know

In this chapter, we've broken down garnishes into five categories. The first we refer to as dropped garnishes, which are some of the simplest and most well-known types of garnish out there. They're typically dropped into the drink at the very end, and they pretty much just sit there, offering very little in terms of flavor or aroma. They are usually consumed once the drink is done.

The second category we'll show you are the visual garnishes. They're a step up in complexity from dropped garnishes, but they're the catalog models of the cocktail world: they look great, and usually smell pretty nice, but they don't offer a whole lot in terms of substance.

Our third class of garnishes, the utilitarian garnishes, are hardworking little options, usually perched on the side of the glass, waiting to be used—just in case you need them.

DROPPED GARNISHES

Seen by the average drinker as more of a bar snack than a crucial drink component, cherries, olives, and onions don't really get much respect these days. You can most often find them sitting at room temperature on a bar top somewhere, bathed in an unidentifiable greasy or sticky liquid, whose only defense against the many dirty fingers that have been plunged within is a bacteria-inhospitable salt or sugar content. But some bartenders, players in a true cocktail renaissance, have left no stone unturned in their attention to detail. At last, these humble dropped garnishes are beginning to get the due respect they deserve.

CHERRIES

I remember fondly my very first cocktail. It was at a Howard Johnson on a road trip with my parents, and my mother included me in the round of drinks they ordered when the waiter came by for the first time. My drink was a Roy Rogers, and when it arrived, I was the happiest seven-year-old in the world, and all because of the garnish: a bright red maraschino cherry skewered by a little green plastic sword.

The archetype of American cocktail cherries is, in fact, that same cherry. While it's ubiquitous (there's one in the back of my parents' refrigerator that I swear is fifteen years old), this mass-market cherry has been bringing artificial color and high-fructose sweetness to crappy drinks since the 1920s.

Fortunately for us, we now have many better options available. A superior version of the American maraschino is one made by Italian producer Luxardo, who makes a liqueur made from Marasca cherries as well. The difference between these and the American version is night and day. Rather than a bleached-and-dyed zombie food product, think of preserved sour cherries packed in a syrup made from Marasca cherry pits. The major selling point these cherries come with is that they are delicious; the only drawback is that a 12.7-oz/360-g jar is pricey.

Another option that many professional bartenders such as myself use are preserved Amarena cherries. Slightly larger than, and of a flavor similar to, the Luxardo maraschinos, these are fresh sour Amarena cherries that have been candied in syrup. They're still fairly expensive but can be found for roughly half the price of the Luxardos.

Improving on Jarred Cherries

One trick I like to employ with both types of cherries is to drain off their syrup and then fill the jar with liquors and let them sit in the fridge before using. To do this, simply drain the liquid from the contents of a 12.7-oz/360-g jar of cherries by suspending a strainer over a container or bowl, then discard. Return the cherries to the jar and add 2 oz/60 ml of cognac or another brandy, ¾ oz/22.5 ml of amaretto, and ¾ oz/22.5 ml of maraschino liqueur. Reseal the jar and shake gently to combine the ingredients. Add a label with the date and store the jar in the fridge for at least 1 month before using.

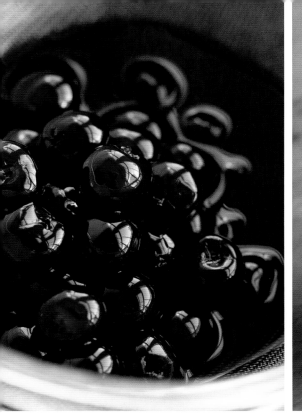

Brandying fresh cherries gives the bartender even finer control over the cocktail. For brandied cherries, most people use sour cherries. Sour varieties (mostly the Montmorency variety) grow only in parts of the Midwest and Pacific Northwest (Michigan, Oregon, and Washington, in particular) for a fleetingly short season. So, many bartenders use a canned Morello cherry, another sour variety. I like the ones from Trader Joe's. But fresh sweet cherries also make a great brandied cherry.

DANIEL SHOEMAKER'S BRANDIED CHERRIES

MAKES ENOUGH TO FILL ABOUT FIVE 1-QT/960-ML CANNING JARS Those who are obsessed with controlling every step of cocktail making often want to make everything possible from scratch. And there is nobody I know in this business who is more obsessed than my friend Daniel Shoemaker, owner of the Teardrop Lounge here in Portland, Oregon. Daniel is a lucky man, because he found a healthy outlet for his obsessive-compulsive nature: he opened a bar at which just about everything is house made, which means we're lucky, too. At Teardrop Lounge, you can get house-pickled onions, house-tinctured roots and barks, house-made Amer Picon, house-carbonated tonic water, house-macerated mango-chipotle hot sauce, and just about anything else you can think of. Among the best of these craft cocktail components are the brandied cherries, for which Daniel generously shares his recipe here.

Oregon is big cherry country, and Daniel gets late-harvest fruit from the Hood River Valley, just east of Portland. The cherries tend to be big, firm, and full of sugar, which is perfect for these garnishes. He usually uses the Lapin variety, which is dark magenta, but you should choose whatever variety looks best in your region. This recipe is for sweet cherries, however, not tart pie cherries, like the Montmorency. It makes a lot, but brandied cherries make great gifts, so you won't regret the abundance.

5 lb/2.25 kg ripe, firm sweet cherries

½ cup/45 g whole juniper berries

½ cup/45 g whole allspice berries

6 cinnamon sticks, lightly crushed

3 whole star anise

5 cups/1.1 kg sugar

8 oz/240 ml fresh lemon juice (see page 22), strained

3 cups/720 ml water

20 oz/600 ml brandy

12 oz/360 ml white rum

8 oz/240 ml bourbon

Clear away anything that you don't want to get spattered with cherry juice. It sprays and it stains, even when you're careful, so wear an old T-shirt. Pull off the stems and punch out the pits of the cherries with a cherry pitter. (A trick that some cooks use is to put their hands and the pitter inside a very large plastic bag as they pit. The bag will corral much of the juice.)

Heat the oven to 200°F/95°C. Place five 1-qt/960-ml canning jars right-side up on a baking sheet and put in the oven for 20 minutes; you can turn off the heat and leave them in the oven until ready to use. In a saucepan, simmer the lids in water to cover for 2 minutes and lay them out on paper towels to drain.

Dump the juniper berries, allspice berries, cinnamon sticks, and star anise in the center of a double layer of cheesecloth and tie into a secure bundle. Fill a large stockpot or canning kettle about one-third full of water and bring to a boil. This will be your water bath for canning the cherries.

Meanwhile, combine the sugar, lemon juice, and the 3 cups/720 ml water in another large stockpot, at least 10 qt/9.5 L. Bring to a simmer, stirring just until the sugar is dissolved. Add the spice bundle, and continue to simmer for about 5 minutes. Add the cherries, stopping when the pot is about half full; you'll be adding another 5 cups/1.2 L of liquid and you'll need to be able to stir the cherries without them spilling out. (You'll probably need to cook the cherries in two or three batches.)

Using the slotted spoon, stir and fold the cherries onto themselves so that they are all soaked in the syrup and are getting thoroughly warmed. You don't want to actually cook the cherries, just let them absorb the syrup. Return the liquid to a simmer; pour in the brandy, rum, and bourbon; and stir to mix. When the liquid is heated through, take the pot off the heat. (Be sure not to boil the liquid because you don't want to cook off too much alcohol.)

Using a wide-mouth funnel or jar filler and a slotted spoon, pack each canning jar with cherries, filling it to the top. Give the jar a good tap on the counter to settle the fruit so there are minimal air gaps. Ladle the hot syrup into the jars up to about ½ in/12 mm from the rim. Place the flat part of the lid on the jar, and screw the band on lightly.

Add the next batch of cherries to the hot syrup remaining in the pot and heat the cherries through. Transfer to jars, top with syrup, and seal the jars.

When all the jars are filled and the lids are on, put the jars into the boiling water bath in batches, as many as will fit without crowding. The water should cover the jars by about 1 in/2.5 cm, so top off with more boiling water if necessary. Boil for 5 minutes, and then retrieve the jars (Daniel uses silicone oven mitts to lift and transfer the jars). Set them on the counter to cool and let the seals form properly. You'll hear a nice pop as the vacuum forms and the lid is sucked down. Tighten the rings of all the jars that have sealed properly. You can store these at room temperature, away from heat and light, for up to 1 year. If you have any jars that didn't seal properly, simply keep them in the refrigerator and use within 2 weeks.

Cherry Pitter

Pitting cherries is unfortunately a painstaking, messy chore. If you're not planning on pitting more than a few cherries, I've found that placing the fruit on the mouth of a clean beer bottle and then running the pit through with a chopstick is a neat little trick and just the kind I like—simple yet effective. Do be careful of the juice, however, which is likely to spray around your work area, and onto your shirt. It stains, whether you're using this improvised method or a cherry pitter.

For bigger batches, you're going to want a cherry pitter. Traditional cherry pitters are nothing more than a stainless-steel plunger suspended over a circular base, through which the pit is ejected while holding the fruit in place. The splatter factor is high with these guys, but fortunately our friends at OXO Good Grips make a handy little model that offers some level of spray control. This is the one I reach for every time.

OLIVES

Who can imagine that iconic image of a martini in neon lights—which has become the universal sign for "Cocktail Bar" all over the world—without an olive on a pick? It's kinda ironic, then, that olives aren't really used in more than one or two cocktails: the martini, of course, and maybe a Bloody Mary. The martini still reigns supreme among classic cocktail enthusiasts, though, so we need to make some choices about our olives.

Stuffed or Not

The first issue is whether to use stuffed or unstuffed olives. The khaki-green olive with the red pimento peeking out is, of course, the classic; most of these are imported from Spain. There are plenty of lowest-common-denominator cocktail olives around, but if you buy a good brand, they can be delicious—briny and meaty, with just a tiny hit of smokiness from the pepper.

Recently, the pimento has seen some competition, with olives getting stuffed by everything from anchovies to Marcona almonds, hot chiles, and even blue cheese. If you're going to stuff something in your olive, the flavor and consistency should harmonize with the cocktail, and a film of cheese grease floating on top of my drink is something I find to be nothing short of repulsive. I leave these cheese-stuffed olives in the snack tray and out of the drinks.

To have the most control over quality, stuff your own olives. Buy some good green—or even black—olives, such as Castelvetrano, Cerignola, or kalamata. Pit them, using a hand-held olive pitter, and then stuff with a whole or half Marcona almond, some fire-roasted sweet peppers or hot chiles, or even a sliver of preserved lemon.

Pitted or Not

If you prefer to serve unstuffed olives, you still need to make a decision about whether to pit the olive or not. While an unpitted olive looks far more attractive than a pitted one, I feel the expectation of most guests is that martini olives are pitted, which could result in an awkward situation should you leave an unpitted olive in someone's drink. Not to mention the other awkward situation: where to place the pit once it's plucked from the mouth.

How Many Olives

The next option to consider is the number of olives to use per drink. Whenever I think about how many olives to use, I remember a quote from bartender Paul Harrington, whose writing is the foundation for everything I know about cocktails today. On his seminal cocktail website Paul said, in the late 1990s, "One olive or onion is elegant, two is proper, and three is a meal." I think that just about sums it up.

To Spear or Not to Spear

The next consideration is whether or not to employ a toothpick. My simple rule is that dropped garnishes in quantities of two or more always need a toothpick, while a single olive or cherry simply sits in the bottom without. When I do use a pick, however, I like to keep the garnishes offset on one end of the pick, giving the guest a little "handle" with which to pick up the snack.

There are many options out there for toothpicks, from the simple to the ridiculous. Cocktail picks range from beautiful bamboo spears to golf tees and plastic buccaneer's swords. But my long-standing choice of garnish toothpick has always been a wood sandwich pick, a perfect size for the larger olives and onions used most often today. You'll find these at suppliers like Country Clean Paper Supplies (www.wesellcoffee.com).

Storing Olives

Dropping a room-temperature olive into an ice-cold martini should be unthinkable, but it's done more often than not. To solve this problem, we keep our olives in the fridge, pre-speared with picks and ready to be used. Another trick we employ at my bar is removing them from their brine and soaking them in dry vermouth. The brine is then fine strained to remove any solids, and bottled with a pour spout, ready to be measured out by the teaspoon for dirty martinis. The olives will last a good 6 months in the fridge.

HOW DO THE PIMENTOS GET INTO THE OLIVES?

You may not have spent a lot of time thinking about how that little sliver of red pepper gets into an olive, but it's an interesting bit of food-production trivia. Because huge volumes of these get produced every year, it would be cost prohibitive to hand-stuff each olive with an actual slice of pepper. Most modern olives are stuffed with a "composite pepper": Roasted pimentos are pureed and bound together with something like guar gum and then cut into strips. The strips are injected into the olives as the pits are being punched out. Neat trick, though do take note that guar gum can trigger reactions in people who have peanut allergies.

ONIONS

It's unclear how and when the Gibson—a drier, more gin-forward variation on the classic martini—was first garnished with its iconic cocktail onion. History has led us to understand that the drink was created in San Francisco sometime in the late nineteenth century at the Bohemian Club for one of its members, Mr. Walter D. K. Gibson. The earliest accounts of the Gibson don't indicate that the onion was the drink's defining characteristic, but rather the near omission of vermouth. That said, there's no challenging the fact that the modern Gibson is garnished with a cocktail onion.

A cocktail onion is similar to an olive in that it's also pickled in a salty, tangy brine and brings some of those same flavor notes to the drink. That's probably why you really only see onions in the same drinks in which you might encounter an olive instead: at the bottom of a martini or perched on the side of a Bloody Mary.

TODD THRASHER'S PICKLED ONIONS

By Todd Thrasher, courtesy of Imbibe *magazine*

MAKES ABOUT ENOUGH TO FILL ONE 1-PT/480-ML JAR Truth be told, I was never a fan of cocktail onions until I tried the onions my friend Todd Thrasher made himself at his bar PX in Alexandria, Virginia. They're a far cry from the foul-smelling specimens available at your local liquor store.

```
1 tbsp pickling spice

24 oz/720 ml warm filtered water

32 oz/960 ml distilled Champagne
vinegar

2 cups/400 g sugar

2 tbsp kosher salt

1 lb/455 g pearl onions, peeled
```

Tie the pickling spice in a sachet of cheese-cloth. Combine the warm water, vinegar, sugar, and salt in a large nonreactive pot over medium heat; stir until the sugar is completely dissolved. Put the pickling spice in the vinegar solution. Add the onions, making sure they are completely covered with liquid. Bring to a boil and continue boiling for only 1 minute (it's important to limit the boil; otherwise the onions will lose their crunchy texture).

Remove from the heat, and transfer the onions and liquid to a clean 1-pt/480-ml glass jar and let cool overnight, covered, at room temperature. The onions will keep in the refrigerator for up to 2 months.

VISUAL GARNISHES

There are some garnishes that we use simply because they look so damn pretty. As I said earlier, of all the garnishes, they truly are the catalog model: they look pretty, they might even smell nice, but they don't really do much else—and at the end of the day they're just there to make the product look good.

FRESH HERBS AND FLOWERS

A tall sprig of fresh herbs rising from a glass, or some delicate flower petals scattered on the surface of a cocktail can be stunning, in the right circumstances. But herb and flower garnishes really are about looks rather than flavor or fragrance. If it's flavor you're going for, you'll need to muddle them or make a syrup with them in order to incorporate them into the drink. Visual perfection is what you're looking for here, so make sure that's the key to your selection.

Choosing Herbs and Flowers for Garnish

The first thing to ascertain is whether your herb or flower is actually edible. Not all herbs are culinary, and some flowers are toxic, and you don't want anything that's been treated with pesticides. So don't just pluck something from a field without knowing exactly what it is.

The best scenario, of course, is to have your own garden, where you can grow organically the herbs and flowers you like to use, and pick them when they're in perfect condition. Most people don't have the space for that, and others aren't quite so dedicated to fresh herbs. (Me, I fall into both camps.) So,

second to that, find a good organic grower at your local farmers' market. Develop a working relationship with them, and plan your menu around the availability of their ingredients. A specialty grocer will often have fresh herbs and edible flowers, but if all you can find are the dreary herbs folded into a plastic clamshell pack, I would seriously consider making a different drink.

The herbs I see most often in cocktails as garnishes are spearmint, rosemary, lavender, cilantro, tarragon, lemon verbena, lovage (which tastes a bit like celery), sage, thyme, and even borage, which has striking blue flowers on slightly prickly stems and tastes like cucumber. Borage was the traditional garnish for a Pimm's cup before cucumber took over because of its much wider availability.

Edible flowers are generally floated on the top of a drink. Blossoms that are appropriate for cocktails include nasturtiums, pansies, hibiscus, roses (the petals), violets, and even squash blossoms, which I have seen beautifully balanced atop some very baroque Bloody Marys over the years.

There are three techniques for garnishing with herbs and flowers:

Composed

Here you're going for delicacy, for example three tarragon leaves arranged in a star pattern on the surface of the drink, or a few tiny rose petals, or a fine chiffonade of sage or basil. You need a cocktail with enough consistency to allow the herbs or petals to float, so in most cases, this type of garnish will be added to the top of an egg-white cocktail.

Sprig

This type of garnish is straightforward. Choose an attractive sprig that's tall enough to stand at least 2 in/5 cm above the rim of the glass. Good choices for this type of garnish are stalkier herbs, such as rosemary, lavender, or something along the lines of a chive blossom or another blooming herb.

Bouquet

I use this method mainly for spearmint, though the technique could also be used for basil, cilantro, parsley, or other leafy herbs. If using mint, pick the top lengths from about 8 sprigs, gather them together by the stems into a tight bunch, and gently squeeze the leaves to lightly crush them and release their fragrance. Then insert the bunch into the drink so that the stems stay securely lodged in the cocktail. If you're using crushed ice, poke a hole in the ice with a chopstick, nestle the bouquet into the hole, and then insert your cocktail straw right through the middle of the herbs. This generous bouquet looks great and also provides a wonderful, fragrant experience as you bring the straw toward your lips to take a sip.

Keeping Herbs and Flowers Fresh

You should give your herbs a quick rinse and then either pat dry gently with paper towels or spin in a salad spinner. Storing fresh herbs can be a challenge, though rosemary and thyme are fairly hardy. I like to wrap herbs loosely in a barely damp paper towel and then tuck that into a plastic storage container and keep it in the fridge. Flowers are even more delicate than herbs. Because you're using flower that have not been sprayed with pesticides, you don't really need to rinse them. Just keep them cool and moist by storing them as you do herbs.

CITRUS TWIST

Looking something like a stubby shoestring, the citrus twist is usually curled over the lip of a glass, such as a highball; tied into a knot and dropped into the drink itself, as in a martini; or, less frequently, stretched over the top of the glass, looking something like the squiggle on a Hostess cupcake.

Twists are attractive, but they don't really add much in the way of fragrance or flavor. For spirit-driven drinks, including a martini, I tend to prefer the wider citrus peel (see page 274), so I can I express the oils over the surface of the drink. The twist is mainly about looks. Choose fruit with thick, pebbly skin for your twists.

Tools for Cutting Citrus Twists

Tucked away in a kitchen drawer, you might find—and be tempted to use—a tool called a zester, which has a row of small holes along the end of a blunt blade. Dragging the blade across a piece of citrus will produce thin strips of zest, but they won't be robust enough or shaped right to use as a twist. The correct tool for this job is called a channel knife, available for cheap at just about any kitchen supply store. A channel knife has one

deep, V-shaped notch on the blunt blade, and it produces a true julienne strip of citrus peel, when used correctly.

My favorite channel knife is the Pro-Touch, with a plastic-handle, made by Messermeister, although Victorinox makes a good model with a wood handle as well.

How to Cut a Twist

First, cut off one end of the fruit to expose the white pith layer, so the knife can get a good purchase on the peel. Place the notch of the channel knife at the exposed edge, dig the blade into the pith, and begin to turn the fruit. Aim the knife so that you're working around the "latitude" of the fruit, not tip to tip, as you would when cutting a wide strip of peel. Peel the length of twist you want, and then trim the ends neatly with a paring knife. With practice, you can remove the entire peel this way, slowly turning the fruit like a lathe as the peel emerges from the slotted blade in one long, continuous spiral.

HORSE'S NECK

Another spiraled citrus-peel garnish in the bartender's repertoire is the nearly extinct horse's neck. Originally designed as the garnish for the drink of the same name, it's essentially the long, wide spiral peel of a whole lemon, wrapped around the inside of a collins glass and finished with either brandy, bourbon, or rye and ginger ale. It's not really that exciting a drink, but the garnish is what makes or breaks it.

Unless you're particularly passionate about drinking your liquor with ginger ale, you're probably going to use the horse's neck as a garnish in other long drinks instead. It works particularly well with orange peel, and I love it in tall tiki-style drinks poured over crushed ice, and, of course, Cafe Brûlot.

How to Make a Horse's Neck

To make the horse's neck, start by trimming either end (stem or stylar) of a citrus fruit with your knife. Using a horizontal, or Y, peeler, carefully peel a wide spiral, starting at the trimmed end, around the entire fruit, sparing no peel. You should be left with a bare lemon in one hand and an entire spiral peel in the other.

There are two options when it comes to getting the peel into the drink. You can curl the peel around the inside of the empty glass and slowly fill with ice while maintaining the peel's placement with a chopstick or bar spoon, or you can slowly guide the peel into the drink, carefully working it between the cocktail and the side of the glass with your chopstick or bar spoon. Be sure to leave the last 1 in/2.5 cm of peel exposed, and try your best to hook it around the rim of the glass. If possible, cut a small notch into the end of the peel to facilitate this.

CITRUS WHEEL

Ironically, the least practical of the citrus garnishes are the ones you see most often in glossy magazines and coffee table cocktail

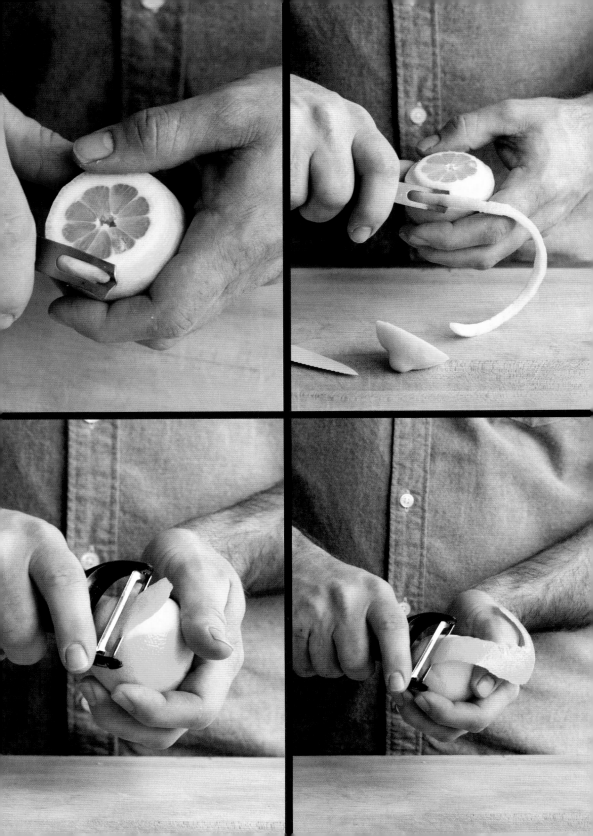

books. Wheels are pretty and make an impact, but they don't really add much to the drink.

There are two types of citrus wheel: thick and thin. A thick wheel sits perched on the rim of the glass looking very pretty, but generally too awkward to be picked up and squeezed. This is why I think of wheels as visual garnishes and not utilitarian. Nobody wants to deal with the mess once a wheel has been squeezed. A thin wheel is designed to be a delicate element that floats on the surface of a blended drink.

Tools for Cutting Citrus Wheels

For normal use, I always rely on a 4-in/10-cm serrated paring knife made by Kuhn Rikon. It comes with a plastic sheath, so I can toss it in my tool bag without worrying about it getting dull or damaging my other equipment. Plus it comes in a variety of bright colors, so I'm usually fairly certain about which one is mine at the end of the night.

For bigger jobs, or for trimming other large fruit, such as grapefruits and pineapples, I rely on what we refer to as the Sandwich Sword: a 9-in/23-cm, serrated, offset bread knife with a plastic handle, like the ones used to halve sandwiches in just about any deli in the world. They're cheap and made by a variety of food-service companies. Once you've handled one for a while, it can be quite nimble and you might be surprised at the accuracy you can effect on even the most delicate of garnishes.

How to Cut Citrus Wheels

For a thick wheel, trim off both ends of the fruit and then cut the whole fruit crosswise into ¼-in/6-mm slices. Cut one small slit just through the rind, but not all the way into the interior. This is where you'll attach the wheel to the rim of the glass. A shallow cut like this allows the wheel to sit proudly on the rim, whereas a deeper cut would mean the wheel slides farther down on the rim, a sloppy and depressing garnish.

To make a thin wheel, cut the fruit crosswise into very thin but even slices. In this case, you do want to cut the slit all the way through to the center of the slice. Pull one side of the slit forward and the other side backward to create "feet" so the slice can balance upright—it should look a bit like a loop on a roller coaster.

For all citrus wheels, as well as wedges (see page 266), it goes without saying that you need to flick out and discard all the seeds.

PINEAPPLE GARNISHES

Even though a pineapple spear or triangle is theoretically edible, its main function is to add visual drama to the drink. For that reason, we always leave the peel on.

How to Cut Pineapple Triangles

Cut off the base and top leaves of your pineapple and discard them. Cut the pineapple crosswise into ¾-in/2-cm slices, to create disks. Cut each disk in half, and then cut the halves into quarters, and the quarters into eighths.

You then need to notch the triangles so that they sit on the rim. To make the triangle sit in plane with the side of the glass, cut your notch straight in from the point. To allow the triangle to sit at an angle on the glass, make your cut partway up one side, rather than directly at the point. The choice depends on the size and shape of glass, and the visual presentation you're going for.

How to Cut Pineapple Spears

Cut off the base and top leaves of your pineapple and discard them. Cut the pineapple in half lengthwise. Lay one half, cut-side down, on the surface and cut in half lengthwise again, to make quarters. Cut each quarter in half lengthwise, to give you eighths. If you've got a large pineapple, make one more cut so that you have a slender spear.

To put a nice finish on the spears, cut off ½ to ¾ in/12 mm to 2 cm of the inner edge of the spear, to remove the hard core. The spear will look more polished and will be much more enjoyable to eat if your guest decides to take a bite.

Storing Pineapple Garnishes

Try not to cut pineapple more than 1 hour ahead, or it will dry out. Store the garnishes in an airtight container in the fridge, and just pull them out as you need them.

UTILITARIAN GARNISHES

This third category of garnish is a little more hard-working than dropped garnishes and visual garnishes. Not only does this garnish need to look appetizing, it also might potentially become integrated into the flavor of the drink at some point, so you're really working it from two angles here.

CITRUS WEDGES

There isn't much in the world I find less satisfying than ordering a gin and tonic, and receiving a healthy dose of bracing gin, a solid glug of tonic water, and a tiny limp chunk of lime floating on top. You're most likely to be served this "garnish," roughly the size of a baby's thumb, at ball games, aboard airplanes, and at just about any bar featuring more than one television.

A proper citrus wedge is freshly cut, glistening with juices, and, with any luck, perfectly balanced on the edge of the glass. It is an option, an accoutrement, a flavorful accessory. The drinker is hopefully going to taste the drink before making the decision to use or discard the citrus garnish, but if it's going to be there, then please, let's make it an attractive option.

You're finishing your cocktail with a big, juicy wedge of lime, and it's just begging to be squeezed into the drink—or is it? There are two ways to go with this, and you just need to decide which way makes sense to you. Even more than a cocktail flavor issue, squeezing is a service and hospitality issue.

Squeezing the wedge for your guest, and then dropping the spent fruit into the drink to release a bit more flavor and to signal the flavors in the drink, means you're doing the work for the guest, and you are the one whose fingers get messy.

But leaving the wedge for your guest to squeeze allows her to make the choice, hopefully after tasting the drink. For many years, I squeezed as a courtesy, but I'd also used the other method, and I'd seen so many guests remove the wedge and not add it to the drink that I've changed my approach. I now balance the wedge on the rim and leave it to the guest to finish the job, thoughtfully provided with a cocktail napkin, of course.

How to Choose Citrus Fruit for Wedges

While you do want your wedge to have a shiny, colorful skin, the most important part of a citrus that is intended for a wedge is its interior. Plump, juicy, and easy to squeeze win out over thick-skinned and pebbly, and often are at odds; it's rare to find a lime or lemon with thick skin that's extremely juicy. Choose fruit that feels heavy for its size, doesn't give too easily when you squeeze it, yet feels like there's not too much skin and pith hiding underneath the surface.

How to Cut a Lengthwise Citrus Wedge

A lengthwise wedge takes advantage of a large surface area of skin, making it hospitable to the drinker who is about to give it a squeeze. It's kind of the ultimate utilitarian garnish—fairly easy on the eyes, but even easier on the fingers. You know what it's for, and it makes no pretense about being other-wise. I find it suitable for drinks such as rum and Cokes.

Trim any excess off of the stem and stylar ends. You're not actually cutting into the fruit; you just want to round the ends, fol-lowing the natural curve of the fruit. You trim off just the actual stem and the nipple on the other end. Next, cut the fruit in half lengthwise. Using the point of your knife, score the inside of each half about halfway through right in the center, cutting all the way through the flesh, but stopping at the peel. This will end up being the notch in each garnish; doing it once on each half means you don't have to score the wedges individu-ally. Cut each half lengthwise in half again, or for larger fruit, cut each half lengthwise into thirds or quarters. Small limes will yield four segments, and large limes, lemons, and oranges will yield up to eight per fruit.

How to Make a Cross-Cut Wedge

A cross-cut garnish is essentially a fat half wheel, and it puts each wonderfully trans-lucent citrus segment on display. To begin, halve the fruit lengthwise. Lay each half cut-side down, and trim off the ends to neaten the shape. Cut crosswise into thick slices. If you're using large oranges or grapefruits, a wedge from a half fruit will be too big, so cut the fruit into quarters, and then cut one crosswise into wedges. Cut a ¼-in/6-mm notch in the center of each wedge, for align-ment in line with the plane of the glass, or at an angle for an offset perch.

WHIPPED CREAM

Whipped cream is a beautiful and elegant garnish used to finish coffee-based cocktails, most famously Irish coffee. To learn how to whip cream, see page 148.

RIMMED GARNISHES

No sports bar or chain Mexican restaurant would be complete without one of those glass-rimmer caddies. You know what I'm talking about; it's a round black plastic thing that folds out to reveal three compartments: one for salt, one for sugar, and one that holds a kind of plastic sponge that you soak with Rose's Sweetened Lime Juice. The bartender mashes the mouth of the glass into the sticky sponge, removes any fruit flies from the rim, and then pounds it into the crusty salt or sugar until the lip is coated in a kind of limey-salty or limey-sugary goo. We had one at the bar I worked in right after college, and I can guarantee you it hasn't been washed since I left.

Getting a perfect salt or sugar rim on the lip of a glass requires careful attention to technique, but once you've mastered it, the process is a snap. The order goes something like this:

1. Invert glass.

2. Moisten rim.

3. Apply salt or sugar.

4. Tap to dislodge excess.

To help give some sense of order to the method, here are some do's and don'ts of preparing rimmed glassware.

DO	DON'T
use freshly cut citrus to moisten the rim of the glass.	prepare a shallow dish of simple syrup or lime cordial, as some books will instruct you to do.
choose a complementary flavor of citrus when moistening the rim. For example, a lime rim for a margarita, lemon or orange for a sidecar.	be tempted to use grenadine or any other syrup for moistening the rim. This will result in a drippy mess.
be meticulous in moistening the rim; any areas touched by citrus juice will be coated in salt and sugar, while any areas not coated will be bare.	use anything but perfectly dried glassware, as any moisture on the glass will pick up salt flakes or sugar crystals in places not intended to be rimmed.
use kosher salt, sea salt, or any other salt with large flakes.	use ordinary table salt or so-called margarita salt, which is nothing more than overpriced kosher salt.
use table sugar, unbleached sugar, or any other dry sugar with large crystals, such as turbinado.	use brown, muscovado, superfine, or powdered sugar.
be vigilant about keeping the rim away from the contents of the drink.	allow salt or sugar on the interior of the glass; only the very top of the rim or in a band around the outside.

There are essentially two types of classic rims: one where the salt or sugar are perfectly balanced on the very tip of the glass, which we call a *lip*; and one where the exterior of the glass is wrapped in a ½- to ¾-in/12-mm to 2-cm belt of salt or sugar, which we refer to as a *band*. The former is best suited to drinks served without ice, as it is easily disturbed; the latter is our default for drinks served on the rocks.

For each, you'll need a shallow bowl or a plate (I prefer a bowl) filled with at least ½ in/12 mm of salt or sugar. After pouring the salt or sugar into the bowl, shake it gently to evenly distribute the contents so that it's completely level; do this every time a new rim is to be produced. Once the salt or sugar begins clumping together and an even distribution is no longer possible, discard and start over with a clean bowl.

How to Rim a Lip

For this you'll need an open piece of citrus cut along the equator. Invert the glass, hold the cut citrus in one hand, and spin the glass so the juice rings just the very edge of the rim. Gently dip the edge of the glass into the dish of salt or sugar and tap. Turn and tap, turn and tap until you've worked your way around the glass, achieving uniform cover-age. Now hold the glass over the sink and tap it with your hand to dislodge any excess. You want a rim that's just a few grains deep, with anything below the edge of the rim free of salt or sugar.

How to Create a Band

The goal here is to create a rim that won't be disturbed when you add the iced drink to the glass—just a little flavoring and texture on the guest's lower lip as she sips the drink. We want to avoid introducing salt or additional sugar to the cocktail itself at all costs.

Slip a slit wedge of citrus (see page 266) over the rim and turn the glass, in essence wiping a band of moisture on the inside and outside of the glass; the band will be as wide as the wedge is deep. Now roll the glass in a dish of salt or sugar so you create a well-defined band on the outside; tap to release any excess.

MARGARITA

MAKES 1 DRINK To salt or not to salt, that is the question. It's believed that originally, the salted rim, which is indelibly linked with tequila, was provided to mask the taste of inferior spirits. While many bartenders have begun to show disdain for the salted rim as we've discovered the beauty of handmade artisan tequilas, the fact still remains that the vast majority of margarita drinkers demand a salted rim with their cocktail. And if that's the way it's going to be, you might as well give them a perfectly salted rim and a perfectly made margarita to go with it.

Salt for rimming the glass

1½ oz/45 ml silver tequila

¾ oz/22.5 ml Cointreau

¾ oz/22.5 ml fresh lime juice

1 tsp/5 ml 2:1 simple syrup
(see page 78)

Ice cubes for shaking

Cracked ice for serving

OLD-FASHIONED GLASS

Rim the lip of the old-fashioned glass with salt (see page 269). Shake the tequila, Cointreau, lime juice, and simple syrup together in a cocktail shaker filled with ice cubes. Strain into the glass filled with cracked ice and serve.

AROMATIC GARNISHES

The most subtle and complex garnishes sit lightly on the surface of the drink, providing an enhanced olfactory experience, but often little to nothing in the way of visual presentation. These are the black diamond garnishes, the advanced level of garnishing that requires some thought and, as always, attention to detail.

CITRUS PEEL

When you gently squeeze a wide swath of citrus peel over the surface of the drink, you express its oils over the surface of the cocktail, adding some perfume to the drink. There are few cocktails that don't benefit from a layer of light, aromatic citrus oil on their surface—especially spirit-driven cocktails. So this is one of the most essential garnishing techniques out there.

Choosing Fruit for Making Peels

Look for larger fruit—which has more surface area—with a rough, pebbled surface (as opposed to smaller, smooth-skinned fruit). This colorful outer skin is called the flavedo, which contains essential oils, wax, fatty acids, and limonene, a fragrance-producing compound. In cooking terminology, this part of the skin is called the zest. This is what we'll be squeezing over the surface of the drink. When selecting fruit, squeeze it gently; it should feel firm and the skin should feel thick. And definitely choose organic if possible; in any case, rinse the fruit well before cutting your garnish.

Tools for Cutting Peels

There are two types of fruit and vegetable peelers on the market: vertical and horizontal. The vertical peeler is the traditional long-handled peeler you've undoubtedly encountered at some point in your life, and its orientation makes it perfectly suited to peeling long vegetables and fruits, such as carrots and cucumbers, as it places the arms and hands into a natural position for doing so.

The horizontal peeler, sometimes called a Y peeler, is designed to comfortably peel round fruits and vegetables, such as potatoes and, in our case, citrus fruits. The handle's orientation places the arms in a more natural position for peeling fruits and vegetables of this size and shape.

My favorite Y peeler is made by OXO Good Grips. They also make a so-called "Pro" version of this peeler, available for a few extra bucks. But I've found it to be less ergonomically comfortable than the standard version, which is the one I use.

Some chefs like using a peeler with a ceramic blade, but not me. They're extremely sharp, and the blade is shallow, which makes it hard to control. Being able to maintain precise control over the blade is important not just for the appearance of your peels, but also for the safety of your fingertips. Not to freak you out or anything, but if you peel enough fruit, the odds are good that one day you're going to lop off the top of one of your fingers. I find that this happens more frequently with ceramic peelers. Not to mention that ceramic blades are fairly fragile and can't stand up to being frequently tossed in a bar bag.

How to Cut a Citrus Peel

Your goal is to create a generous, even ribbon of peel, without jagged edges and with enough of the white pith underneath to give the peel some structure and firmness. Hold the fruit firmly in your nondominant hand and firmly drag the peeler lengthwise—from stem to stylar—in one firm stroke. Try not to stop and start, which can create rippled edges. Peeling tip to tip gives you the longest peels and also uses the fruit's surface more efficiently, for maximum yield.

How to Garnish with a Peel

Simply dropping a piece of pared citrus peel into a drink does nothing but add a spot of color—its oil needs to be forced out so that the oil coats the surface of the drink. Position the peel over the drink, colored-side down. Squeeze the short ends together between your thumb and middle finger, rolling the peel slightly to intensify the curve along its full length. If you look closely and catch the right amount of light on the surface of the drink, you can see exactly how much oil you're expressing while you do this.

I like to use the leftover peel to wipe the rim of the glass for an added dimension of flavor as the rim touches the lips. Holding the base of the glass with the nondominant hand to prevent spillage, simply rub the colored side of the peel around the lip of the glass several times until it's well coated with oil.

At this point, you've reached that age-old bartender's dilemma again: to drop or discard (this comes up when garnishing with wedges, too; see page 266). Some drinks benefit from the peel sitting in the cocktail and continuing to provide further depth and flavor as the drink sits. I find that the old-fashioned (see page 82) is one of those drinks.

For others, a big swath of peel is only going to get in the way, cluttering the otherwise clean, neat presentation of the cocktail. I find that the Sazerac (page 278) falls in that category, and so for that drink, I leave it out. Whichever method you choose, be prepared to explain your reasoning to your guests, as these can be very polarizing choices in the cocktail world.

THE FLAMED ORANGE PEEL

One popular trick behind the bar today dates back to 1970 in Los Angeles, was revived by Dale DeGroff in New York in the 1980s, and continues to be popular among bartenders everywhere, and that's the flamed orange peel. Reportedly invented by bartender Pepe Ruiz for the flame of love cocktail created for Dean Martin, the trick involves holding an orange peel close to an open flame and briefly igniting the volatile oils over the surface of the drink.

Begin with a large, thick swath of orange peel, about 1 in/2.5 cm by 2½ in/6 cm. Holding a lit match or lighter between the peel and the surface of the cocktail, squeeze the oils so they pass through the flame and onto the drink's surface. From there it's business as usual, wiping the rim of the glass with the orange peel and deciding whether to drop or discard.

You'll often see bartenders "warming up" the peel by heating it first with the fire source, but I suspect that's a lot of show and not much science. The warming is a mystery to me. Flaming the orange peel should be a bit of bar magic—it must catch the guest completely by surprise. The bartender has to execute it in one fluid motion. When done properly, the guest just catches it out of the corner of their eye; then they smell the orange oil. Warming turns it into a science project and makes the guest nervous and uneasy about what should be sleight of hand.

SPICES

While many spices make their way into various ingredients of cocktails—such as liqueurs, syrups, and tinctures—for garnishing, the two most common spices you'll use are nutmeg and cinnamon.

It should go without saying at this point, but I'll just mention it again to drive home the point: Any spice you use in a cocktail needs to be freshly grated or ground, in order to deliver the fragrance and flavor you want. Never, ever buy preground spices from the grocery store, and always beware of the little salt shaker full of three-year-old preground nutmeg that's kept under bars all over the world.

Nutmeg is easy. The hard, round whole nutmegs stay fresh for a long time, and grating them is easy as long as you have a Microplane grater.

For cinnamon, I use the Ceylon soft-stick cinnamon, which is very crumbly and delicate, unlike the rock-hard rolls of cassia cinnamon, which is from a different plant altogether. Ceylon is true cinnamon; it has a potent fragrance and sweet-spicy flavor. To garnish with cinnamon, I just grate it directly over the drink.

When using both of these spices, I like to grate so that the spice falls in one concentrated spot on the surface of the drink, rather than creating a more widespread light dusting. You can make an attractive pattern if you simply hold the grater close to the surface of the drink and grate in short strokes.

Microplane makes an actual nutmeg grater, which has a slim curved plate, against which you grate the nutmeg. I personally don't care for these, because you end up hollowing out a little groove, eventually making the nutmeg difficult to use. Any of the fine-gauge flat graters work well; you just grate through the whole nutmeg. For cinnamon, this basic grater works best as well.

SPRAYS

Perhaps the most esoteric and complex garnish is a spritz of something sprayed over the surface of the cocktail. Absinthe, vermouth, bitters, Islay Scotch, mezcal, orange blossom water and rosewater, and herbal liqueurs are all beautiful accompaniments and interesting ways to give a fragrant finish to a drink.

For all of your sprays, just use a generic atomizer bottle—one that's never held anything nonpotable, such as perfume—and fill with the liquid of your choice. Be sure to label the bottle.

Most atomizers are inexpensive and readily available on the Internet. Since one brand isn't much better than another, I recommend simply finding one that matches the look of your bar.

SAZERAC

MAKES 1 DRINK Sometimes it's helpful to think of a garnish in an uncommon way. I like to think of the absinthe rinse found in a traditional Sazerac cocktail as an aromatic garnish that's placed *underneath* the drink. It incorporates into the finished product but also retains some aromatics along the inside collar of the glass.

The classic methodology is to pour a small measure of absinthe into the glass, swirl it, and then dump it out, which coats the glass evenly, but is also a waste of absinthe and is slightly messy. At our bars we like to use an atomizer filled with absinthe to neatly and evenly coat the inside of the glass.

2 oz/60 ml rye whiskey
1 tsp/5 ml 2:1 simple syrup (see page 78)
3 dashes Peychaud's bitters
1 dash Angostura bitters
Ice cubes
Absinthe (in an atomizer bottle) for garnish
1 lemon peel for garnish

FROZEN ROCKS GLASS

Stir the whiskey, simple syrup, and bitters together in a mixing glass. Add ice cubes and stir until chilled. In the frozen rocks glass, spray absinthe until the entire interior surface is evenly coated. Strain the cocktail into the glass, twist the lemon peel over the surface, and discard the peel before serving.

BITTERS DROPLET ART

If a spray of bitters over the surface of a drink is a beautiful aromatic presentation, a few drops can be both aromatic and visually appealing at the same time. This is an advanced-level garnishing technique, along the lines of something a pastry chef might employ.

Reserve this technique for drinks that contain egg whites, as the foam on the drink's surface is the only thing that will support a few drops of bitters so they don't quickly dissipate into the drink.

How to Make Decorative Bitters Art

Despite the fact that bitters bottles are outfitted with a tiny pour spout, you don't ever want to pour directly from the bottle unless you're looking for a sloppy mess. It's impossible to control the exact amount of bitters, or where it will land, as the force of the tipping contents can cause the bitters to squirt out in an arc. I've seen bartenders successfully employ a free-pour bitters bottle to achieve a beautiful straight line across the top of an egg-white cocktail, but the following is the only way to consistently place precise droplets in the foam.

Transfer your bitters to a small eyedropper, available at any cosmetics or craft supply store. They're cheap and readily available, and much like atomizers, I've never seen one particular brand that's head and shoulders above the rest.

Carefully place your drops on the drink, and then drag a toothpick or the point of a sharp knife through drop. Moving from the center of a drop outward will make a "tail"; dragging all the way through will make a heart shape; and dragging through several dots will connect them into a little garland.

INDEX

A

absinthe
  glasses for, 238
  history of, 238
  Sazerac, 278
  serving, 238
  as spray, 278
  Vesper, 195–96
Adkins, Erik, 88, 107
agave syrup, 76, 77
aging, barrel, 132
Alexander Cocktail, 146
Allen, Ethan, 32
Amco, 19
Angostura bitters, 137
Antoine's, 241
apple brandy and applejack
  Autumn Leaves, 135
  Jack Rose, 100
  Philadelphia Fish House
    Punch, 111
apple cider
  apple seeds and, 39
  choosing apples for, 38–39
  equipment for, 38
  Flannel Shirt, 40
  pasteurized, 38
  storing, 39
apricot brandy
  Hotel Nacional Special, 107
atomizers, 278
Autumn Leaves, 135

B

Baker, Charles H., 107, 122
baker's sugar, 75

Bamboo, 118
band, creating, 268, 269
Barnard, W. G. "Papa," 228
barrel aging, 132
bar spoons, 189, 203–4
bartending
  as craft, 185
  physicality of, 190
  speed and, 191, 193
batching, 196–97
Beachcomber Bar, 229
Bellini, 49
bin Laden, Osama, 91
bitters
  commercial, 136–37
  definition of, 136
  droplet art, 281
  history of, 136
  House Orange Bitters, 138
  measuring, 188
  nonpotability of, 136
  as spray, 278
blending, 227–28
Blue Blazer, 239–40
Bohemian Club, 256
Bolívar, Simón, 137
Bond, James, 195
Bonzer jiggers, 189
Boston shaker
  choosing, 213–14
  dry shake alignment for, 158
  opening, 215, 218
bourbon
  Daniel Shoemaker's Brandied
    Cherries, 252–53
  House Old-Fashioned, 82
  Mint Julep, 176
  Revolver, 140
Bourbon & Branch, 140

brandy. See also apple brandy
  and applejack; apricot brandy;
  cognac
  Daniel Shoemaker's Brandied
    Cherries, 252–53
Breville Juice Fountain Elite, 33
Brooke, Joseph, 241
brown sugar, 75, 77
Buck's Club, 71
Buddha's hand, 27
Buena Vista Cafe, 150
building in the glass, 225

C

cachaça
  about, 237
  Caipirinha, 237
Café Brûlot, 241–42
Caipirinha, 237
Canadian whisky
  Maple Old-Fashioned, 83
carbonation, 53–55, 57
Caribe Hilton, 229
caster sugar, 75
Cavendish, Henry, 53
channel knives, 260, 262
Chapman, John, 32
cherries
  Daniel Shoemaker's Brandied
    Cherries, 252–53
  as garnishes, 250
  improving on jarred, 250–51
  pitting, 253
chiles, infusing with, 124
Chinese Five-Spiced Dark
  Rum, 128
cinnamon
  Cinnamon Tincture, 134
  as garnish, 277
Cipriani, Giuseppe, 49

citrus. *See also individual fruits*
  bulk-buying, 16–17
  choosing, 16–17
  history of, 14–15
  horse's neck, 262
  juice, 17, 22–25
  muddling, 235
  peels, 274–75, 277
  twists, 260, 262
  varieties of, 27–28
  wedges, 266–67
  wheels, 262, 264
Clinebell Equipment Company, 170
Clyde Common, 154, 193
Clyde Common Eggnog, 154
cobbler shaker, 213
Cocktail Kingdom, 172, 204, 206, 208, 213, 235, 240
cocktails
  history of, 81
  sugar syrups in, 81
  three elements of good, 10
Coco López, 229
coconut cream
  Piña Colada, 229
coffee
  Café Brûlot, 241–42
  Irish Coffee, 150
  Spanish Coffee, 243, 245
coffee liqueur
  Revolver, 140
  Spanish Coffee, 243, 245
cognac
  Café Brûlot, 241–42
  Japanese Cocktail, 113
  Philadelphia Fish House Punch, 111
  Sidecar, 220

Cointreau
  Margarita, 272
  Sidecar, 220
  Thyme-Infused Cointreau, 127
  White Lady, 161
Colliau, Jennifer, 88–89, 112
Collins, John, 54
compound syrups
  advantages of, 89
  fruit in, 97
  Ginger Syrup, 103
  Grenadine, 98, 100
  Gum Syrup, 90–91, 93
  herbs in, 94
  Mint Syrup, 96
  Oleo Saccharum, 108
  orgeat, 112
  Pineapple Syrup, 103
  Quinine Syrup, 59
  Raspberry Syrup, 102
confectioners' sugar, 75
Conigliaro, Tony, 132
Cook, James, 54
Country Clean Paper Supplies, 255
Craddock, Harry, 161, 185
cream
  choosing, 145
  sell-by date for, 147
  storing, 147
  types of, 146
  whipped, 147–48, 267
cream whipper, infusing with, 127
crème de cacao
  Alexander Cocktail, 146
crème de pêche
  Philadelphia Fish House Punch, 111

Cuffs & Buttons, 157
Cynar Flip, 153

D
Daiquiri No. 3, 28
dairy products. *See also* cream
  choosing, 145
  role of, in cocktails, 144
  sell-by date for, 147
  storing, 147
  types of, 146
Daniel Shoemaker's Brandied Cherries, 252–53
Dark and Stormy, 68
dashes, 186, 188
Death + Company, 83
DeGroff, Dale, 277
Demerara sugar, 75–76, 77
dilution, 201–2
dissolution, 119
dram, 186
Drambuie
  Kingston Club, 42
drops, 186
dry ice, 168
dry shake, 157, 158

E
eggs
  choosing, 145
  Clyde Common Eggnog, 154
  cracking, 152–53
  Cynar Flip, 153
  freshness of, 152
  measuring, 152
  raw, 152
  separating, 154, 156

White Lady, 161

whites, preparing and storing, 156–57

Estopinal, Kirk, 136

Exacto-Pour testing set, 193

F

fat washing, 120

Fizz Giz, 57

flaming drinks
  Blue Blazer, 239–40
  Café Brûlot, 241–42
  with orange peel, 277
  Spanish Coffee, 243, 245

Flannel Shirt, 40

flavor, complexities of, 119–20

Fleming, Ian, 195

flips
  Cynar Flip, 153
  history of, 153

flowers
  as garnishes, 259–60
  storing, 260

food mills, 33

food processors, 33

Franklin, Benjamin, 53

free pouring, 191, 193–94

French 75, 71

fruit. *See also* juices; *individual fruits*
  in compound syrups, 97
  muddling, 235
  purees, 46

G

Galatoire's, 241

garnishes. *See also individual garnishes*
  aromatic, 274–75, 277–78, 281
  dropped, 250–56

rimmed, 268–69

role of, 248

utilitarian, 266–67

visual, 259–60, 262, 264–65

Gibson, 256

Gibson, Walter D. K., 256

gill, 186

gin
  Alexander Cocktail, 146
  Clover Club, 102
  French 75, 71
  Gin and Tonic, 58, 62
  Improved Holland Cocktail, 196–97
  Martini, 210
  Tom Collins, 54, 56
  Vesper, 195–96
  White Lady, 161

ginger
  Dark and Stormy, 68
  Ginger Beer, 65–66
  Ginger Syrup, 103
  juice, 45
  storing, 45

glass, as unit of measure, 185

glasses
  for absinthe, 238
  for Irish Coffee, 150
  for martinis, 195
  mixing, 204, 206
  oversized, 195
  rimmed, 268–69

Gonzalez, Giuseppe, 136

Gracia, Ricardo, 229

Grand Marnier
  Café Brûlot, 241–42

granulated sugar, 75

grapefruits
  choosing, 16–17
  Daiquiri No. 3, 28
  juice, 17, 24
  varieties of, 27–28

Grenadine, 98, 100
  Jack Rose, 100

Gum Syrup, 90–91, 93

H

Hamilton Beach, 20

Harry's Bar, 49

Hawthorne strainer, 208, 219

hemicellulose, 132

Hemingway, Ernest, 28

herbs
  in compound syrups, 94
  as garnishes, 259–60
  infusions with, 126–27
  muddling, 230
  storing, 260
  tinctures with, 133, 134

honey, 76, 77

horse's neck, 262

Hoshizaki ice machines, 172

Hotel Nacional Special, 107

House Old-Fashioned, 82

House Orange Bitters, 138

Huber's Cafe, 243

I

ice
  behavior of, 165
  for blended drinks, 227–28
  block, 170
  carbonation and, 55
  clarity of, 165–66
  cracked, 172, 174
  crushed, 174
  cubes, 170, 172
  dilution and, 201–2
  dry, 168
  handling, 168, 170
  history of, 164
  importance of, 164

large-format, 170, 172
making, 166, 168
obtaining, 166, 168
for punch, 178
role of, 165
spears, 172
spherical, 181
storing, 168
transporting, 168
types of, 170, 172, 174
Improved Holland Cocktail,
    196–97
infusions
    with chiles, 124
    Chinese Five-Spiced Dark
        Rum, 128
    choosing ingredients for,
        120–21
    fat washing and, 120
    flavor and, 120
    goal of, 120
    with herbs and spices, 126–28
    Limoncello, 130
    making, 121
    Nocino, 129
    processes involved in, 119
    storing, 122
    straining, 122
    Tequila por Mi Amante, 122
    Thyme-Infused Cointreau,
        127
    tinctures vs., 133
    wood, 132
ingredients, importance of, 10
Irish whiskey
    Irish Coffee, 150

J

Jack Rose, 100
Japanese Cocktail, 113
jiggers, 185, 188–89

juicers, 19–20, 33
juices
    apple, 38–39
    citrus, 17, 22–25
    ginger, 45
    pineapple, 42
    pomegranate, 44
    techniques for, 22–23, 34, 36
    tomato, 43
Julep, Mint, 176
julep strainer, 208

K

Kahlúa
    Spanish Coffee, 243, 245
Kingston Club, 42
knives
    channel, 260, 262
    paring, 264
    serrated, 264
Kold-Draft ice machines, 172
Kuhn Rikon, 264
kumquats, 27

L

lemons. See also citrus
    choosing, 16–17
    Clover Club, 102
    Flannel Shirt, 40
    French 75, 71
    Ginger Beer, 65–66
    Jack Rose, 100
    juice, 17, 24–25
    Limoncello, 130
    Oleo Saccharum, 108
    Philadelphia Fish House
        Punch, 111
    Sidecar, 220
    Tom Collins, 54, 56

varieties of, 27
    White Lady, 161
Lewis bags, 174
Lillet blanc
    Vesper, 195–96
limes. See also citrus
    Caipirinha, 237
    choosing, 16–17
    Daiquiri No. 3, 28
    Hotel Nacional Special, 107
    juice, 17, 24
    Kingston Club, 42
    Margarita, 272
    Mojito, 233
    Queen's Park Swizzle, 226
    varieties of, 27
Limoncello, 130
lip, rimming, 268, 269
Luxardo, 250

M

MacElhone, Harry, 71
mandarins, 28
maple syrup
    calories in, 77
    grades of, 77
    Maple Old-Fashioned, 83
    in simple syrup, 77
maraschino liqueur
    Daiquiri No. 3, 28
    Improved Holland Cocktail,
        196–97
Margarita, 272
Marrero Pérez, Ramón
    "Monchito," 229
Martin, Dean, 277
Martini, 210
Mayahuel, 83
McGarry, Malachy, 71

measuring
American system for, 186-87
eggs, 152
history of, 185-86
importance of, 185
metric system for, 187, 195-96
speed and, 191, 193
tools for, 188-91
Messermeister, 262
metric system, 187, 195-96
mezcal
Oaxaca Old-Fashioned, 83
Microplane, 277
mint
Mint Julep, 176
Mint Syrup, 96
Mojito, 233
Strawberry-Mint Shrub, 114
Mister Mojito, 235
mixers, 52
mixing glasses, 204, 206
Mojito, 233
muddling, 230, 235
muscovado sugar, 76, 77

N

Nepove, David, 235
Nocino, 129
Norpro, 19, 219
nutmeg, 277

O

Oaxaca Old-Fashioned, 83
old-fashioned
history of, 81
House Old-Fashioned, 82
Maple Old-Fashioned, 83

Oaxaca Old-Fashioned, 83
Rum Old-Fashioned, 82
Oleo Saccharum, 108
Philadelphia Fish House
Punch, 111
olives, 254-55
onions
as garnishes, 256
Todd Thrasher's Pickled
Onions, 256
oranges. *See also* citrus
bitters, commercial, 137
choosing, 16-17
House Orange Bitters, 138
juice, 17, 24
peel, flamed, 277
varieties of, 27-28
orgeat
about, 112
Japanese Cocktail, 113
osmosis, 119
OXO, 189, 213, 219, 253, 274

P

Parisian shaker, 214
Pazuniak, Maks, 136
peaches
Bellini, 49
puree, 46
Pearl-Kimmel, Stephanie, 118
peelers, 274
peels, citrus, 274-75, 277
Pegu Club, 157
Pépin, Jacques, 152
Perlage System, 70
Peychaud, Antoine Amédée, 137
Peychaud's bitters, 137
Pike, Justin, 193-94
Piña Colada, 229

pineapple
choosing, 42
garnishes, 265
Hotel Nacional Special, 107
juice, 42
Kingston Club, 42
Piña Colada, 229
Pineapple Syrup, 103
Plinth, Charles, 54
pomegranates
choosing, 44
Grenadine, 98, 100
juice, 44
storing, 44
pony, 185
pouring
free, 191, 193-94
overhanded vs. underhanded,
189-91
powdered sugar, 75
Priestley, Joseph, 53-54
The Prizefighter, 140
punches
history of, 14-15
ice for, 178
Philadelphia Fish House
Punch, 111
PX, 256

Q

Queen's Park Hotel, 226
Queen's Park Swizzle, 226
quinine
history of, 58
Quinine Syrup, 59
Quinine Tincture, 59

R

Ra Chand, 20
Raspberry Syrup, 102
  Clover Club, 102
raw sugar, 75-76
recipes
  choosing, 10
  scaling up, 196-97
Regan, Gary, 136, 224
Revolver, 140
Reynolds, Blair, 112
Reynoso, Henry, 146
Ricket, E., 90
rimmed garnishes, 268-69
rolling, 225
Rösle, 213
Ruiz, Pepe, 277
rum
  Chinese Five-Spiced Dark
    Rum, 128
  Daiquiri No. 3, 28
  Daniel Shoemaker's Brandied
    Cherries, 252-53
  Dark and Stormy, 68
  Hotel Nacional Special, 107
  House Orange Bitters, 138
  Mojito, 233
  Philadelphia Fish House
    Punch, 111
  Piña Colada, 229
  Queen's Park Swizzle, 226
  Rum Old-Fashioned, 82
  Spanish Coffee, 243, 245
rye whiskey
  Autumn Leaves, 135
  Sazerac, 278

S

salt rim, 268-69
Sandrof, Ben, 153
Santer, Jon, 140
Savoy, 185
Sazerac, 278
Schweppe, Johann Jacob, 54
Scotch
  Blue Blazer, 239-40
  Flannel Shirt, 40
Scoville scale, 124
Seattle muddle, 224
seltzer water, 54
shaking
  dilution and, 201-2
  for egg-white cocktails,
    157-58
  equipment for, 213-14
  goals for, 213
  stirring vs., 200
  straining and, 219
  technique for, 214-15, 218
sherry
  Clyde Common Eggnog, 154
Shoemaker, Daniel, 252
shrubs
  history of, 114
  making, 114
  Strawberry-Mint Shrub, 114
Sidecar, 220
Siegert, Johann Gottlieb
    Benjamin, 137
simple syrups
  choosing sugar for, 75-77
  in cocktails, 81
  goal of, 74
  making, 78, 80
  measuring ingredients for, 78
  storing, 80
  strength of, 78

Slanted Door, 88, 107
Small Hand Foods, 89, 112
Sodastream, 57
soda water, 54, 57
Solomon, Chad, 157
Spanish Coffee, 243, 245
spears
  ice, 172
  pineapple, 265
speed pourers, 191
spices
  as garnishes, 277
  infusions with, 126, 127-28
  tinctures with, 133, 134
Spill-Stop pour spouts, 191
sprays, 278
Stenson, Murray, 193-94
stirring
  bar spoons for, 203-4
  dilution and, 201-2
  goals of, 203
  mixing glasses for, 204, 206
  shaking vs., 200
  straining and, 208
  technique for, 206, 208
straining, 122, 208, 219
strawberries
  Strawberry-Mint Shrub, 114
  Tequila por Mi Amante, 122
Strega liqueur
  Autumn Leaves, 135
subsidence, 121
sugar. See also simple syrups
  rim, 268-69
  types of, 75-77
Sunkist, 20
superfine sugar, 75
Swissmar bar spoon, 204
swizzle sticks, 226
swizzling, 226

T

tangerines, 28

Teardrop Lounge, 252

technique, importance of, 10

tequila
 Clyde Common Eggnog, 154
 infusing, with chiles, 124
 Margarita, 272
 Oaxaca Old-Fashioned, 83
 Tequila por Mi Amante, 122

Thomas, C., 90

Thomas, Jerry, 56, 81, 82, 112, 153, 185, 239, 240

Thoreau, Henry David, 164

Thrasher, Todd, 256

Thyme-Infused Cointreau, 127

tinctures
 choosing alcohols for, 133
 Cinnamon Tincture, 134
 infusions vs., 133
 intensity of, 133
 making, 134
 Quinine Tincture, 59

Tiny Tavern, 8

Todd Thrasher's Pickled Onions, 256

tomato juice, 43

Tom Collins, 54, 56

tonic water
 Gin and Tonic, 58, 62
 history of, 58
 making, 58

toothpicks, 255

Tovolo ice trays, 170, 172

triangles, pineapple, 265

Triple Sec
 Spanish Coffee, 243, 245

Tudor, Frederic, 164

turbinado sugar, 75-76, 77

twists, citrus, 260, 262

U

ultrapasteurization, 145

V

vermouth
 Autumn Leaves, 135
 Martini, 210
 as spray, 278

Vert, Constantino Ribalaigua, 28

Vesper, 195-96

Victorinox, 262

Vitamix, 228

vodka
 Cinnamon Tincture, 134
 infusing, with chiles, 124
 infusing, with herbs, 126
 Limoncello, 130
 Nocino, 129
 Vesper, 195-96

W

walnuts
 Nocino, 129

Ward, Phil, 83

Waring, Fred, 229

Waring ice-crushing machine, 174

wedges, citrus, 266-67

wheels, citrus, 262, 264

whipped cream
 as garnish, 267
 making, 147-48

whiskey. *See* bourbon; Canadian whisky; Irish whiskey; rye whiskey; Scotch

White, Neyah, 114

White Lady, 161

white sugar, 75, 77

wine
 Bellini, 49
 French 75, 71
 Nocino, 129
 sparkling, 70

wineglass, as unit of measure, 185

WMF, 213, 214

Wondrich, David, 111

Y

Yarai mixing glass, 206

Y peelers, 274

yuzu, 28

Z

zesters, 260

Zig Zag Café, 194